A Midwest Gardener's Cookbook

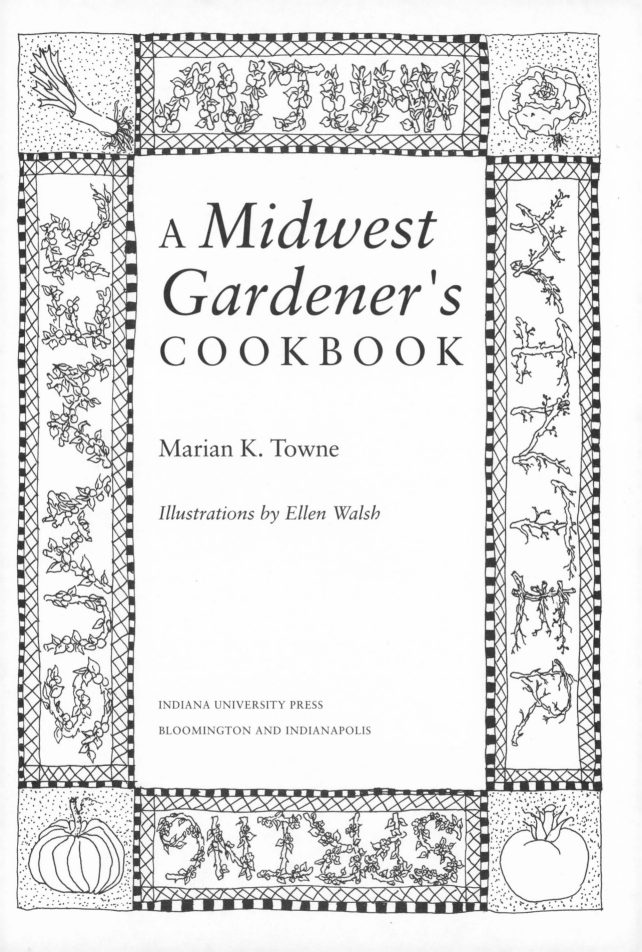

A *Midwest Gardener's* COOKBOOK

Marian K. Towne

Illustrations by Ellen Walsh

INDIANA UNIVERSITY PRESS

BLOOMINGTON AND INDIANAPOLIS

The paper used in this publication meets the minimum requirements of
American National Standard for Information Sciences—Permanence of Paper
for Printed Library Materials, ANSI Z39.48–1984.

MANUFACTURED IN THE UNITED STATES OF AMERICA

Library of Congress Cataloging-in-Publication Data

Towne, Marian Kleinsasser.
A Midwest gardener's cookbook / Marian K. Towne;
illustrations by Ellen Walsh.
p.   cm.
Includes bibliographical references and index.
ISBN 0–253–21056–9 (pbk.: alk. paper)
1. Cookery (Vegetables) 2.Cookery (Fruit) 3.Cookery, American—
Midwestern style. I. Title.
TX801.T69 1996
641.6'5--dc20   95-39893

1 2 3 4 5 01 00 99 98 97 96

CONTENTS

PART THREE   AUTUMN

PREFACE

A Midwest Gardener's Cookbook is the product of more than fifty years of cooking according to seasonal principles. I grew up during the Great Depression on a farm in southeastern South Dakota where we had to rely for our "daily bread" upon nature, hard work, and the help of relatives and friends, particularly after the death of our mother when I was not yet four years old.

We ate primarily what we could raise ourselves and what others shared with us from their bounty. What was grown beyond our daily needs we preserved for future use, canning (and later freezing) up to four hundred quarts of food each year and storing other produce such as potatoes and squash in an unheated cellar.

Wherever my family and I have lived since I married and left South Dakota—Kansas, Illinois, Ohio, Indiana—whether in city or town, we have always managed to have some kind of garden, even if only a postage stamp–size tomato patch in the backyard of a Chicago townhouse.

This cookbook has been organized according to the growing seasons, from spring to winter, and alphabetically within each season those fruits, vegetables and herbs then in plentiful supply. For it is at that time that the home gardener (or careful shopper at farmers' markets) is able to secure the freshest, most nutritious, and least expensive produce. Whenever spinach is in season, for example, the home gardener needs to have close at hand (without looking in ten cookbooks) at least ten recipes for using spinach in a variety of ways so that one's family will not get bored with the vegetable before the season is past. When zucchini are abundant the gardener wants to make good use of his/her harvest and know of ways to preserve it for winter.

PART ONE

Asparagus
Chard
Chives
Dandelions
Green Onions
Lettuce
Mint
Mulberries
Parsley
Peapods
Peas
Radishes
Rhubarb
Spinach
Strawberries
Violets

Asparagus

Since asparagus is the first crop harvested in many areas, it has come to be a universal symbol of spring. When served with eggs, it is inevitably associated with Easter and new life.

Asparagus is attractive also because it is highly nutritious while being low in calories, making it just the right vegetable for spring when our thoughts turn to shedding some winter weight. It is high in vitamins A, B, and C as well as potassium. Four stalks have only 10 calories and a cup of chopped asparagus only 30 calories.

Snap off the lower part of the stalk and keep the trimmings for soup stock. When bending a stalk of asparagus, it will snap naturally between the fresh upper part and the woody lower part. It is rarely necessary to trim or scrape stalks of fresh home-grown asparagus or wild asparagus. Steam for about 12 minutes in salted water.

Asparagus Salad Vinaigrette

Drain and chill steamed asparagus. Serve with French dressing or vinaigrette, the classic proportions of which are 3 or 4 parts of olive oil to 1 part of lemon juice, lime juice, or vinegar. Add salt and pepper to taste. If the dressing is stored in the refrigerator, remove the garlic clove (if you use it) after 24 hours. Add fresh herbs only if the dressing is to be used at once, since they become unpleasantly strong if left in the oil for a long period of time. This recipe is a good way to store and use leftover cooked asparagus.

Asparagus and Beet Salad

leftover steamed asparagus spears
canned sliced or diced beets, drained
spicy French dressing
Bibb or other leaf lettuce

Pour French dressing over cooked asparagus spears and beets which have been placed in separate dishes. Chill in refrigerator for several hours. Remove asparagus from marinade and place on lettuce on salad plates. Top with beets. Pass additional dressing, if desired.

Asparagus Stem Soup

woody stems saved from several bunches of asparagus
1 medium onion, chopped
2 medium potatoes, peeled and sliced
stems of 1 small bunch parsley, minced
1 clove garlic, minced
2 T. butter
1 qt. milk
salt and pepper to taste

Sauté asparagus stems, onion, potatoes, parsley, and garlic in butter on low heat for about 15 minutes, covered. Season. Slowly bring milk to boiling point in separate pan. Meanwhile, purée vegetables in blender. Discard solids, if any are present. Combine milk and puréed vegetables. Heat slowly. Serve in shallow bowls. Garnish with asparagus tips cooked lightly in butter.

Microwaved Fresh Asparagus

1 lb. fresh asparagus
¹/₄ c. water

Arrange prepared asparagus spears in a flat microwave casserole with tougher stem ends toward the outside. Add water and cover with plastic wrap. Microwave on high for 5 to 7 minutes. Let stand covered 3 to 5 minutes before serving.

Variation: Add 4 thin slices of peeled fresh ginger root to the water in which asparagus is microwaved. Remove the ginger before serving drizzled with butter.

Asparagus Shortcake

1 lb. fresh asparagus
4 T. butter
4 T. flour
2 c. milk
1 t. salt
¹/₈ t. pepper
4 hard-cooked eggs

Clean and cut asparagus into half-inch lengths, reserving woody ends for soup. Steam asparagus until tender. Make white sauce by melting butter and stirring in flour. (A metal potato masher held firmly to the bottom of the pan while making circular motions works superbly.) Add milk gradually and stir over low heat until thickened. Add steamed asparagus and 2 sliced, hard-cooked eggs. Serve over hot biscuits (shortcake style) or over toasted corn bread or sliced bread toast. Garnish with remaining hard-cooked eggs, sliced. (This is an excellent luncheon dish to serve after Easter when you have an ample supply of cooked, colored eggs and when asparagus is in season.)

Variation: Sprinkle grated Cheddar cheese over top.

Chicken-Asparagus Casserole

1 lb. fresh asparagus, cut into 1-inch pieces
2 T. butter
2¹/₂ c. chopped cooked chicken
1 can (10 ¹/₂ oz.) condensed cream of mushroom soup
³/₄ c. milk
¹/₂ t. salt
¹/₂ t. marjoram

Heat oven to 400°. Sauté slightly the asparagus pieces in butter. Combine asparagus, chicken, mushroom soup, milk, salt, and marjoram in 2-quart casserole. Bake in preheated oven about 12 minutes, or until mixture bubbles.

Top with corn bread batter prepared from a mix or prepare a recipe of corn bread according to cornmeal box directions, using 1 c. cornmeal. Batter should be lumpy. Spread batter over hot chicken mixture in casserole and bake about 30 minutes, or until topping is golden brown. (This casserole was prepared by Violet Whitmer for our family when her friend and Marian's mother-in-law, Margaret Towne, died. Violet later became Mrs. Arthur Towne.)

Asparagus combines well with other ingredients, so that you could serve it every day for a month when it is plentiful and not tire of it. Some suggestions are:

Asparagus Quiche, made with Swiss cheese and bacon.

Asparagus with Horseradish Sauce, adding 1 T. prepared horseradish to 1 c. sour cream.

Asparagus with Ham Bits.

Asparagus with Mushroom Sauce.

Asparagus with Pine Nuts and/or Capers.

Asparagus with Lemon-Tarragon Butter.

Asparagus–Pork Sausage Strata.

Asparagus Omelet.

Asparagus Benedict: Place asparagus spears over sautéd chicken breast on toasted English muffin. Top with warm poached egg and warm Hollandaise sauce.

Chard

Sometimes called Swiss chard, this leafy green vegetable is usually too large and strong-flavored for salads but may be cooked as one would spinach. Sow seeds in early spring. Very young leaves are suitable for tossed green salad. When it is young and tender, it may be chopped (both leaves and stalks) and sautéd in bacon drippings, butter, or oil and flavored with salt, black pepper or red pepper flakes, and vinegar or lemon juice.

As the vegetable matures, the stalks become celery-like. At this point chard stalks may be substituted for celery in soups, sauces, or casseroles. However, do not substitute it, uncooked, for celery in salads, as it turns brown. If chard is served as a vegetable at the mature stage, sauté the chopped or diced chard stalks until tender and then add the green leaves, coarsely shredded.

Chard will replenish itself throughout the growing season if harvested from the outer leaves continuously. Often chard may be harvested around Thanksgiving time if a heavy frost is late in coming. (In 1994 I harvested it from the Towne family garden on New Year's Eve.) Simply remove the old leaves from the root still growing in the ground and new leaves will appear from the center. Leave the old leaves in the garden as mulch or weed retardant or put them in a compost pile.

Like spinach, chard may be frozen for winter use by sautéing first the stalks, then the green leaves, and packing it, when cool, into air-tight plastic containers.

Chard, like kale and carrots, winters well in the garden in warmer climates. Cover the plants with leaves or straw and harvest as desired. The live plants may also be brought into a sunny basement or greenhouse in large containers which allow for sufficient soil to sustain the roots. Harvesting the leaves can then proceed throughout the winter.

Chard Soup

1 small onion, chopped
1 clove garlic, minced
1 lb. chard
4 T. olive oil
5 c. water
2 large potatoes, peeled and cubed
1 t. salt

In soup pot sauté onion, garlic, and chard stems in oil. Add water and potatoes. Bring to a boil and simmer, covered, for 20 minutes. Cool. When cool, purée vegetables in blender. Cut chard leaves into coarse shreds and put back into pot with liquid. Add salt. Bring all to boil and cook until chard is soft. Serve immediately. Serves 4.

Chard and Rice Casserole

1 c. white rice
$^1/_2$ c. minced onion
$^1/_3$ c. olive oil
1 lb. chard
1 clove garlic, minced
$^1/_4$ c. chopped fresh basil

Boil rice in 2 c. salted water for 10–12 minutes or until water is absorbed. Meanwhile, in a skillet sauté onion in oil until soft and golden in color. Add chard and garlic and sauté over high heat for 5 minutes or until chard is wilted. Stir in basil and cooked rice. Remove pan from heat. Season with salt and pepper to taste.

Variation: Use brown rice and add $^1/_2$ cup grated Cheddar cheese at the end. Stir until cheese melts and holds mixture together. Soy sauce may also be added.

Stir-Fried Chard with Ginger and Chili

1 lb. chard
2 T. oil
2 thin slices ginger root, peeled,
   slivered, and chopped
1 whole dried red chili pod or 1 fresh
   jalapeño pepper, seeds removed, and minced
1 clove garlic, minced
$^1/_4$ c. chopped onion
$^1/_4$ t. salt

Wash and trim chard. Cut stems in thin slices and leaves in large pieces.

Heat wok or deep frying pan, add oil, and, when hot, toss in ginger, chili pepper, garlic, and onion. Allow to sizzle briefly. Add salt. Add thin slices of chard stems. When crisply tender, toss in chard leaves. Stir-fry briefly. Cover to allow greens to cook briefly. Serve over brown rice or as a vegetable accompaniment to meat. Serves 2–4.

Chard and Pasta

1 lb. pasta (linguini, vermicelli, or spaghetti)
2 T. olive oil
1 dried red chili pod, minced
1 clove garlic, minced
1 lb. chard, stems and leaves separated
$^1/_4$ t. salt
Parmesan or Romano cheese, grated

Cook pasta until *al dente*, drain, and keep warm in colander set in original pasta-cooking pot. Cover to retain heat.

Heat oil and add chili and garlic, stirring for 2 minutes. Add chard stems which have been sliced thin. Cook for 2 minutes, stirring often. Add chopped chard leaves and cook until wilted. Stir in salt.

Combine hot pasta and greens in large, warm serving bowl and sprinkle with cheese. Serve with crusty French bread.

Chard may be substituted in recipes calling for bok choy, and large chard leaves may be substituted for cabbage leaves for Pigs in Blankets or cabbage rolls. Simply wilt the leaves as you would cabbage leaves for ease in handling.

Chives

Chives belong with onions, leeks, and garlic in the allium family. The thin, grass-like leaves have a delicate taste of onion and are usually used to flavor cream cheese, salads, omelets, and mixed vegetables. Ed Becker, gardener extraordinaire, likes to put snipped chives on his tomato and cottage cheese for lunch.

If both the leaves and the flower, which looks like a mauve pincushion, are picked continuously, the plant will grow more vigorously and have a better flavor. However, never snip randomly from the top of your chives plant but cut whole blades, being careful to leave a half inch to allow for regrowth through early fall. Chives may suddenly die out and disappear, so if you have a healthy plant in your garden, divide the bulbs in the autumn and give some to a friend to prevent overcrowding. (That friend may later reciprocate with a clump of chives for your garden if yours die out. But keep them free of weeds and you should never have to resort to growing chives from seed.) If you are growing chives indoors on a sunny windowsill, you have the added advantage of their being close at hand when needed.

Chives growing in the garden tend to flatten out when pounded by heavy rains. To minimize grit in chives coming from a heavy downpour, give them a plastic collar. Take a large plastic flower pot, cut out the bottom, and set the pot over the plant, bottom end up. This collar will keep chives clean so all you need do is snip the leaves and give them a quick rinse before using.

Cooking destroys texture, color, and delicate flavor, so always add chives to a finished dish.

Sauce Vinaigrette

1 T. *finely chopped onion, preferably*
   green onion, Bermuda, or Vidalia
1 T. *snipped chives*
1 T. *finely chopped parsley leaves*

1 t. *salt, or to taste*
freshly ground black pepper to taste
4 T. *white vinegar*
8 T. *olive oil*

Mix all seasonings with the vinegar and let stand for several minutes before combining with oil. Mix thoroughly before serving. Makes 1 cup.

Lemon-Chive Dressing

$^1/_3$ c. *lemon juice*
$1^1/_2$ t. *salt*
1 t. *Dijon-style mustard*
pepper to taste
$1^1/_4$ c. *olive oil*
2 T. *snipped chives*

In a bowl combine first 4 ingredients. Add oil in a stream, whisking. Whisk the dressing until it is well blended. Before serving, add chives. Makes $1^2/_3$ cups.

Chive-Parsley Sauce for Cooked Vegetables

$^1/_4$ c. *butter*
1 T. *minced chives*
1 T. *minced parsley*

Melt butter in small saucepan. Stir in chives and parsley. Serve over cooked potatoes, cauliflower, or zucchini. Store any remaining sauce, covered, in the refrigerator. To reheat, melt slowly and gently to retain delicate flavor.

Chives and Sour Cream Dip

$1^1/_2$ c. *sour cream, plain yogurt, or combination thereof*
2 T. *finely chopped chives*
2 T. *minced parsley leaves*
salt and pepper to taste, if desired

Mix ingredients and chill for at least 1 hour before serving. Serve with cut raw vegetables, crackers, or chips.

Cream-Style Chive Dressing

¹/₂ c. cottage cheese
1 c. plain yogurt
¹/₄ c. red wine vinegar
¹/₄ c. chives, finely chopped

Purée cottage cheese in blender until smooth. Add yogurt and vinegar. Process until fully blended. Transfer mixture to serving bowl and mix in chives.

Dandelions

Every spring a young man's fancy turns to thoughts of . . . greens! There is a primal urge toward salads, native or domestic, probably because our bodies crave vitamin A and iron after the long winter. If you have a natural lawn, uncontaminated by your neighbors' spraying, you may be able to harvest a delicious, inexpensive salad from nature's bounty. Or you may harvest young, tender dandelion leaves on your morning walks in wooded areas before yellow flowers appear.

If harvesting from your own uncontaminated crop in your own yard, cut off (or, better yet, dig out!) the dandelion plant at the root crown for ease in handling, especially washing. Use only tender, new leaves before flowering begins because flowering causes the leaves to become bitter and tough, unless they are boiled. Throw remainder of the plant on the compost pile.

Wash thoroughly under cold running water or in several baths of cold water to remove any dirt or grit. Dry first by turning upside down on the drainboard or allow to drip suspended from a wire basket. Then roll up and dry in a dish towel and, if possible, chill for several hours, still wrapped, until ready to prepare.

Wilted Dandelion Greens

4 slices bacon
¹/₄ c. cider vinegar
4 chopped green onions
1 t. sugar
2 quarts dandelion greens, loosely packed

Fry bacon until crisp. Remove from pan and drain on absorbent paper, such as a clean brown paper bag. To hot bacon drippings add vinegar, green onions, and sugar.

Crumble bacon over dandelion greens. Pour hot dressing over greens. Toss and serve at once on warm plates. May be served with hot crusty bread and hard-cooked eggs for excellent luncheon dish. Serves 4.

Variation: Add drained sliced beets. They counteract the somewhat bitter taste of the dandelion.

Sautéd Dandelion

1 lb. young dandelion greens
2 T. olive oil
1 clove garlic, minced
juice of 1 lemon
salt and freshly ground pepper to taste

Wash and drain dandelion leaves. Cut up greens. Heat oil in skillet. Add dandelion and garlic, season with salt and pepper. Sauté for a few minutes before adding lemon juice, and serve hot. Serves 6. Serve with smoky sausages.

Spring Greens Soup

2 lbs. chard, rinsed and stemmed
1 T. olive oil
2 green onions, chopped
1 clove garlic, minced
1/2 t. chopped chili pepper
1 1/2 lbs. dandelion greens, rinsed and stemmed
2 c. chicken broth
1 c. peeled and cubed potatoes
1/2 t. sugar
1/2 t. salt
1/4 t. pepper
2 T. chopped fresh mint, plus mint for garnish if desired
1 c. milk
1 c. yogurt, plus yogurt for garnish if desired
1 c. crumbled feta cheese

In large pot over medium heat, place chopped chard stems, oil, scallions, garlic, and chili pepper, and cook 3 to 5 minutes or until wilted. Add dandelion greens and chard leaves. Cook until wilted. Add chicken broth, potatoes, sugar, salt, and pepper. Cover and simmer 45 minutes. Remove pot from heat and let cool slightly. Add mint, milk, and yogurt. Purée in blender. Serve warm, garnished with heavy sprinkle of crumbled feta cheese, mint, and additional yogurt, if desired. Serves 8.

Potato and Dandelion Salad

1 lb. new red potatoes (waxy potatoes are preferred to avoid mushiness in salad)
¹/₂ c. water
2 T. olive oil
2 T. cider vinegar
¹/₄ t. salt
¹/₄ t. pepper
¹/₂ lb. thin-sliced cooked turkey kielbasa sausage
1 T. finely chopped green onion
1 T. chopped parsley
1¹/₂ T. red wine vinegar
¹/₂ t. Dijon-style mustard
salt and pepper to taste
3 T. olive oil
2 c. washed and well-dried young dandelion greens (stemmed)

To prepare potato salad, microwave potatoes with water in microwave-safe casserole on high for 7–10 minutes, covered. Allow potatoes to stand until they may be handled. Drain. Potatoes may be peeled if desired, but retaining peelings is more nutritious. Cut into chunks and place in serving bowl. Pour mixture of oil, vinegar, salt, and pepper over warm potatoes and allow to marinate for at least half an hour at room temperature.

Before serving, place kielbasa slices in slightly overlapping arrangement in microwave-safe casserole and microwave on high for 3 to 4 minutes or until warmed. Gently fold kielbasa, green onion, and parsley into potatoes.

For the dandelion salad, whisk together vinegar, mustard, salt, and pepper in bowl. Gradually whisk in oil. Toss dandelion greens in dressing. Arrange dandelion salad around rim of platter. Put potato salad in center and serve. Serves 4.

Pioneers used dandelion roots as a source of vitamin C during long winter months. They also roasted the roots and used them for a coffee-like drink free of caffeine, much as chicory or parsnip roots may be roasted and ground.

Dandelion Coffee (Decaf)

Dig up roots, trim off leaves and stems and any small rootlets. Wash off earth and scrub roots well. Put in warm place to drain and dry.

Cut larger roots in half and into shorter lengths. Spread pieces on shallow roasting tin and bake in hot oven (400°) for 30 minutes until roots are brown and dry throughout. Allow to cool before grinding. Spread grounds on baking sheet and roast for 7 minutes in moderate oven (350°).

To prepare, put 5 to 6 T. of grounds in warm jar or pitcher. Pour on 1 pint boiling water, stir, and let steep for 1 hour. Strain into pan or microwave-safe mug to reheat.

Dandelion Wine

Pick dandelion blossoms in early morning when dew is present,
using only perfect, open blossoms.

4 qts. dandelion blossoms
4 qts. boiling water
3 lbs. brown sugar
3 diced oranges, juice, skin, seeds and all
3 diced lemons, juice, skin, seeds and all
1 cake yeast

Combine blossoms and boiling water in 2-gallon or larger open crock. Cover with cheesecloth to keep out dust, and let stand at room temperature for 3 days.

Strain and discard blossoms. Place liquid in large saucepan, add sugar, oranges, and lemons. Boil for 30 minutes.

Cool to lukewarm. Pour into crock and add yeast. Cover. Let stand for 3 weeks or until bubbling stops.

Filter through fresh cheesecloth and bottle. Age for at least 4 months, the longer the better.

Green Onions (Scallions)

My father, John P. Kleinsasser, recorded in his diary (immortalized in my book, *Bread of Life: Diaries and Memories of a Dakota Family, 1936–1945*) when I was three years old that he feared I had eaten too many green onions. My ravenous appetite (which, unfortunately, has not abated) probably attested to my body's craving for some green spring tonic after a bleak South Dakota winter. I can remember wonderful breakfasts consisting entirely of green onions, radishes, home-made cottage cheese, homemade bread, and butter.

Scrambled Eggs and Green Onions

8 green onions, thinly sliced
2 T. butter
6 eggs
salt, pepper, and paprika

Sauté onions in butter in skillet for about 2 minutes. Beat eggs slightly with fork and season with salt and pepper. Add to onions and cook over low heat, stirring as egg sets. When all is set, sprinkle with paprika. Serves 4.

Green Onion Soup

1 quart chicken broth
2 t. oil
2 eggs, well beaten

³/₄ c. sliced green onions, including
    green tops
1 T. soy sauce

Heat broth. Using medium skillet, heat oil and pour in eggs. Cook omelet-style until lightly browned on bottom, then turn and gently cook other side. Turn out on plate and cut into thin strips about 2 inches by ¹/₄ inch. Add with onion and soy sauce to boiling chicken broth, simmer 1 minute, and serve. Serves 3 to 4.

Creamed New Green Onions

Sauté sliced green onions in butter, add flour and milk to make a white sauce, and flavor with salt and pepper or nutmeg. Serve on toast points and garnish with fresh parsley.

Garden Sauce with Green Onions

¹/₄ c. chopped green onion
1 T. butter
1 can (10 ¹/₂ oz.) cheese soup
¹/₂ c. sour cream
1 t. lemon juice

In saucepan, cook onion in butter until it is tender. Add remaining ingredients. Heat, stirring occasionally. Makes about 1¹/₂ cups. Good served over asparagus.

Spring Garden Cottage Cheese Salad

To creamed cottage cheese add sliced green onions with tops, sliced red radishes, chopped parsley, and pepper to taste. Serve on fresh leaves of garden lettuce, spinach, and/or young chard. (Later in the season add green pepper, carrot, tomato, cucumber, or whatever is in season and in great supply.)

Cheese and Sausage Strata

¹/₂ lb. bulk pork sausage
³/₄ c. sliced mushrooms
¹/₄ c. sliced green onions
¹/₂ lb. Velveeta or other pasteurized
    processed cheese, cubed

4 c. bread cubes
1 c. milk
4 eggs, beaten

Brown sausage and drain. Add mushrooms and onions and continue cooking for 5 minutes. Drain. Set aside to cool 10 minutes. Stir together sausage mixture, cheese cubes, and bread cubes. Place in greased 8-inch square baking dish. Beat milk and eggs and pour over sausage mixture. Cover. Refrigerate for several hours or overnight. Preheat oven to 350°. Remove cover. Bake 50 to 55 minutes or until golden brown. Let stand 10 minutes before serving. Serves 6. (Adapted from Velveeta cheese ad.)

Macaroni and Egg Salad

6 hard-cooked eggs, chopped

2 c. cooked, drained, and cooled elbow macaroni (about $^3/_4$ c. uncooked)

$^1/_2$ c. chopped carrots

$^1/_2$ c. chopped celery

$^1/_2$ c. thawed frozen peas

$^1/_3$ c. thinly sliced green onion

$^3/_4$ c. cottage cheese

$^1/_4$ c. plain yogurt

2 T. grated Parmesan cheese

1 T. prepared mustard

1 t. lemon juice

$^3/_4$ t. celery salt

$^1/_2$ t. dried marjoram

$^1/_2$ t. ground pepper

In large mixing bowl combine eggs, macaroni, and vegetables. Toss lightly until thoroughly mixed. Measure remaining ingredients into blender container and process until smooth. Stir into egg-macaroni mixture until moistened throughout. Chill. Serves 6 as a main dish salad.

Rice Primavera

1 c. sliced fresh mushrooms

$^1/_2$ c. sliced green onions

$^1/_2$ c. chopped celery

3 T. butter

3 c. water

$1^1/_2$ c. uncooked long grain white rice

5 t. instant chicken-flavored bouillon granules

$1^1/_2$ t. Italian seasoning (oregano, basil, etc.)

$^1/_2$ c. grated Parmesan cheese

$^1/_2$ c. chopped red bell pepper

$^1/_2$ c. frozen green peas

$^1/_2$ c. shredded carrot

In large saucepan cook mushrooms, onions, and celery in butter. Add water, rice, bouillon, and Italian seasoning. Bring all to boil. Reduce heat, cover, and simmer for 25 minutes. Add cheese, pepper, peas, and carrot. Cook 5 minutes more or until rice is tender and liquid is absorbed. Serves 8–10. (Adapted from Wyler's bouillon ad.)

Bavarian Party Dip and Spread

¹/₂ c. minced green onions
1 T. butter
1 lb. Braunschweiger sausage
3 oz. cream cheese
¹/₄ t. black pepper

Sauté onions in butter for 8–10 minutes, stirring frequently. Remove from heat and drain. Remove casing from sausage and mix meat with cream cheese until smooth. Mix in onion and pepper. Serve as a spread on crackers or thin-sliced party rye bread, or as a dip accompanied by fresh raw vegetables such as carrots, celery, broccoli florets, radishes, cauliflower, and cherry tomatoes. (Adapted from Kahn's Braunschweiger label.)

Lettuce

One of the easiest vegetables to grow is leaf lettuce, especially the variety Black Seeded Simpson. When producing, it is so abundant that one is hard-pressed to use all of it unless one learns to use lettuce in ways other than in salads or sandwiches.

In addition to Black Seeded Simpson, which flourishes only in cool weather and then bolts, like spinach, many gardeners are planting Bibb lettuce for its beautiful dark green leaves held loosely together. Oakleaf lettuce and curly endive or chicory have met with some popularity as well. The latter tends to be somewhat bitter, so a little goes a long way when added to other greens. Arugula, ceriola, radicchio, mâche, sorrel, and mustard greens are now coming into favor. The home gardener is able to experiment with these out-of-the-ordinary greens. All of these lettuces are more nutritious than the traditional head of iceberg lettuce, transported for hundreds of miles and stored for months before reaching the salad bar.

In the South Dakota Hutterite Mennonite community where I grew up, the spring "Salat" was invariably made with a 3-gallon milk pail of leaf lettuce well picked over (considered child's work), well washed, doused with fresh cream (sometimes directly from the cream separator spout), flavored with vinegar, salt, and sugar, and garnished with sliced hard cooked eggs. When I became a city dweller, the fresh cream gave way to cultured sour cream or yogurt mixed with mayonnaise-type salad dressing, and flavorings included sliced green onions and sliced radishes (red or white). Sometimes it was served with thin slices of ham (cut julienne-style) and homemade croutons and sprinkled with Parmesan cheese.

Caesar salad *aficionados* are steering clear of undercooked eggs in the dressing because of the danger of salmonella poisoning. Instead they are turning to commercially prepared Caesar dressing and adding anchovies and sesame seed to the romaine lettuce.

Lettuce and Strawberries Salad

2 heads Bibb lettuce or other firm leaf lettuce, such as romaine
2 c. fresh strawberries
1/2 sweet onion or 1/2 c. green onions, diced
1/4 lb. feta cheese
Strawberry Vinaigrette Dressing (recipe follows)
1/4 c. toasted almond slices

Wash lettuce in cool water and pat dry. Tear into bite-size pieces. Put in bowl, cover with cloth, and refrigerate until ready to serve.

At serving time, add whole or quartered strawberries and thin-sliced onions. Sprinkle top with crumbled feta cheese.

Add just enough dressing to coat greens. Toss to mix. Sprinkle each serving with toasted almond slices. Serves 4 to 6.

Strawberry Vinaigrette Dressing

1/2 c. strawberry vinegar (or balsamic or red wine vinegar in which strawberries
have been steeped)
2 T. honey
1 t. minced chives
1/8 t. salt
1/8 t. pepper
3 T. olive oil

Combine vinegar, honey, chives, salt, and pepper. Mix well. Gradually whisk in oil.

Wilted Lettuce

6 c. leaf lettuce
2 hard-cooked eggs, diced
4 slices bacon
1/3 c. chopped onion

2 T. sugar
1/2 t. salt
3 T. cider vinegar
6 radishes, thinly sliced

Wash lettuce, drain well, pat dry, and tear into bite-size pieces. Place in salad bowl. Add diced egg. Cook bacon until crisp in microwave and drain off fat. Crumble bacon into lettuce mixture. In the drippings sauté onion. Add sugar, salt, and vinegar. Heat until boiling. Pour dressing over lettuce and toss to coat. Add radishes for garnish. Serves 4.

Lettuce with Croutons

1½ c. cubed white or brown bread
2 T. oil or butter
2 cloves garlic, minced
½ t. salt
½ t. dry mustard
freshly ground pepper to taste

2 T. wine vinegar
¼ c. salad oil
5 to 6 c. fresh torn mixed lettuces,
　　whatever is available
Parmesan or Romano cheese, grated

Sauté lightly or brown in oven the cubed bread in oil. Set aside.

Combine in salad bowl the minced garlic, salt, dry mustard, ground pepper, wine vinegar, and oil. Set aside. When ready to serve, add freshly torn green lettuces. Toss and serve. Sprinkle with croutons and cheese.

When the lettuce crop has been abundant and your family has tired of lettuce salad at every meal, try using it in soup and casseroles.

Lettuce Soup

1 lb. leaf lettuce (such as Black Seeded
　　Simpson, just before it bolts)
2 T. butter
1 T. grated onion

2 T. flour
4 c. milk or chicken stock
¾ t. salt or to taste
¼ t. paprika

Clean and wash lettuce. Place in covered saucepan with moisture clinging to lettuce leaves. Cook over low heat for about 6 minutes. Drain excess water and purée in blender.

Melt butter in saucepan. Add onion and sauté for 3 minutes. Stir in the flour and cook until blended. Gradually add milk or stock. Add seasonings, then lettuce. Heat soup well and serve with grated Parmesan cheese. Serves 4.

Lettuce and Rice

4 slices cured bacon, diced
½ c. chopped onion
½ c. chopped green pepper
3 c. shredded lettuce

1 c. cooked rice
2 c. canned tomatoes
salt and pepper to taste

Cook bacon until crisp, drain off excess fat, and add onion and green pepper. Sauté until tender. Add lettuce and cook lightly, until lettuce is wilted. Add rice and tomatoes and cook until heated through. Add seasonings to taste. Serves 4–6, depending upon appetites. This dish is a fine accompaniment to cold sliced ham. It is even better when served with hot crusty bread.

Stir-Fried Lettuce

2 T. olive oil
1 piece (1 inch) ginger root, peeled, grated, or sliced thin
1 clove garlic, minced
6 c. mixed lettuces (Bibb, Belgian endive, or whatever is available)
1 T. soy sauce
1 T. sesame seeds

Heat oil in wok or deep skillet over medium heat. Add ginger root and garlic. Stir for 10 seconds. Add lettuces and turn them quickly to mix with the oil. Cook and turn until wilted, depending upon the "structural integrity" of the lettuces, but no longer than 2 minutes. Turn into warm serving bowl, toss with soy sauce, and sprinkle with sesame seeds. Serves 4.

Mint

Like chard, mint in the home garden may be enjoyed for three seasons. However, we are considering it a product of spring, when its first flavorful leaves appear to delight our palates.

There are many different kinds of mint, both wild and cultivated. We have two varieties in our garden: the spearmint, with its narrow, slightly toothed, shiny leaves; and the peppermint, with its much stronger smell and flavor. The spearmint is preferred in the home garden, for it is most often used in mint sauces, jellies, and as a dried herb. The peppermint is good for herbal tea, as an aid to digestion. We thank our son Jon for planting it south of the garage, where it has flourished beyond our wildest hopes (and desires)! Often farm women in dry western areas plant it beneath the pump or hydrant, where it will always get watered.

Minty Lamb Burgers

1 lb. ground lamb
1 small onion, coarsely grated
1 t. finely minced garlic
1/4 c. chopped fresh mint

salt and freshly ground pepper to taste
4 toasted hamburger buns
4 tomato slices
1/3 c. plain yogurt for garnish, if desired

Mix ground lamb with onion, garlic, and chopped mint. Season to taste. Form into 4 patties. Pan fry, grill over hot coals, or broil on high for about 4 minutes per side. Serve lamb patties immediately on toasted buns topped with tomato slice and dollop of yogurt, if desired. Garnish with sprig of fresh mint. Serves 4.

Minty Chicken Curry

2 T. cooking oil

1 medium onion

1 piece (1-inch) peeled and minced fresh ginger root

1 clove garlic, minced

1 medium green bell pepper

$1/2$ c. chopped celery

1 T. curry powder (or more, if desired)

1 t. cumin powder

2 medium tomatoes or unpeeled red apples

2 c. cooked chicken, bones, skin, and fat removed

2 c. defatted chicken broth

1 c. plain yogurt

3 c. cooked white or brown rice

$1/2$ c. chopped fresh mint

$1/4$ c. golden or brown raisins

$1/4$ c. toasted slivered almonds (optional)

8 fresh mint sprigs for garnish

Heat oil in heavy frying pan. Add onions, ginger, garlic, bell pepper, and celery. Sauté over low heat for 5 minutes. Sprinkle with curry powder and cumin. Cook for 1 minute, stirring constantly. Add tomatoes or apples (chopped) and chicken pieces. Add chicken broth and cook for 10 minutes slowly. Place yogurt in small bowl and slowly whisk in 1 T. of the liquid from curry mixture. Gradually stir it back into the curry. Heat through but do not boil. Stir in chopped mint. Serve over rice. Sprinkle with raisins and almonds, if desired. Garnish with mint sprigs. Serves 4.

Minted Citrus Carrots

juice of 1 medium orange

juice of 1 medium lemon

$1/4$ c. freshly chopped mint

$1/8$ t. freshly ground pepper

3 large carrots, peeled and shredded

In a small bowl, whisk juices, mint, and pepper together. Toss with shredded carrots and refrigerate. Serve cold. Serves 4. (From Ariana Kaufman, my grand-daughter, at age 10.)

White Bean Salad

1 lb. Great Northern beans

1 medium onion, quartered

1 carrot, quartered

1 rib celery, quartered

1 small ham bone or $1/4$-lb. bacon

1 clove garlic, crushed

Dressing (recipe follows)

1 t. pepper

$1^1/4$ c. chopped green bell pepper

1 medium onion, thinly sliced

$1^1/2$ c. chopped, loosely packed mint leaves

Soak beans in cold water overnight. Discard soaking liquid. Place beans in large pot with quartered onion, carrot, celery, ham bone and 1 crushed clove garlic. Add enough cold water to fill pot half full. Bring to a boil, lower heat and simmer 1 to 1½ hours or until beans are tender. Drain and save cooking liquid and onion, carrot, celery, and ham bone for bean soup at a later time.

When ready to serve the salad, put cooked and drained beans in serving dish. Add coarsely chopped green pepper, onions, and fresh mint. Pour dressing over beans and toss to blend. Serve at room temperature.

(For a quicker meal, use two 16 oz. cans or jars of Great Northern beans. Drain in a colander and rinse under stream of cool water to remove canning liquid. Proceed as with cooked beans.)

Dressing for White Bean Salad

1 clove garlic
1 t. coarse salt (kosher)
³/₄ c. oil
¹/₄ c. white wine vinegar
¹/₂ t. sugar

Crush garlic with teaspoon of coarse salt. Put garlic in a jar with oil, vinegar, sugar, and black pepper. Shake to mix well.

New Potatoes with Peas and Mint

3 lbs. small new red potatoes, unpeeled
1¹/₂ c. fresh shelled peas (or frozen peas, defrosted)
¹/₂ c. sour cream
¹/₂ c. mayonnaise
1 T. freshly grated lemon zest (colored portion of rind)
¹/₂ c. finely chopped fresh mint
salt and freshly ground pepper to taste
lettuce leaves, washed and patted dry
mint sprigs for garnish

Microwave potatoes in ¹/₂ c. water in microwave-safe casserole (covered) for 7 minutes or until just tender when pierced. Drain water and allow to air dry. When potatoes are slightly cooled, cut into chunks.

Cook peas in lightly salted boiling water just until tender, drain, and air dry.

Whisk together sour cream and mayonnaise in mixing bowl. Add lemon zest, mint, salt, and pepper.

Toss dressing together with potatoes and peas. Refrigerate for 2 or more hours.

Serve on lettuce leaves in large shallow bowl, garnishing with mint sprigs. Serves 8.

Cabbage and Mint Slaw

4 c. finely shredded cabbage
$^1/_2$ t. salt
6 green onions, chopped, using most of green tops
$^1/_2$ c. fresh mint leaves, chopped
freshly ground black pepper to taste
$^1/_2$ c. mayonnaise-type bottled slaw dressing, such as Marzetti's

Mix all ingredients together in large bowl and refrigerate overnight. Serve on lettuce leaves. Serves 6–8.
Variation: Add 1 raw red apple, diced.

Minted Mixed Melon Champagne Compote

12 c. mixed melon balls (fresh or frozen)
1 c. lightly packed fresh mint leaves thinly sliced
3 T. sugar, superfine
3 T. brandy
3 c. chilled champagne
fresh mint sprigs

Mix first 4 ingredients in punch bowl and refrigerate 30 minutes. Spoon fruit mixture into dessert goblets. Pour champagne over fruit. Garnish with mint sprigs. Serves 12 at dessert buffet. (From Woodbury Vineyards, Dunkirk, New York.)

Mint Tea

8 leafy sprigs fresh mint
boiling water

sugar to taste
mint sprigs for garnish if served over ice

Place mint leaves in a large teapot. Cover with boiling water. Add sugar. Serve hot or cold over ice, garnished with mint sprig.

Peppermint Tea

2 rounded t. chopped peppermint, fresh or dried (instructions follow)
1 c. boiling water

Put chopped peppermint in small pot. Pour on boiling water. Cover and infuse for 7 minutes. Strain into cup.

To Dry Peppermint

Cut stems of mint and tie into small bundles. Hang them upside down in a warm, airy kitchen. When dry and crisp, strip the leaves from the stalks and crumble them into screw-top jars. Store away from light.

To Dry Peppermint (Alternate Method)

Peppermint may be dried overnight in a gas range oven with a pilot light by laying the stalks on a paper-lined baking sheet. By morning the leaves will be dry enough to strip off the stalks and put into jars.

Mint Ice Cubes

4 c. water
1 c. sugar
24 mint leaves

Boil water and sugar 5 minutes and cool. Press each mint leaf between fingers to release essence and place 1 in each compartment of ice cube trays. Pour sugar water mixture over each leaf and freeze. Use cubes in regular or mint-flavored iced teas. Tea will become sweeter and mintier as cubes melt. Yields 2 trays or 24 cubes.

Mint Julep

1 T. chilled Simple Syrup (recipe follows)
2 to 4 sprigs fresh mint
crushed ice
3 oz. bourbon (6 T.)
powdered sugar
lemon slice
fresh mint sprig

Pour simple syrup into bottom of a 10-ounce glass. Add mint and crush with back of spoon. Fill glass with crushed ice. Add bourbon and stir gently. Add more crushed ice to fill glass. Top with sprinkling of powdered sugar. Garnish with lemon slice and mint sprig. Makes 1 large drink.

Simple Syrup

Add 1 c. sugar to 1 c. boiling water. Stir until sugar is dissolved. Chill thoroughly.

Mint Jelly

This makes a handsome Christmas gift when accompanied by something red (cranberry relish, for example).

1 big bunch (handful) of mint
2 lbs. windfall green apples (full of pectin)
5 c. water
juice of 1 lemon
4 T. finely chopped mint leaves
2 c. sugar
green coloring (optional)

Thoroughly wash mint. Wash apples and cut into quarters but do not peel or core. Put mint, apples, water, and lemon juice in large saucepan and bring to a boil. Cover and cook gently until apples are soft.

Drip through a jelly bag or double thickness of muslin for 2–3 hours or overnight.

Measure liquid into steel pan. To each 2½ c. liquid, add 2 c. sugar. Bring slowly to boil, stirring until sugar is dissolved. Stir in finely chopped mint leaves. Boil rapidly for 15 minutes, until liquid jells when dripped onto cold saucer. Skim and add two drops of green coloring, if desired. Pour into sterilized jelly glasses and seal. Good served with lamb.

Variations: Ripe crab apples may be used with powdered pectin, following the recipe in the box. For a "pulpier" jelly, strain rather than drip the liquid through a jelly bag. Also, vinegar may be substituted for the lemon juice if a stronger flavor is desired, with lamb, for example.

Mint Sauce

Makes a good Easter gift to serve with leg or breast of lamb.

1 c. cider vinegar
1 c. water
½ c. honey
¼ c. dried mint leaves

Combine vinegar, water, and honey. Bring to boil. Add mint leaves, cover, and let steep 5 minutes. Put into bottles. Makes 2½ cups. Serve with lamb.

Yogurt-Mint Marinade

1 c. plain yogurt
¼ c. minced fresh mint leaves
2 T. oil
1 T. lemon juice

1 T. minced green onion
1 t. honey
1 t. salt

In shallow dish with cover combine all ingredients. Use to marinate meat (such as beef or lamb) in refrigerator overnight before grilling for shish kebab or shashlik (lamb on sticks).

Golden Tea Spritz

1 quart boiling water
4 T. instant tea
¹/₂ t. dried mint (crushed) or 6 sprigs crushed fresh mint
12 whole cloves
1 c. sugar
1 quart cold water
¹/₂ c. lemon juice
2 lemons, thinly sliced
24 oz. bottled carbonated water, chilled
1 pint lemon sherbet

Pour boiling water over tea, mint, cloves, and sugar. Let stand 5 minutes. Strain. Add water, lemon juice, and lemon slices. Refrigerate. When ready to serve, pour in carbonated water. Add scoops of sherbet. Makes 18 servings from punch bowl or pitcher.

Tabbouleh

¹/₂ c. cracked bulgar wheat
¹/₄ c. finely chopped fresh mint leaves
¹/₂ c. finely chopped parsley leaves*
¹/₂ c. chopped green onions with tops
1 medium tomato,** chopped
3 T. olive oil
4 T. lemon juice or juice of 2 lemons
¹/₂ t. salt
grinding of fresh pepper, to taste

Place cracked wheat in bowl and barely cover with boiling water. Let stand 30 minutes or until all water is absorbed. Wheat should be tender but firm to bite. If wheat is too dry, add a little more boiling water. If excessive water is added, drain and press the wheat. Let wheat cool thoroughly. Then mix with remaining ingredients. Refrigerate until ready to serve. Serves 6 when spooned onto lettuce leaves.

*Do not discard parsley stems but chop them fine and add to soups or sauces.
**When cucumbers, zucchini, and tomatoes are in season, add more tomatoes and other vegetables to the salad.

Mint as a Repellent

Fresh mint sprigs placed on a windowsill seem to reduce indoor fly population. Transplanting some of the herb to your cucumber patch results in fewer cucumber beetles. However, watch out because mint is very invasive and you could have another pest on your hands!

Mint as Medicine

Mint is a popular folk remedy for indigestion because it is thought to make belching easier by relaxing the muscle at the top of the stomach. Of all the remedies for an upset tummy, mint tea is probably one of the most pleasant.

Ten Other Uses for Mint

1. Add a few sprigs fresh mint to homemade apple sauce.
2. Add sprigs of fresh mint to glasses of iced tea.
3. Add sprigs of fresh mint to fruit or vegetable salads.
4. Add fresh mint leaves to cottage cheese salads.
5. Brew sun tea outdoors by placing several hands full of mint in large jar of water and setting it in the sun.
6. Sprinkle chopped mint over cooked vegetables such as green peas, buttered carrots, green beans and potatoes.
7. Add crumbled dry mint to dried-pea soup when serving it.
8. Add mint (fresh or dried) to Greek salad of lettuce, tomatoes, black olives and feta cheese in an oil and vinegar dressing.
9. Add mint to sour cream and/or yogurt for a vegetable dip.
10. Sprinkle fresh chopped or dried mint over the top of hummus (Middle East garbanzo bean or chickpea dip eaten with pita bread) before serving.

Mulberries

Thanks to the birds, mulberry trees are found all over the Midwest along fences and roadsides. The birds may think they have a monopoly on the fruit, but usually there is enough of the dark red to black or whitish-violet fruit to serve both birds and humans.

Unfortunately, many humans scorn mulberries, looking upon them as a scourge responsible for stained laundry and car hoods during the summer. This is the classic opportunity to "turn a lemon into lemonade."

Mulberry Juice Cocktail

1 c. ripe dark mulberries
1 t. lemon
1 t. honey
cold water or carbonated water, to taste
sprig of mint

Press mulberries through colander to extract juice. Add lemon and honey. Pour over ice in glass. Add cold water or carbonated water and serve with sprig of mint.

Mulberry Cobbler

4 c. mulberries
¹/₂ c. honey
2 t. lemon juice
³/₄ c. dry oatmeal
¹/₂ c. flour (white, whole wheat, or mixed)
¹/₂ c. butter

In buttered baking dish place mulberries, honey, and lemon juice. Combine oatmeal and flour. Cut in butter and sprinkle this mixture over the fruit mixture. Bake in preheated (375°) oven for 35 minutes. Serve warm with ice cream.
Variation: Sprinkle 1 t. cinnamon over top before baking.

Mulberry Muffins

1 c. dark mulberries
1 c. white flour
1 c. whole wheat flour
2 t. baking powder
¹/₂ t. salt
1 egg
¹/₂ c. milk
¹/₄ c. oil
¹/₂ c. honey

Combine dry ingredients. Mix wet ingredients in another bowl. Combine the liquid and dry ingredients, mixing only enough to moisten the dry ones. Fold in mulberries.

Fill 12 paper-lined muffin tins ²/₃ full and bake in preheated 400° oven for 20–25 minutes or until golden brown. Turn out of pan as soon as they are done. Best eaten while still warm.

Mulberry-Rhubarb Pie

pastry for 2 9-inch crusts   *³/₄ c. sugar*
2 c. mulberries, fresh or frozen*   *3 T. flour*
1 c. rhubarb, sliced

Combine all ingredients and pour into pie shell. Arrange top crust. Cut slits for steam to escape, seal and flute edges. Bake at 375° for 1 hour or until golden brown.

---

*To Freeze Mulberries: Simply shake from tree, sort, wash, drain, and freeze whole in plastic containers. Then, when the snow flies and you don't mind heating up your kitchen, you can bake a pie or cook up a batch of jam, as my sister Ruth Pollman does.

Mulberry-Rhubarb Jam

Shake dark ripe mulberries from tree by tapping lightly on the branch and catching on old sheets reserved for that purpose. If you have a mulberry tree like my Grandma Tieszen's, which produced berries an inch long, you won't have to shake long. Sheets may be laid on the ground or, if you have enough help, the sheets may be held under the branch to be shaken. Pick out leaves, twigs, green berries, or bird droppings before transferring mulberries from sheet to pan. When you have shaken desired amount, pour mulberries on stain-proof kitchen table or on paper-covered table. Carefully sort good berries from refuse. You need not stem the berries, because the tiny green stems will cook up. Do not be concerned about eating the seeds either, unless your doctor says you should be.

Wash berries in several baths of water, letting the refuse float to the top and removing it from the berries. Drain using a large sieve or colander. Purée cleaned berries in blender.

Measure carefully the pulp and sugar to be used for each jar of liquid pectin or box of powdered pectin, following the recipe for Strawberry-Rhubarb Jam. You will be surprised at how good the jam is! (This jam was a staple in my farm home in South Dakota, where the drought was often so severe that only wild plum, chokecherry, and mulberry trees survived. One year my sister Pearl was so ambitious that she preserved 8 gallons of the jam, according to my father's diaries, as recorded in my *Bread of Life: Diaries and Memories of a Dakota Family, 1936–1945.*)

Mulberry Jam Sweetheart Cookies

2¹/₂ c. sifted all-purpose flour   *1 egg*
1 t. baking powder   *1 t. vanilla*
¹/₂ t. salt   *1 c. uncooked oatmeal*
³/₄ c. soft butter   *Mulberry-Rhubarb Jam (see recipe*
³/₄ c. sugar   *above)*
2 T. milk   *confectioners' sugar (optional)*

Sift flour, baking powder, and salt into bowl. Add soft butter, sugar, milk, egg, and vanilla. Beat until well blended. Stir in oatmeal. Knead to form a bowl. Chill in refrigerator or freezer.

Divide dough in half and roll out each half to ¼-inch thickness on board or canvas sprinkled with confectioners' sugar or flour. Cut into heart or other shapes.

For peek-a-boo cookies, cut a design in the middle of half the cookies. Place plain cookies on a lightly greased cookie sheet. Top each plain cookie with a teaspoon of Mulberry-Rhubarb Jam. Cover with a cutout cookie and seal or flute edges.

Bake at 375° about 15 minutes. Yields 2 dozen peek-a-boo cookies.

Mulberry Jam Bars

Follow recipe above for cookies. Instead of rolling out the dough, crumble half of it into bottom of greased 8 x 14-inch baking pan. Pat down firmly. Spread Mulberry-Rhubarb Jam (recipe above) over the cookie crumb layer in pan (1 c. to 1½ c. jam, or enough to cover). Sprinkle remaining cookie crumb dough over top of jam layer. Bake at 375° for 20–25 minutes or until crumb dough is golden and jam begins to bubble up along sides. Cool on wire rack and cut into squares. Serve cold or warm with whipped topping or ice cream. Serves 10 to 12.

Parsley

Because parsley is a biennial and may be kept as a perennial if the flower stalks are cut when they appear, we assume you will have parsley in your garden in spring. However, if you are planting it for the first time in the spring (and it is a good idea to sow some every spring), you will wait patiently for it to germinate. In that respect it is like the carrot, its cousin. Because of its late germination, it is a good idea to start some indoors and, if planting seed outdoors, to mark the row by seeding radishes "sparsely with the parsley" and pulling the radishes as they mature.

Parsley may also be seeded outdoors in late fall. Then, in late summer, you can "pot up" young plants for wintertime use from a sunny windowsill. Just be careful not to overwater the plants.

Parsley is an excellent source of potassium. In addition, it contains a lot of chlorophyl, making it a natural breath freshener, especially after onions and garlic. Therefore, *never* think of parsley only as a garnish to be left on the platter or on your plate. Furthermore, parsley is rich in vitamin C, three times richer than orange juice. So, when you run out of that favorite breakfast drink, serve parsley with your morning eggs!

Like mint, parsley is such an all-around flavor enhancer that it is good with almost every food, with the exception of fruits and sweets.

Parsley is best when used fresh. But if you have an oversupply and wish to dry it for winter use, hang it upside down in a room with warm circulating air or place it in a gas oven with a pilot light. However, there is a better way of preserving the fresh taste and color of parsley. Freeze it!

Freezing Parsley

If you have a large supply of parsley, freeze it (chopped, minus stems) in an ice cube tray. Remove the cubes to a plastic bag and store in the freezer until needed. One cube is the right amount for a hamburger or 2-egg omelet.

Fresh parsley may also be frozen by itself by submerging sprigs of parsley head down in each section of the ice cube tray before the cubes turn to ice. They may then be stored in a plastic bag in the freezer.

Gremolata (Parsley Sauce)

1/4 c. finely chopped fresh parsley
1 t. minced garlic (or more or less, to taste)
1 T. finely grated lemon zest

Combine all ingredients and sprinkle on broiled fish about 5 minutes before it is done, or spread a bit on an omelet before adding the filling and folding. Mix it with mayonnaise for a sandwich spread or serve as a topping for baked potatoes.

Blender Parsley Sauce

2 c. parsley sprigs
1 small dill pickle
2 T. chopped chives

1/3 c. mayonnaise
1/3 c. sour cream

Put all ingredients in blender container. Cover and blend until parsley is chopped and sauce is green. Turn into a small saucepan and heat over low heat, stirring occasionally, about 2 to 3 minutes. Serve over hot cooked vegetables such as asparagus, chard, shelled peas or Sugar Snaps, or radishes. Makes 3/4 cup.

There are many varieties of parsley, but the two most popular are the curled parsley, seen most often as a garnish, and the Italian parsley, with flat leaves, preferred in spaghetti and other Italian dishes.

Spaghetti al Pesto

2 T. salt
4–6 quarts boiling water
1 lb. dried spaghetti (or other pasta)
2 c. firmly packed Italian (flat) parsley
  leaves
2 T. fresh basil leaves
3 cloves garlic

3/4 c. olive oil
3 T. butter
1/2 c. freshly grated Romano cheese
1/2 c. freshly grated Parmesan cheese
11/2 t. salt
1/4 t. pepper

Add 2 T. salt to rapidly boiling water. Gradually add spaghetti so that water continues to boil. Cook, uncovered, stirring occasionally until *al dente* (firm to the bite). Drain in colander.

While pasta is cooking, combine remaining ingredients in blender. Blend at high speed until mixture looks almost like a paste but with some specks of parsley still visible. Toss with drained spaghetti until it is completely coated.

Green Rice

2 c. hot cooked rice
1 c. grated Cheddar cheese
1 c. chopped parsley
1/4 c. oil

2 c. canned evaporated milk
1 onion, grated
1 clove garlic, minced
1 t. salt

Mix cheese with hot rice. Add remaining ingredients, mixing thoroughly. Bake in greased casserole at 350° for 45 minutes.

(This is a "complete" dish because the cheese and milk make it a high-protein although meatless meal. Using brown rice will make it even more nutritious. From Noma Genne, Hyde Park Union Church, Chicago.)

Cold Green Sauce

1 c. mayonnaise
1/2 c. sour cream
2 small dill pickles (or 1 large)
3 c. parsley leaves

Whirl ingredients in blender until finely chopped and sauce is green. Store in airtight refrigerator jar. Serve with fish or roast beef or on sliced tomatoes, cold hard-cooked eggs, or boiled potatoes. Makes 2 cups.

Variation: Dill and chives may be used to make up some of the 3 cups of "green."

Parsley Raita

1 c. fresh parsley, chopped
1/2 t. salt
pinch cayenne pepper

2 T. minced green onion
2 1/2 c. plain yogurt

Crush parsley with mortar and pestle to release essential juice of parsley. Add salt and pepper. Let mixture sit for a few minutes. Add onion and yogurt. Let raita mellow for 1/2 hour in refrigerator and serve very cold as accompaniment to curries or lentils and rice. Fresh sliced tomatoes may also be added to this favorite Indian "salad."

Parsley Butter

2 T. chopped parsley leaves
1 stick softened butter
1 t. lemon juice

Add parsley to softened butter and lemon juice. Use over any hot vegetable. Store in covered dish in refrigerator.

Peapods

One of my fondest memories from childhood is picking the first Tiny Marvel green peas and eating them fresh out of hand. My sister Ruth and I sometimes had "picnics" under the trees with a gallon can of peapods. A less fond memory is the laborious shelling of peas so that our entire farm family might have the spring delicacy of new potatoes and creamed peas. You see, we did not know about the Chinese snow peas and Drs. Lamborn and Park of Twin Falls, Idaho, who later developed the Sugar Snap Pea by crossing a regular snow pea with a one-in-a-million mutant shell pea plant.

Thanks to the good doctors, almost anyone with a trellis or a woven wire fence can grow Sugar Snap peas with ease. Sugar Snaps, like snow peas, flourish in cool, damp weather and may be eaten raw and cooked or frozen for later use.

Sugar Snaps are fatter than snow peas and have strings which are easily pulled off. To prepare for freezing, string them and then blanch in boiling water for 2 or 3 minutes. Then chill in ice water for 3 to 5 minutes. After blanching, lay pods separately on trays and freeze immediately. When they are thoroughly frozen, package them in small plastic bags or containers to seal and freeze further. After Sugar Snaps have been frozen, use them only in cooked dishes.

However, when the Sugar Snaps are fresh, you will want to enjoy them raw on party trays with dips, in salads and as a snack. They make a perfect vegetable to pack in a lunch pail for a finicky eater. Hardly anyone can resist the crunchy peapod.

Sugar Snap Dip

¹/₂ lb. (about 30 pods) fresh Sugar Snaps
1 c. sour cream or plain yogurt
4 green onions, sliced with some of green tops
¹/₄ t. powdered ginger
1 t. Worcestershire sauce

String all of the snap peas. Combine other ingredients and arrange peapods on platter radiating out from center of bowl of dip.

Snap Pea Stir-Fry

2 c. Sugar Snap peas (8 oz.)
2 T. soy sauce
1 t. cornstarch
$^1/_3$ c. water
2 T. cooking sherry
1 t. sugar
1 T. oil

Remove strings from snap peas. In a small bowl blend soy sauce with cornstarch. Stir in water, sherry, and sugar. Set aside. In wok or skillet, heat oil. Stir-fry peas, lifting with spatula in an up-and-over motion, about 2 minutes or until crisply tender. Stir soy mixture and add to wok. Cook and stir until thickened and bubbly. Serve over rice.

Variations: Snap peas may be sautéd with green onions, fresh mushrooms, almonds, or red bell pepper strips. Flavor with soy sauce and serve over rice.

Green Pea Soup

This is a good recipe for those who still grow conventional peas, for it utilizes some of the pods as well as the peas.

2 lbs. green peas in pod
1 onion
$^1/_4$ c. butter
sprig of mint
sprig of parsley
1 quart chicken stock

salt to taste
peppercorns to taste
1 T. flour
$^1/_2$ c. half and half or evaporated milk
chopped mint

Shell and wash peas. Select $^1/_4$ of the best pods and wash. Sauté peas and sliced onion in butter. Add pods, mint and parsley sprigs, chicken stock, salt, and peppercorns. Simmer gently until peas are tender, 25–30 minutes. Remove mint and parsley sprigs and strain the soup. Return soup to pan.

Mix flour smoothly with the half and half. Add to soup and bring to a boil for 1 to 2 minutes. Correct the seasoning. Add extra evaporated milk if desired. Top with chopped mint just before serving.

When my husband had a sabbatical in Berkeley during the early 1980s we sampled a lot of Chinese cooking in San Francisco. Amazingly to us, peapods were rarely included in Chinese cooking there. He considered snow peas essential to a Chinese dinner, and finally rebelled when one lunch consisted entirely of various fungi.

Snow peas, also called Chinese peapods, are very versatile. Their crisp texture makes them perfect for salads.

Snow Pea and Mushroom Salad

$^1/_4$ lb. snow peas, stem end removed
$^1/_4$ lb. fresh mushrooms, sliced thin
2 T. soy sauce
1 t. sugar
2 t. sesame seed oil

Blanch stemmed snow peas in boiling salted water for 2 to 3 minutes. Drain and cool by running cold stream of water over them in colander. Toss with mushrooms. In another bowl mix soy sauce, sugar, and oil until sugar is dissolved. Chill vegetables and dressing separately until ready to serve. Toss chilled dressing with salad just before serving.

Snow Peas in Basil Vinaigrette

2 T. lime juice
2 T. balsamic vinegar
2 green onions, sliced thin
3 T. olive oil
1 clove garlic, minced
1 T. chopped fresh basil
$^1/_4$ t. salt
freshly ground pepper
1$^1/_2$ lbs. snow peas, trimmed
$^1/_4$ c. toasted sliced almonds

Combine lime juice and vinegar in small bowl. Add green onions and let steep 5 minutes. Whisk in oil, garlic, basil, salt, and pepper. Set aside.

Bring to boil 3 qts. water. Add snow peas. Stir once. Cook $^1/_2$ minute. Drain and cool under cold water. Drain.

Toss with vinaigrette and almonds just before serving. May be served hot or cold.

Coleslaw with Snow Peas

$^1/_3$ c. salad oil
3 T. cider vinegar
1 T. Dijon mustard
2 t. sugar
1$^1/_4$ t. celery seed
1 t. salt
$^1/_4$ t. ground black pepper

1 large red pepper
1 large green pepper
1 large carrot
$^1/_2$ lb. snow peas
1 small head green cabbage (about 1$^1/_2$ lbs.)

In large bowl whisk oil, vinegar, mustard, sugar, celery seed, salt, and pepper. Set aside.

Cut peppers into thin strips. Grate carrot. Cut peapods diagonally in half. Slice cabbage thin with sharp knife or on a cabbage cutter. (Do not use bitter core.)

Add vegetables to dressing in bowl and toss to coat well. Refrigerate covered to blend flavors. Serves 8.

Pasta Salad with Snow Peas

1 lb. mostaccioli or rigatoni pasta,
    uncooked
1/2 c. oil
1/2 t. dill seed, lightly crushed with
    pestle and mortar
1/2 t. red pepper flakes
salt and black pepper to taste

1 green bell pepper, sliced thin
2 small yellow summer squash, sliced
    thin
2 c. snow peas, blanched
1 c. sliced mushrooms
8 green onions, sliced thin
1/2 c. red wine vinegar

Cook pasta *al dente* and drain. While still warm, toss with 9 T. of the oil and the spices in large bowl.

Heat remaining 3 T. oil in large skillet. Sauté peppers until crisply tender, about 4 minutes. Add to pasta.

Combine remaining vegetables with pasta. Sprinkle red wine vinegar over top, toss well, and refrigerate until serving time. Serves 4 as main dish.

Peas

My neighbor, Rory Walsh, announced to her mother last June as they were munching peas at a nearby U-Pick farm that among the vegetables she would grow in her garden when she grew up would be peas! How wonderful to think of an adolescent already planning her vegetable garden. May she find unending pleasure in her gardening.

This tiny legume is popular worldwide and a good source of protein. Whether it is eaten canned (a preference of older people who grew up with the canned-pea taste), frozen (an early association with Birds-Eye), or dried, the pea is the world's leading processed vegetable, according to the Produce Marketing Association. But for my money, the fresh pea just popped out of its pod can't be beat in terms of flavor and texture.

Crunchy Pea Salad

1¹/₂ c. fresh peas (shelled)
1 c. diced celery
1 c. chopped cauliflower
¹/₄ c. sliced green onion
1 c. cashews
¹/₂ c. sour cream
1 c. "ranch" dressing

Combine all ingredients. Chill before serving on lettuce leaves. Garnish with bacon bits, if desired. (Adapted from Hidden Valley Ranch Dressing ad.)

Peas and Radishes

3 c. shelled peas (from approximately 2¹/₂ lbs. fresh peas)
¹/₄ c. mayonnaise
1 T. chopped parsley
1 T. tarragon vinegar
³/₄ t. salt
¹/₈ t. pepper
²/₃ c. radishes
lettuce leaves

Microwave shelled peas in microwave-safe casserole (covered) with 3 T. water on high for 8 minutes or until tender. Drain. Rinse under running cold water to cool.

While peas are cooking, mix mayonnaise, parsley, vinegar, salt, and pepper. Slice radishes.

Add peas and sliced radishes to mayonnaise mixture. Toss to coat. Cover and refrigerate.

Serve over lettuce leaves. Serves 6 as an accompanying salad.

Microwaved Peas and Radishes

1 c. shelled peas
1 c. radishes, sliced
2 T. water
¹/₂ c. milk
1 T. all-purpose flour

¹/₄ t. dried dillweed
¹/₈ t. salt
¹/₈ t. lemon pepper
fresh dill sprig (optional)

In microwave-safe casserole combine fresh peas and sliced radishes. Add water and zap on high for 5 to 7 minutes or until tender. Drain. Cover and keep warm.

In 2-cup glass measuring cup combine milk, flour, dried dillweed, salt, and lemon pepper. Microwave, uncovered, on high for $1^1/_2$ to $2^1/_2$ minutes or until bubbly, stirring every half minute. Stir into hot vegetables. Top with fresh dill sprig. Serves 4 as a side dish.

Chilled Dilly Pea Soup

2 c. fresh shelled peas
2 green onions, sliced
2 c. defatted chicken broth
$^1/_2$ t. dried dillweed
1 c. plain yogurt or sour cream
yogurt, sour cream, or green onion for garnish

In a microwave-safe casserole combine peas, sliced onions, $^1/_4$ c. of the chicken broth, and dillweed. Zap on high (covered) for 8 to 10 minutes or until tender. Do not drain. Uncover and cool slightly before adding remaining chicken broth.

In a blender process pea mixture until smooth. Transfer to bowl and cover to chill.

At serving time, blend in the cup of yogurt or sour cream. Garnish each serving with additional yogurt, sour cream and/or green onion slices. Serves 4 as a side dish.

Radishes

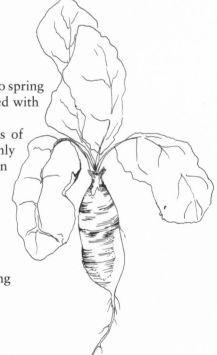

Often considered only a garnish or a bright addition to spring salad, radishes may be cooked as a vegetable and served with cream sauce or may be added to stir-fry.

Nothing is cheerier than harvesting new red globes of radishes from the early garden. However, they like only cool, damp weather and soon burst their globes or turn pithy. So radishes must be watched carefully and harvested at their prime. They do keep well in the refrigerator, however, if the leaves are removed and they are stored in plastic bags. Do not store them in water, since the water will leach the minerals and vitamins out of the radishes.

It is noteworthy that radishes may be cooked according to any recipe for turnips.

Radish Coleslaw

5 c. shredded cabbage
1/3 c. minced onion
1/2 c. diced celery
1 c. thinly sliced radishes

Combine ingredients in a large bowl several hours before serving, if possible. Just before serving, toss with salad dressing of choice. Serve at once. Serves 6.

Radish Tea Sandwiches

Spread thinly sliced party rye bread with cream cheese. Top with thin slices of radish marinated in mayonnaise. Garnish with parsley leaf.

Spring Salad Sandwich Topped with Vegetables

Spread dense, dark rye bread with mayonnaise. Spoon seasoned cottage cheese on bread and top with slices of cucumber and radishes. Garnish with green pepper strips.

Vegetables with Curried Yogurt Dipping Sauce

2/3 c. plain yogurt
1/3 c. sour cream
1 T. curry powder
1 t. salt
1 t. lemon juice
pepper to taste

Mix above ingredients in a small bowl and set in center of serving platter. Arrange raw vegetables such as radishes and peapods around the bowl and serve.

Cooked Radishes

Slice new, tender radishes or peel and slice older, larger radishes. Drop into boiling salted water to cover. Simmer, uncovered, 6 to 8 minutes or until tender. Drain, correct the seasoning, and serve with a cream sauce.

Cold Cream Sauce for Cooked Radishes

1 c. part-skim ricotta cheese
2 T. plain yogurt
¹/₄ t. salt

Combine cheese, yogurt, and salt in blender and whirl until the mixture is very smooth with no trace of graininess, about 1 minute. Scrape into a small bowl, cover, and refrigerate until ready to use.
Variation: Add ¹/₄ t. curry powder to cream sauce.

Sautéd Radishes and Green Onions with Ginger

2 T. ginger root
³/₄ lb. radishes
12 green onions
3 T. butter
salt and pepper to taste

Peel and grate ginger root to make 2 T. Thinly slice entire green onions. Heat butter in skillet and sauté white end of green onions for 2 minutes. Add ginger root and sauté for 1 minute. Slice radishes and add them to mixture. Sauté for 4 minutes. Season with salt and pepper. (Sliced green onion tops may be folded in after seasoning or reserved for use in another recipe.)

Curried Creamed Radishes

2 c. radishes, trimmed
1 T. butter
1 T. flour
¹/₄ t. curry powder
³/₄ c. milk
salt

Cut washed and trimmed radishes in half. Cover with water and cook, covered, for 10 minutes. Drain. Melt butter and stir in flour and curry powder. Add milk and cook, stirring, until thickened. Add radishes and heat. Season to taste with salt. Serves 4.

Radish Relish

1 lb. red radishes, cut in half	1 c. white vinegar
1 medium onion, quartered	3/4 c. sugar
1 medium carrot, cut into 1/2-inch pieces	3/4 c. water
2 T. whole allspice	1 t. mustard seed
1/4 t. whole cloves	1/2 t. salt

In food processor combine half the radishes, half the onion, and half the carrot pieces. Cover and process until finely chopped. Remove from processor and repeat with remaining vegetables.

Tie allspice and cloves in mesh bag. In microwave-safe casserole combine vegetables, spices, vinegar, sugar, water, mustard seed, and salt.

Microwave, covered, on high for 7 to 9 minutes or until boiling. Stir. Cook, covered, 7 more minutes or until vegetables are tender. Allow to cool, uncovered. Makes 1 qt. relish. Will keep in refrigerator for weeks or may be preserved by processing in clean half-pint jars for 15 minutes by hot water bath method, starting to time when the water boils. May be served chilled or at room temperature. A good accompaniment to all meats and poultry.

Pickled Radishes

When you have a bumper crop of radishes and are tired of using them in all other ways, pickle them for the winter.

1 T. pickling spice
1 c. cider vinegar
1/2 c. sugar
2 t. salt
3/4 c. water
5 cups red radishes

Tie pickling spice in mesh bag. In 2-quart saucepan over medium heat bring vinegar, sugar, salt, spices, and water to a boil. Reduce heat and simmer, covered, for 10 minutes to blend flavors. Meanwhile, trim stems from radishes. Cut large radishes in half. Place trimmed radishes in large bowl.

Pour hot vinegar mixture over radishes. Cover and refrigerate overnight. May be served from shallow relish bowl or processed in hot water bath in half-pint jars for 15 minutes, starting the timing after water boils.

Rhubarb

An excellent spring tonic, rhubarb keeps well when refrigerated or frozen. In recent years cooks have added less sugar when stewing rhubarb, so experiment with its effect on your taste buds. Never cook rhubarb in an aluminum pan. Stainless steel is best. To freeze, simply cut fresh rhubarb into pieces about a half inch long and freeze fresh in a heavy plastic bag. Then remove from the bag as much as you need for your recipe as you use it throughout the year. Rhubarb needs to be pulled for the stalks to be replenished, so pull away and prepare. Be careful not to eat the leaves, however, as they are poisonous. Just throw them on the compost pile!

Rhubarb-Strawberry Molded Salad

1 3-oz. package strawberry-flavored gelatin
1 c. boiling water
1 c. stewed rhubarb, sugared to taste
1 c. sliced fresh strawberries

Dissolve gelatin in boiling water. Stir until dissolved. When cooled, stir in stewed rhubarb. When gelatin begins to set, stir in strawberries. Pour into individual molds or glass refrigerator dish. Refrigerate until firm. Unmold individual molds onto lettuce leaf or cut individual servings and remove with spatula to leaf. Top with dab of mayonnaise and garnish with a whole strawberry.

Rhubarb-Vegetable Salad

3 c. diced rhubarb
1 ³/₄ c. water
¹/₂ c. sugar
1 3-oz. package lime gelatin
¹/₄ t. salt
2 T. chopped green pepper
¹/₂ c. finely shredded cabbage
1 c. chopped celery

Cook rhubarb in water for 5 minutes. Add sugar. Stir the mixture into gelatin. Add salt and vegetables. Pour all into individual oiled molds and chill until firm.

Rhubarb Dressing

³/₄ c. sugar

¹/₃ c. wine vinegar

1 T. onion juice

¹/₂ t. dry mustard or ground ginger

1 c. salad oil

1 c. Rhubarb Purée (recipe follows)

1 T. poppy seeds

salt and pepper to taste

Combine sugar, vinegar, onion juice, and mustard. Gradually add oil, beating until smooth. Beat in rhubarb purée and poppy seeds. Season with salt and pepper. Cover and chill until serving time. Serve over fresh fruit salad.

Rhubarb Purée

juice of 1 large orange

¹/₄ c. sugar

1 lb. rhubarb, chopped

Combine orange juice, sugar, and rhubarb in stainless steel or enameled saucepan. Cover and simmer 5 to 8 minutes or until rhubarb is tender. Purée in blender. Use 1 c. for dressing recipe above.

Rhubarb-Nut Bread

²/₃ c. oil

1 egg

1 c. sour milk (made by adding ¹/₂ t. lemon juice to sweet milk)

1 t. vanilla

1 t. baking soda

¹/₂ t. salt

2¹/₂ c. flour

1¹/₂ c. brown sugar, packed

1¹/₂ c. fresh rhubarb, diced

¹/₂ c. pecans, chopped

¹/₂ c. granulated sugar

1 t. cinnamon

Mix together oil, egg, milk, and vanilla. Stir together dry ingredients. Stir in rhubarb and pecans. Add oil mixture and stir to mix well.

Put into greased and floured 9 x 5-inch loaf pan. Combine ¹/₂ c. granulated sugar and cinnamon. Sprinkle this mixture on top of batter. Bake at 325° for 40 minutes. Let cool slightly before turning out and standing upright. (This bread keeps in the refrigerator for days and freezes well.)

Rhubarb Punch

To prepare rhubarb juice for punch: Pour 1 qt. boiling water over 2 c. tender rhubarb which has been washed and cut into small pieces but not peeled. Simmer 30 minutes or until tender. Let stand overnight in this juice. Next day drain and strain juice. For one quart of juice add ³/₄ c. sugar.

To make punch, use following recipe:

1 qt. rhubarb juice
3 c. pineapple-grapefruit drink
1 package cherry-flavored drink powder, mixed with appropriate amount of water, adjusting for amount of ice used

Combine. When ready to serve, add 2 c. lemon-lime soda or ginger ale.

Rhubarb-Strawberry Dessert

1 3-oz. package strawberry-flavored gelatin
1 c. boiling water
1 c. vanilla or strawberry ice cream

1 c. stewed rhubarb, flavored with sugar to taste
1 c. sliced fresh strawberries

Pour boiling water over gelatin and stir until dissolved. When cooled, beat in with rotary mixer the ice cream until frothy. Add rhubarb and strawberries. Pour into stemmed glasses and chill until firm in refrigerator. Before serving, place a dab of whipped topping on each dessert and garnish with a whole fresh strawberry. (This is a good way to use up ice cream which has been in the freezer a bit too long.)

Rhubarb Surprise Pie

Crust and Filling

1 c. flour
1 t. baking powder
¹/₂ t. salt
2 T. butter
1 beaten egg

2 T. milk
3 c. raw diced rhubarb
1 3-oz. package strawberry-flavored gelatin

Mix together flour, baking powder, salt, and butter. Add beaten egg and milk and mix well. Press mixture onto bottom and sides of greased 9-inch pie plate to form crust. Toss together the rhubarb and gelatin and fill crust with this mixture.

Topping

¹/₂ c. flour
1 c. sugar

¹/₂ t. cinnamon
¹/₄ c. butter, melted

Combine above ingredients and sprinkle over top of pie.
Bake at 350° for 50 minutes. (From Marie Kleinsasser, Glendale, Arizona.)

Quick Rhubarb Upside-Down Cake

1 stick butter

1 c. brown sugar

2 c. diced rhubarb, fresh or frozen

¹/₂ t. cinnamon (optional)

1 box yellow cake mix (2-layer size)

Melt butter in 8 x 14-inch heatproof glass loaf pan in 375° oven. Add brown sugar and spread uniformly over bottom of pan. Sprinkle diced rhubarb uniformly over brown sugar. Sprinkle cinnamon over rhubarb. Prepare cake mix according to package directions and spread over rhubarb. Bake for 30–45 minutes, depending upon whether thawed or frozen rhubarb is used, or until browned on top. Serve warm with vanilla ice cream.

Rhubarb Custard Pie

3 c. rhubarb pieces

pastry for 2 9-inch crusts

1 c. sugar

2 T. flour

¹/₈ t. salt

2 eggs, beaten

Wash rhubarb stalks and cut into half-inch pieces before measuring. Line a pie pan with pastry. Mix sugar, flour, salt, and eggs. Add to rhubarb and turn into pie pan. Cover with top crust, press edges together, and trim. Gash top to let steam escape. Bake in quick oven (425°) for 10 minutes. Reduce heat and continue baking in moderate oven (325°) for 30 minutes.

Rhubarb Cobbler

Base

1 c. sugar

¹/₃ c. pancake mix or Bisquick

1 t. grated lemon peel

4 c. rhubarb

Heat oven to 375°. For base, combine sugar, pancake mix or Bisquick, and lemon peel. Add rhubarb and toss lightly. Place in 9-inch square glass baking dish.

Topping

³/₄ c. pancake mix or Bisquick

²/₃ c. sugar

1 egg, beaten

¹/₄ c. melted butter

For topping, combine mix and sugar. Stir in egg until mixture resembles coarse crumbs. Sprinkle evenly over rhubarb base. Drizzle with melted butter. Bake in preheated oven 35–40 minutes. Serve with ice cream.

Stewed Rhubarb (Oven Method)

If you are already using your oven, you may conserve heat by cooking rhubarb in the oven instead of over surface burner. For 1½ lbs. diced rhubarb, use only 1½ T. of water and ⅔ c. sugar. Place ingredients in a 1½ quart casserole and bake, covered, at 375° for 30 minutes or until tender, stirring once.

Stewed Rhubarb (Microwave Method)

Use same proportions of rhubarb, water, and sugar as in oven method above. Place in microwave-safe casserole with cover and process on High for 10 minutes, turning casserole once if you do not have a rotary tray.

Rhubarb Daiquiri

1½ c. chopped rhubarb
½ c. sugar
2 T. water
⅔ c. light rum
3 c. ice cubes
1 T. lime juice

Combine rhubarb, sugar, and water in stainless steel or enameled saucepan. Bring to boil. Cover and simmer for 5 minutes. Allow to cool. Combine rhubarb mixture with other ingredients in a large glass pitcher or small punch bowl. Stir and serve immediately in glass cups or tumblers. Serves 4 to 6.

Spinach

Unfortunately, some people still reject spinach as a vegetable because they remember it coming from tin cans and associate it with Popeye and Olive. It is best served fresh in salads with other greens, I believe. Simply wash it carefully and tear the large dark green leaves into bite-size pieces. Stems may be cooked with larger leaves as a vegetable, allowing approximately 1 pound for 3 servings. Stems also are good diced and added to vegetable soup.

Spinach may be prepared "wilted," as the recipes for Wilted Lettuce or Dandelion Greens indicate. It also makes a fine cream soup, following directions for Lettuce Soup above. Any recipe with "Florentine" in its name indicates spinach is present, often as a garnish. For example, spinach added chopped and raw to an omelet (along with sliced mushrooms and sautéed onions) makes a delicious Omelet Florentine. (I remember this first prepared for a Fairview Presbyterian Church committee meeting by a young medical student, Frank Green, now a cardiologist.)

Spinach, when growing in abundance, may be easily frozen and stored in small plastic containers after it has been thoroughly washed and sautéd for just a few minutes, as you would for serving it as a vegetable. This process reduces the spinach in bulk so drastically that a winter's supply will take up amazingly little space in the freezer.

Cream of Spinach Soup

1 quart fresh spinach
3 c. boiling water
¹/₂ t. salt
2 c. Thin White Sauce (recipe follows)

Wash and pick over spinach. Put in stainless steel saucepan with salt and boiling water. Simmer for 20 minutes. Press through sieve or purée in blender. Add 2¹/₂ c. of the liquid and pulp to hot white sauce. Mix well. Serves 4.

Thin White Sauce

2 T. butter
2 T. flour
2 c. milk

Melt butter and blend in flour. Add milk and heat slowly until desired consistency is attained. (I prefer using a metal potato masher firmly held to the bottom of a stainless steel skillet to speed the process. My first experience with this recipe was when Vivian Hofer and Alverna Schulz, partners in a Freeman [South Dakota] Academy cooking class, prepared spinach soup in 1950.)

Spinach and Egg Soup Parmesan

2 T. butter
1 clove garlic, minced
4 thin but large slices Italian bread
¹/₄ c. grated Parmesan cheese

3 c. chicken broth
1 lb. fresh spinach, cooked
4 poached eggs

Blend butter with garlic. Spread on bread. Sprinkle slices with cheese and heat in 375° oven for 10 minutes or until crispy.

In saucepan combine chicken broth and cooked and drained spinach. Simmer 3–5 minutes. Ladle into large but shallow soup bowls. Float slice of cheese toast on soup and top with poached egg. Serve immediately. Serves 4.

Spinach, Radish, and Green Onion Salad

6 c. fresh spinach
1¹/₂ c. sliced radishes
1 c. sliced green onions
¹/₄ c. Tomato Ketchup Salad Dressing (recipe follows)

Combine spinach, radishes, and green onions until well mixed. Toss with dressing. Serves 8.

Tomato Ketchup Salad Dressing
This dressing will keep several weeks in the refrigerator.

1 c. vegetable oil
¹/₃ c. vinegar
¹/₂ c. ketchup
¹/₄ c. sugar

2 t. dry mustard
1 t. salt
1 t. Worcestershire sauce
¹/₂ t. pepper

Measure ingredients into blender. Cover. Blend at high speed about 1 minute. Serve over salad greens. Makes about 2 cups. 1 T. = 1 serving. (From my mother-in-law, Margaret Shug Towne.)

Spinach-Strawberry Salad

1¹/₂ lbs. fresh spinach
1 pint fresh strawberries
¹/₄ c. sugar
2 T. sesame seed
1¹/₂ t. minced onion
¹/₄ t. Worcestershire sauce
¹/₄ t. paprika
¹/₂ c. oil
¹/₄ c. vinegar

Wash and pat dry spinach. Tear into bite-size pieces. Wash, hull, and halve strawberries. Place sugar, sesame seed, and onion in blender container. Add Worcestershire sauce and paprika. With blender running, add oil and vinegar in a slow, steady stream until thoroughly mixed and thickened.

Drizzle only enough dressing over spinach and strawberries to satisfy. Serve immediately. Serves 6 to 8. Reserve remaining dressing for future use.

Spinach Salad in a Wok

1 lb. spinach	2 oranges
1/2 lb. bean sprouts	Soy Dressing (recipe follows)

Remove stems from spinach and reserve for soup. Rinse leaves and pat dry with paper towels. Tear leaves that are too large in half. Sort bean sprouts, rinse and pat dry. Peel oranges and slice in rings or wedges. Heat half of Soy Dressing in wok or pan. Add spinach and toss quickly just until leaves are partially wilted. Remove from heat. Add sprouts and orange slices. Serve immediately with remaining dressing, as desired.

Soy Dressing

1 c. oil	1 t. minced ginger root, peeled
1/4 c. lemon juice	1/2 t. salt
1/4 c. soy sauce	1/2 t. minced garlic
2 T. sugar	1/8 t. hot pepper sauce
2 T. sesame seeds	

Combine all ingredients and stir well. Makes about 1 1/2 cups.

Herbed Spinach Bake

This is an ideal buffet dish. It can be assembled ahead of time and baked just before dinner. I have contributed this to "potlucks" in Kansas, "tureens" in Ohio, and "pitch-ins" in Indiana.

1 lb. fresh spinach, cooked in water remaining on leaves from final rinse	1/3 c. milk
	2 T. chopped onion
1 c. cooked rice	1/2 t. Worcestershire sauce
1 c. shredded sharp Cheddar cheese	1 t. salt
2 eggs, slightly beaten	1/4 t. crushed rosemary or thyme leaves
2 T. butter	(dried)

Pour mixture into 10 x 7-inch greased baking dish. Bake at 350° for 20–25 minutes or until knife inserted halfway between center and edge comes out clean. Cut into squares. Serves 6.

Spinach Lasagne

1/2 lb. lasagne noodles	1 t. oregano
2 T. oil	seasoned salt
1 c. chopped onion	1/2 c. dry bread crumbs
2 cloves garlic, crushed	1 c. shredded mozzarella cheese
2 c. tomato sauce	2 eggs, beaten
1 lb. fresh spinach, cooked in water remaining on leaves after final rinse	

Cook lasagne noodles according to package directions. Drain, being careful to keep them whole.

Heat oil in heavy pan. Add onions and 1 clove garlic. Cook until golden. Stir in tomato sauce.

Drain cooked spinach, reserving ³/₄ c. of the spinach liquid. Add liquid to tomato sauce. Add oregano. Simmer 15–20 minutes.

Combine cooked spinach with remaining garlic, bread crumbs, ¹/₂ c. of the cheese, beaten eggs, and seasoned salt to taste.

Arrange half the pasta in a greased 11 x 13-inch baking dish. Top with half the spinach mixture. Spoon on half the sauce mixture. Repeat the layers. Cover with foil and refrigerate several hours or overnight.

Bake in 350° oven 30–40 minutes. Remove foil and sprinkle with remaining cheese. Bake 15 minutes longer. Serves 6 to 8. This can be frozen after baking the first 40 minutes, before sprinkling on the remaining cheese. To serve, thaw completely, sprinkle on remaining ¹/₂ of cheese and bake 20 minutes or until hot.

Greek Spinach Pie (Spanakopita)

3 lbs. fresh spinach

12 green onions, finely chopped

¹/₂ c. olive oil

¹/₂ c. minced parsley

¹/₂ c. chopped fresh dill or 2 T. dry
   dillweed

salt and freshly ground pepper to taste

¹/₂ c. half and half or evaporated milk

1 lb. feta cheese, crumbled

8 eggs, beaten

olive oil for brushing pan

¹/₂ lb. filo pastry leaves (available in
   frozen food sections)

1 c. melted butter combined with ¹/₂ c.
   olive oil

Preheat oven to 375°. Wash spinach, cut off stems, dry thoroughly and chop. In large skillet, sauté green onions in olive oil until tender. Combine spinach, parsley, and dill, and add to green onions over high heat. Sauté 2 minutes, stirring occasionally with wooden spatula. Remove from heat, season with salt and pepper, add half and half, feta cheese, and eggs, and mix well.

Brush a 9 x 13-inch baking pan with olive oil and line it with 5 filo leaves, brushing each leaf with mixture of melted butter and olive oil. Fill with spinach mixture and top with remaining filo leaves. Cut into square pieces with a sharp knife before baking. Bake 45 minutes.

This is definitely a party dish. It may be served hot or cold as an appetizer (cut into small squares) or as a main dish (cut into larger squares). Serves 8 to 16. (From Teri Peterson and Eric Limbach, Berkeley, California.)

Baked Spinach Balls

3 lbs. fresh spinach, chopped, cooked
    and drained thoroughly

2 c. herbed stuffing mix (or make your
    own from dried bread toasted in
    buttered herbs)

2 medium onions, chopped fine, or 12
    green onions, chopped

5 eggs, beaten

3/4 c. melted butter

1/2 c. grated Parmesan cheese

1/2 t. garlic, minced

1/2 t. salt

1 t. thyme

1/4 t. pepper

Squeeze excess liquid from cooked spinach using your hands. Combine drained spinach with remaining ingredients. Stir to mix completely. Roll mixture into 1-inch balls with your hands. Place on baking sheets. Bake in 350° oven for 15 minutes. Serve warm, although they are good at room temperature.

This is a good recipe to make ahead, when spinach is in abundance from garden, to be served at a party later. To make ahead, place unbaked spinach balls on a foil-lined baking sheet and freeze. Remove from freezer and immediately put into a heavy plastic freezer bag. Return to freezer until ready to use. Thaw on baking sheet and bake according to above directions. Makes about 10 dozen. Serve as hors d'oeuvres (with toothpicks).

Spinach Topping for Pizza

Place 12-inch frozen, refrigerated, make-your-own, or Boboli pizza round (bread dough) in oiled or floured pizza pan and make the topping using:

2 T. olive oil

1 clove garlic, minced

3 1/2 c. crushed fresh tomatoes or canned
    tomatoes, drained

2 t. oregano

1 1/2 t. basil

1/4 t. salt

1/4 t. pepper

3 lbs. spinach, chopped, cooked slightly,
    and well drained

2 1/2 c. shredded mozzarella cheese

1 c. grated Parmesan cheese

2 c. fresh mushrooms, sliced (optional)

To make sauce, heat oil in large saucepan. Add garlic and sauté 2 minutes. Stir in tomatoes, oregano, basil, salt, and pepper. Simmer 30 minutes or until thick.

Mix spinach, cheeses, and mushrooms together in large bowl. Spread spinach mixture onto dough on pizza pan. Top with tomato sauce and bake at 450° for 25–30 minutes. (The way I make pizza, this is enough topping for several pizzas.)

Spinach Pesto

2 cloves garlic, peeled

1 c. fresh parsley sprigs

2 T. pine nuts (pignoli) or walnuts

1 lb. fresh spinach, chopped

1/2 c. olive oil

1 T. dried basil leaves

1/2 t. salt

1/4 t. pepper

2/3 c. grated fresh Parmesan or Romano
    cheese

Using a blender, mince garlic. Add parsley and nuts. Pulse to chop fine. Add spinach, olive oil, basil, salt, and pepper. Purée 30 seconds. Add cheese. Pulse to blend. Thin with additional olive oil if necessary. Transfer pesto to a glass jar. Keeps in refrigerator 2 weeks or can be frozen.

To serve, toss ½ cup pesto with 4 servings of hot cooked pasta or float a tablespoon of it atop a bowl of minestrone soup. Makes 1½ cups. (Jan Becker extends pesto by adding cottage cheese just before serving on pasta.)

Spinach Quick Bread

1 ¾ c. flour
1 T. baking powder
2 T. sugar
½ t. salt
¼ t. nutmeg
1 egg, slightly beaten

1 c. milk
1 lb. fresh spinach, chopped, cooked, and squeezed dry
½ c. grated sharp Cheddar cheese
2 T. melted butter

Stir together flour, baking powder, sugar, salt, and nutmeg. Combine egg, milk, drained spinach, cheese, and butter. Stir into flour mixture until just blended.

Spoon into well-greased loaf pan. Spread top evenly. Bake in a 375° oven for 50–55 minutes or until bread tests done with a toothpick inserted into the middle. Cool 10 minutes on a rack. Turn upside down and remove from pan. Cool on rack again. Serve warm with cream cheese.

Variation: Batter may be used for muffins instead of bread, in which case bake at 400° for 20–25 minutes. Yields 12 muffins. Be sure to grease muffin tins or use paper liners.

Strawberries

Nothing is better than vine-ripened, home-grown strawberries, except, perhaps, vine-ripened, home-grown tomatoes. While we usually think of strawberries as being used in delectable desserts, they also make fine salads, one treat I was introduced to in California during the early 1980s. I was recently served strawberries in a tossed salad in an Italian restaurant, Amici's, on the east side of Indianapolis.

Strawberries on Bibb Lettuce

Arrange Bibb lettuce leaves on chilled salad plates. Drizzle mayonnaise thinned with lemon juice and a pinch of sugar over lettuce. Arrange halved strawberries (cut from tip to stem end to retain beautiful heart shape) over lettuce and serve.

Strawberry Dressing

1 c. puréed strawberries
2 T. red wine vinegar
2 T. sugar

¹/₄ c. oil
salt and pepper to taste

Stir together all ingredients and serve over fresh greens.

Easy Strawberry Appetizer or Dessert

In a large bowl place clean, red-ripe strawberries, stems attached. Surrounding the bowl of strawberries place small bowls of powdered sugar, plain yogurt, chocolate sprinkles, sour cream, or whipped cream as in a Lazy Susan.

For appetizer, serve with plain wheat crackers.

For dessert, serve with small crisp cookies.

Strawberry Tea Punch

2 quarts strong brewed tea, cooled
1 can (6 oz.) frozen lemonade concentrate
¹/₂ c. sugar
1 pint fresh or frozen strawberries

Stir sugar, lemonade concentrate, and strawberries into cooled tea. Serve over ice in punch cups or glasses. Serves 8 to 10.

Strawberry Yogurt Sauce

1 c. plain yogurt
1 c. sliced fresh strawberries
1 T. sugar
¹/₄ t. almond extract

Place all ingredients in blender and purée. Chill 1 to 2 hours and serve over chilled fresh fruit in season or over slice of angel food or pound cake. Makes 1¹/₂ cups.

Fresh Strawberry Sundae Sauce

¹/₂ c. light corn syrup
1¹/₂ c. fresh crushed strawberries

In a small bowl, stir together corn syrup and fruit. Cover and refrigerate. Serve over ice cream or cake. (This is a recipe children can prepare with some guidance. They will enjoy the outcome too!)

Italian Strawberry Ice

2 quarts strawberries
1 c. sugar
1 c. water
juice of 1 small lemon

Wash and hull berries; then purée in blender. Boil sugar and water together for 5 minutes. Cool. Combine with berry purée; then stir in lemon juice. Freeze, stirring occasionally, to a mush. Serves 4 to 6.

Strawberry Shortcake

2 c. flour
2 T. sugar
1 T. baking powder
1 t. salt
6 T. shortening (or ²/₃ stick butter)
²/₃ c. milk

Cut shortening into mixed dry ingredients with pastry blender. Stir in milk to make soft dough. Pat half of the recipe into greased 8-inch round layer cake pan. Dot with butter. Pat out other half on top. Bake at 450° for 12 to 15 minutes.

Remove from oven when cake is golden brown and allow to cool. Split layers apart. Spoon sweetened unchilled strawberries between layers and on top. Serve warm with whipped cream. Serves 8.

Frozen Strawberry Whip Dessert

2 ²/₃ c. cookie crumbs
¹/₂ c. melted butter
3 egg whites
1 c. sugar
1¹/₄ c. frozen strawberries, thawed
1 pt. whipped topping or vanilla ice cream

To form the crust, combine cookie crumbs and melted butter in small bowl. Press into a 10-inch pie pan or a 10-inch square glass baking dish, reserving ²/₃ c. crumbs. Bake for 8 minutes in a 350° oven.

For the topping, beat egg whites until stiff. Add sugar and berries. Beat for 15 minutes. Fold in whipped topping or ice cream. Pour on the crust. Sprinkle the top with remaining ²/₃ c. cookie crumb mix. Cover with foil and freeze. Serves 9–12. (From Camille Raimondi, Hyde Park Union Church Business and Professional Women, Chicago.)

Nonfat Strawberry Dessert

¹/₂ c. cold water
¹/₂ c. instant nonfat dry milk
1 T. lemon juice
1 pt. fresh strawberries, hulled and sliced

Place cold water in bowl of electric mixer. Add dry milk and beat until very stiff. Fold in lemon juice and strawberries, a few at a time, with spoon. Pour into a 1-quart freezing tray. Freeze until firm, about 4¹/₂ hours. Cut into desired portions and serve. Serves 4 to 6.

Fresh Strawberry Pie

1 9-inch pie shell, baked
1 c. crushed strawberries
fresh strawberries (about 1 pint)
1 c. sugar
1 T. cornstarch

Mix and boil until clear the crushed strawberries, sugar, and cornstarch. Arrange fresh whole hulled strawberries in bottom of a baked pie shell, stem side down for the first layer, and fill in the spaces with berries tip side down. Pour cooled filling over strawberries and chill. Serve with whipped cream or whipped topping. "Gild the lily" by placing a whole fresh berry with stem atop each serving. (From Cousin Annie [Mrs. Jacob L. Hofer, Jr.] of Dolton, South Dakota. After the death of my mother in 1937, our family enjoyed many Sunday dinners at Annie's ample board.)

Freezer Strawberry Jam

2 c. mashed strawberries (using a metal potato masher)
4 c. sugar
1 box powdered fruit pectin
³/₄ c. water

Mix strawberries and sugar well. Set aside 10 minutes. Stir powdered fruit pectin with water in steel saucepan. Bring to boil, stirring constantly. Boil 1 minute. Remove from heat. Stir mixtures together until sugar is completely dissolved. Pour into containers. Cover. Let stand at room temperature 24 hours. Store in freezer. After opening, store in the refrigerator. Makes four 8-oz. containers. (Exact measurements are essential for jam to set.)

Strawberry Punch

4 c. sliced strawberries
6 c. white grape juice
1 28-oz. bottle club soda, chilled

Blend 3 cups of the strawberries in blender. Combine with grape juice and remaining sliced berries in a punch bowl or large pitcher, preferably clear glass. Before serving, add club soda. Stir gently. Pour over ice in 8-oz. glasses or punch cups.

Strawberry Daiquiris (Non-alcoholic)
From Ellen Walsh, who serves these to her four children on Friday evenings when the family unwinds from the week's demands.

2 c. frozen strawberries
$^1/_3$ c. superfine sugar
$^1/_3$ c. orange juice
1 T. lemon juice
4 fresh strawberries and mint sprigs for garnish

In blender or food processor, combine strawberries, sugar, orange and lemon juices. Process until smooth. Pour into 4 wine glasses. Garnish each glass with a whole strawberry and mint sprig. Serve with straws. Serves 4.

Violets

Each spring my backyard is carpeted with violets. Unfortunately, they vanish too soon. But I have found ways to enjoy their beauty immediately while preserving them for those dark and cold winter days when we wait for spring to return.

Leaves and stems of violets are rich in vitamin A and may be eaten raw in salads or added to soups and stews. Like okra and sassafras leaves, violet greenery (an oxymoron if there ever was one!) is a thickening agent.

Violet blossoms are rich in vitamin C and may be plucked off the plant as a natural vitamin tablet during your morning walk in the garden. Blossoms may also be added to salads, as you would nasturtiums, but add them last as a garnish so as not to damage their delicate beauty.

Violet Tea

1 handful violet blossoms
boiling water
honey or sugar (optional)

Place handful of violet blossoms in bottom of tea pot. Add boiling water and allow to steep until desired strength is achieved. Strain tea into delicate tea cup. Add honey or sugar if desired.

Violet Blossom Jelly

2 c. violet blossoms picked from chemically untreated lawn
boiling water to cover

Wash violet blossoms in water bath. Remove any bugs or debris. Place in crockery bowl and pour on boiling water. Allow to steep overnight. Strain into a stainless steel kettle, measuring the amount of liquid required for recipe for apple jelly printed on commercial powdered pectin recipe folder. Discard violet blossoms. Follow recipe for apple jelly. Seal in half-pint jelly jars with lids and rings.

Violet-Flavored Yellow Tea Cake

Follow recipe for Rose Geranium Cake in Part IV, Winter, placing violet blossoms instead of rose geranium leaves at bottom of greased cake pan and pouring over them the yellow cake batter prepared with cake mix. Bake according to directions, cool on wire rack and turn out on cake plate. (Enough violet blossoms should be used to ensure that there is at least one for each serving of cake.)

PART TWO

Basil	Elderberries
Beans	Gooseberries
Beet Greens	Grape Leaves
Blackberries	Ground Cherries
Blueberries	Kohlrabi
Cantaloupe	Mesclun
Cherries	Mustard Greens
Chokecherries	Nasturtiums
Collards	Okra
Corn	Peaches
Cucumbers	Raspberries
Currants	Summer Savory
Daikon Radish	Summer Squash
Daylilies	Tomatoes
Dill	Watermelons
Eggplant	Zucchini

Basil

The popular annual herb basil may be grown indoors but flourishes outdoors in summer's warmth into a handsome, bushy plant. Very tasty when served with tomatoes, it also benefits the growing tomatoes when placed beside them in the garden because it repels insects and disease and actually improves both the growth and flavor of tomatoes.

Basil should never be allowed to go to seed. Pinch it often to keep the white or purplish flowers from forming. Thus, you need a lot of recipes for using basil during the summer, or else you should freeze and dry it for year-round use.

Frozen basil can be used only in cooked dishes because the leaves will turn black, just as if they were frozen outdoors by the frost. Flowering heads may also be frozen, but they will be much stronger in flavor than the leaves are.

If you miss the opportunity to freeze surplus basil, try dried basil for pesto, though it is inferior to the pesto made with the fresh or frozen herb. I dry basil leaves in my gas range oven, which has a pilot light. I strip leaves from stems after washing and shaking off excess moisture. Then I place them on paper-lined cookie sheets, turn them occasionally, and crush only when completely dry.

My experience drying herbs in the microwave oven has met with mixed reviews, so I do not recommend it. It is difficult to prevent herbs from becoming overheated and thus tasting scorched. But microwave directions say it can be done by brushing clean, not rinsing, the herbs, placing them between paper towels, and treating them on high for 2 to 3 minutes. If they are not dry when checked, they may be treated again for 30 seconds.

Red Wine–Basil Vinaigrette

2 medium cloves garlic, peeled and crushed
2 T. Dijon-style mustard
$^{1}/_{2}$ c. red wine vinegar
1 t. freshly ground black pepper
1 c. olive oil
$^{1}/_{2}$ c. slivered basil leaves
$^{1}/_{2}$ c. chopped parsley

In a small bowl whisk garlic, mustard, vinegar, and pepper together. Pour oil into bowl in a slow stream, whisking constantly until vinaigrette is slightly thick. Fold in basil and parsley. Serve over mixed greens with fresh tomatoes and cucumbers. Yields $1^{1}/_{2}$ cups dressing.

Tangy Pesto Sauce

$^1/_2$ c. fresh basil leaves, loosely packed

1 t. olive oil

1 t. fresh lemon juice

1 small clove garlic

1 T. pine nuts (pignoli) or walnuts

2 T. cold water

1 T. freshly grated Parmesan cheese

Combine basil, olive oil, lemon juice, garlic, nuts, and 2 T. cold water in blender. Pulse until smooth. Scrape into bowl and stir in the Parmesan. Cover surface with plastic wrap to prevent darkening. Serve over summer harvest vegetables or hot, drained pasta. Serves 4.

Variation: Jan Becker adds 2 to 3 rounded tablespoons of cottage cheese to the pesto before tossing it with pasta. She freezes the pesto in plastic-lined cupcake tins and then melts the frozen pesto in the top of a double boiler before adding the cottage cheese and tossing it with pasta.

Freezer Pesto

4 c. firmly packed basil leaves

3 large cloves garlic

$^1/_2$ c. olive oil

$^1/_2$ t. salt

$^1/_3$ c. pine nuts

Parmesan cheese

Pick over basil leaves, discarding any that are blackened. Rinse well in several changes of water. Dry thoroughly in a salad spinner or on absorbent towels or paper.

In a food processor chop garlic. Add basil leaves, oil, and salt. Process on medium speed a few seconds, until mixture is a fine paste. Pour into a 2-cup jar and cover with thin layer of olive oil. Refrigerate or freeze until ready to use.

To serve, in a processor chop $^1/_3$ c. pine nuts. Add a few tablespoons of the pesto base and continue processing until nuts are very finely chopped. In a large serving bowl, combine pesto, nut-pesto mixture, and $^1/_2$ to $^3/_4$ cup grated Parmesan cheese. Drain pasta, turn into serving bowl with pesto, and toss with freshly ground pepper. Serve additional cheese (Parmesan or cottage) on the side.

Pesto Sauce from Dried Basil

$^1/_4$ c. chopped parsley

$^1/_4$ c. dried basil leaves

1 c. freshly grated Parmesan cheese or mixture of Parmesan and Romano

$^1/_3$ to $^1/_2$ c. olive oil

3 or more cloves garlic, minced

2 T. lemon juice

crushed pine nuts (pignoli) or walnuts (optional)

Combine all ingredients but lemon juice in blender and whirl until thick paste is formed. Add lemon juice.

Pesto may be used in making quiche, pizza, or in minestrone soup. I have also added it to flavor spaghetti sauce, butters, tossed mixed vegetables, and omelets.

Tuna with Cucumbers and Pesto

2 cans (7 oz. each) tuna in oil, well-drained
1 medium cucumber, seeded and diced
3 T. mayonnaise
1 heaping T. freezer pesto

In small mixing bowl flake tuna with fork into large pieces. Add cucumber, mayonnaise, and pesto. Blend lightly until mixed. Serve on lettuce leaf with lemon wedge. Serves 3 to 4. (Make shortly before serving.)

Pesto–Cream Cheese Butter

1 8-oz. package cream cheese, at room temperature
1 c. (2 sticks) butter, at room temperature
¹/₂ c. pesto

Combine cream cheese, butter, and pesto. Use as spread on thin slices of French or sourdough bread, toasted, or on crisp raw vegetables such as carrot slices, celery sticks, etc. (Recipe may be doubled, shaped in a mold, and decorated with fresh basil leaves for a buffet table.)

Garden Vegetable Soup with Basil Pistou

1 c. dry navy beans
1 ham bone
1 large onion, diced
1 c. diced celery
2 potatoes, peeled and diced
2 medium carrots, diced

2 tomatoes, peeled and chopped
1¹/₂ c. coarsely chopped cabbage or chard
1 c. green beans
Pistou (recipe follows)

Soak beans overnight, drain, and cover with fresh water. Add ham bone, onion, celery, potatoes, and carrots. Cook until almost tender. Add tomatoes, cabbage or chard, and green beans. Simmer ¹/₂ hour longer.

To serve, ladle soup into bowl. Pass pistou to stir into each serving. Serve with crusty French bread.

Pistou

3 c. lightly packed fresh basil leaves
1 c. grated Gruyère cheese (4 oz.)
2 cloves garlic
1 t. lemon juice
$^1/_4$ t. salt
$^1/_2$ c. olive oil

Place basil, cheese, garlic, lemon juice, and salt in blender container or in mortar. Cover and process until smooth, or pound with pestle to a smooth paste. Add olive oil, a little at a time, until mixture is consistency of soft butter. Makes 1 cup.

Pesto Quiche

$^1/_4$ c. prepared pesto (fresh or frozen)
1 (9-inch) deep-dish pie shell
1 clove garlic
1 large onion
3 T. butter
3 eggs
1 c. milk
$^1/_2$ c. ricotta cheese
$1^1/_2$ c. grated Parmesan cheese

Bake pie shell in 350° oven for 5 minutes. Peel and mince garlic and onion. Sauté in butter until translucent. Lightly beat eggs. Mix milk with ricotta, then combine with eggs, garlic, onion, and prepared pesto. Turn into crust and sprinkle Parmesan cheese evenly over the top. Bake on top shelf of oven at 350° for about 40 minutes or until puffed and lightly browned.

Beans, Green or Yellow Wax

For many of the world's people, beans are a staple. Even in the United States, cooks living in some areas would not consider putting a meal on the table without serving beans in some form. This fact was brought home in conversation with a Presbyterian minister who had grown up in a German community in Pennsylvania. Potatoes and bread had been staples in his home, but when he went to his first summer parish in Tennessee, he found beans on the tables of all who invited him for Sunday dinner. When he asked one woman why she always cooked beans, she looked nonplussed. "Why," she said, "I never thought of it. We always have beans."

My husband, also a Presbyterian minister, tells of the hospitality shown him by an elderly woman in a remote log cabin in West Virginia. She had nothing to offer him but coffee and canned beans. "Nothing would do but that I stay and share what she had," he remembers.

Green beans used to be called string beans for the threads that had to be removed. However, nurseries have bred the strings out of the beans for the most part, making preparation and eating more enjoyable.

Complementary planting experts advise planting beets with bush beans. Marigolds, nasturtiums, and summer savory deter beetles, they say. They also advise against planting onions and garlic with beans since the strong-smelling bulbs stunt the growth of beans.

Green and wax beans are best picked while still tender and young, before the bean seeds begin bulging in the pod. Avoid picking beans when plants are wet from dew or rain; otherwise, rust spots will develop on the plants and beans.

If beans are picked regularly and carefully while pods are still comparatively young, the bushes will bear throughout the summer. If the plants seem to dry up during the heat of summer, do not pull them out immediately. Often they will be rejuvenated by late-summer or early-autumn rains and begin bearing again.

Fresh beans may be cooked whole, slivered, French-cut on the bias (diagonally), or simply cut in inch-long pieces. Uniformity in size makes the vegetable more attractive. Simmer beans (uncovered) no more than 20 minutes if you wish to retain good color. Add salt only after the beans have been cooked. (Adding salt adds cooking time and causes loss of nutrients.)

Microwaving beans with a few tablespoons of water in a microwave-safe covered casserole on high for 4–5 minutes helps to preserve nutrients.

Young, tender beans are very good eaten raw. In fact, my husband prefers them that way, especially warm from the plant and eaten out of hand. Therefore, do not neglect to offer them whole on a relish tray with dip or diagonally cut in green garden salads.

Common flavorings include butter and basil, cream sauce, mushrooms, toasted slivered almonds, bacon and onions, or tomato sauce. Marjoram and summer savory also complement beans nicely.

Fresh Bean Salad

After beans (green, purple, yellow wax, or combination) have been cooked *al dente,* drain the water into the stock pot. While beans are still warm, toss with French or vinaigrette dressing. Chill. Before serving on a lettuce leaf, toss beans with chives or sliced green onion. (Purple beans turn green when cooked.)

Wilted Bean Salad

After beans have been lightly cooked, drain the water into the stock pot. While beans are still warm, pour over them the dressing for Wilted Dandelions (Part I, Spring). Serve with French or other hot crusty bread.

Scandinavian Green Beans

Serve this with tuna or salmon, spooning sauce over fish. Or it may be served as a main-dish salad with salad greens.

2 cups green beans	$1/4$ t. ground allspice
$1/4$ c. white vinegar	dash of pepper
1 T. oil	$1/4$ c. pickled cocktail onions
1 t. dillweed or seed	$1/4$ c. thinly sliced radishes

Lightly cook green beans and drain, reserving 2 T. of cooking liquid, to which add vinegar, oil, dillweed, allspice, and pepper. Mix well and add to beans. Let marinate for at least 1 hour. At serving time, add cocktail onions and radishes. Toss lightly. Serves 6 as a buffet dish or 4 as a main-dish salad.

Four-Bean Salad

This is a good recipe to prepare for a church supper, or any time you have a crowd to feed.

2 c. cooked dark red kidney beans	1 small onion, finely chopped (about $1/2$ c.)
2 c. cooked small green lima beans	$1/2$ large green bell pepper, finely chopped (about $1/2$ c.)
2 c. cooked fresh green beans, cut up	
2 c. cooked yellow wax beans, cut up	2 t. prepared mustard
1 c. chopped celery	$1/2$ t. salt
$1/2$ c. cider or white vinegar	$1/8$ t. pepper
$1/2$ c. sugar	$1/2$ c. oil

Drain beans (and rinse, if canned, then drain again); place in large bowl. Add chopped celery. Prepare marinade: Boil vinegar and sugar until sugar is dissolved. Stir in onion, green pepper, mustard, salt, and pepper. Immediately remove from heat and pour over beans. Cover and set aside to marinate in refrigerator for several hours or several days. Stir occasionally. When ready to serve, pour on $1/2$ c. oil and mix well. Yields 9 c. salad for 18–25 servings. (From Mary Jane Sadler, Findlay, Ohio.)

Variation: You may substitute cooked navy (white) beans for the limas and pinto beans for kidney beans. Or, simply make it a three-bean salad instead of a four-bean salad.

Dilled Beans and Carrots

$3/4$ c. boiling water	4 small to medium carrots, peeled and cut into 3-inch strips
$1/2$ t. salt	low-calorie bottled Italian dressing
1 t. sugar	
$1/2$ t. dill seeds	
$1/2$ lb. fresh green beans, trimmed and left whole (2 c.)	

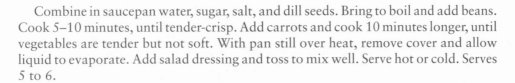

Combine in saucepan water, sugar, salt, and dill seeds. Bring to boil and add beans. Cook 5–10 minutes, until tender-crisp. Add carrots and cook 10 minutes longer, until vegetables are tender but not soft. With pan still over heat, remove cover and allow liquid to evaporate. Add salad dressing and toss to mix well. Serve hot or cold. Serves 5 to 6.

Green Beans with Nippy Dressing

1¹/₂ lbs. French-cut green beans
¹/₄ c. mayonnaise
2 T. prepared mustard
2 t. prepared horseradish
paprika

Cook beans until crisp-tender. Mix mayonnaise, mustard, and horseradish together. Fold into hot beans and serve garnished with paprika. Serves 4 to 6.

Rosemaried Green Beans

1 lb. fresh green beans, sliced
1 t. salt
¹/₄ t. rosemary leaves
2 T. French salad dressing

Place beans in saucepan with half-inch depth boiling water, salt, and rosemary. Bring to boil and cook, uncovered, for 5 minutes. Cover and continue cooking until crisp-tender. Drain if necessary. Add dressing and toss lightly. Serve hot or cold.
Variation: Omit the French dressing, and serve the beans hot with 1 T. butter and rosemary leaves.

Deviled Green Beans

1 lb. fresh green beans, sliced
2 T. butter
1 t. prepared mustard
1 t. Worcestershire sauce

Place beans in saucepan with half inch of boiling water. Bring to boil and cook, uncovered, for 5 minutes. Cover and continue cooking until crisp-tender. Drain if necessary. Mix butter, mustard, and Worcestershire and add to cooked beans. Heat until mixture coats beans. Serve hot.

Sweet-Sour Green Beans

2 c. cooked yellow wax beans (reserve liquid)
1 T. light brown sugar
1 T. lemon juice
1 T. butter
salt

Into 1-quart steel saucepan turn the beans and liquid in which they have been cooked. Heat thoroughly and drain. In the empty saucepan over low heat, stir together the sugar, lemon juice, and butter until butter melts. Add beans and mix well. Add salt if desired and reheat. Serves 4–5.

Strankel Zup (Fresh Bean Soup)

This is a traditional Hutterite Mennonite dish which my children, now adults, still speak of fondly. It can also be made with canned or frozen green beans during the winter but is never quite so good as when it is made with fresh beans from the garden.

Cook until tender a smoked ham bone or several ham hocks with chopped onion and chopped celery. (Chopped Swiss chard stalks in season may be substituted for celery.) During the last half hour of cooking add 2 c. cubed potatoes or unpeeled new potatoes, 1/2 c. grated carrots, 3 or 4 sprigs parsley or summer savory (also known as *pepar krut*), and 4 c. cut green and/or yellow wax beans. When all are tender, serve with dollop of sour cream.

Variation: Bay leaf may also be cooked with beans. Milk, half and half, yogurt, or evaporated milk may be substituted for sour cream.

Stewed Green Beans

2 T. peanut oil
1/2 lb. bacon, cut in half-inch pieces
1 1/2 T. green onion, julienned
1 t. peeled ginger root, julienned
1 T. soy sauce

1 t. salt
1/2 c. water
1 lb. green beans, trimmed and cut in 1-inch lengths (may be more mature beans)

Heat oil in wok or large saucepan over medium heat. Reduce heat somewhat, and add bacon, green onions, and ginger root. Stir-fry until bacon is crisp. Add soy sauce, salt, and water. Bring to boil. Add beans, mix well, and cover. Reduce heat and simmer 20 minutes or until hardly any liquid remains. Serve hot over rice. (A Chinese friend of mine says this recipe serves 4 Americans or 8 Chinese!)

I refuse to publish the bean casserole brought to too many church suppers in which canned mushroom soup and canned French-fried onions predominate. However, a good casserole to take to a pitch-in (known in other regions as a potluck or tureen) is the following:

Bean and Onion Bake

3 c. sliced onions
$^1/_3$ c. butter
$^1/_4$ c. flour
$1^1/_2$ t. salt
$^1/_4$ t. dry mustard
dash pepper

2 c. milk
1 c. shredded Cheddar cheese ($^1/_4$ lb.)
3 c. green beans (cooked crisp-tender
   and drained)
2 T. fine dry bread crumbs
$^1/_2$ t. marjoram

Sauté onion slices in butter until they are limp. Blend in flour, salt, mustard, and pepper. Add milk and stir constantly until mixture thickens. Blend in $^3/_4$ c. cheese. Fold in green beans. Turn into shallow 2-quart casserole.

Combine and mix remaining $^1/_4$ c. cheese, bread crumbs, and marjoram. Sprinkle mixture over top. Place in moderate oven (350°) for 30 minutes or until thoroughly heated. Serves 10.

Snappy Dilly Beans (Canned)

4 lbs. whole green beans (thin, long
   beans preferred)
yellow mustard seed
dill seed
instant minced garlic

crushed red pepper
5 c. vinegar
5 c. water
$^1/_2$ c. pickling (kosher) salt

If necessary, cut beans into lengths to fill half-pint jars. Pack into hot sterilized jars. Place $^1/_4$ t. each mustard seed and dill seed and $^1/_{16}$ t. each crushed red pepper and minced garlic in each half-pint jar.

Combine vinegar, water, and salt. Heat to boiling. Pour boiling liquid over beans, leaving half-inch head space. Adjust caps. Process 25 minutes* in boiling water bath. (Start counting time after water in canner returns to boiling.) Remove jars. Set jars upright, several inches apart, on a wooden rack to cool. Makes 14 half pints. Serve as a pickle on a relish tray.

---

*1989 USDA recommendations are 10 pounds of pressure for 20 minutes for pints.

Mustard Bean Pickle (Canned)

3 lbs. yellow wax beans
6 T. yellow mustard seed
6 T. celery seed
6 cloves garlic
3 c. cider vinegar
2 c. water
5 T. salt
2 T. sugar
2 T. prepared horseradish (not cream style)
2 t. red pepper sauce

Wash and trim beans. Drain. Put mustard seed in piece of cloth and pound to crush slightly, or crush with mortar and pestle. Divide mustard and celery seeds and garlic among 6 pint "Mason" or canning jars. Fill jars to $1/2$ inch of top with prepared beans.

Put remaining ingredients in steel saucepan. Boil 2–3 minutes, or until salt and sugar dissolve. Pour hot solution over beans. Carefully run knife between beans and jar to release air. Add more solution if needed to cover beans. Wipe top and threads of jar. Put dome lid on jar. Screw band tight. Process 25 minutes* in boiling water.

Have water steaming but not boiling when jars are lowered into it. Quickly bring to boiling and begin counting processing time. Let pickle season 2–3 weeks before using.

———————

*1989 USDA recommendations are 10 pounds of pressure for 20 minutes for pints.

Canning Green or Yellow Wax Beans

Because of the low acid content of beans, they must be preserved under pressure (10 pounds of pressure for 20 minutes for pints and 25 minutes for quarts).

Beans may be canned whole if they are young and tender, or cut in uniform pieces or French cut if they are older. I recommend the cold pack for ease in handling. Add 1 t. salt per quart and fill with boiling water, leaving a half-inch head space. Adjust lids and process.

Freezing Green or Yellow Wax Beans

Beans must be blanched before freezing. Plunge whole beans into boiling water for 3 minutes, cool in ice water, drain and pack. For cut beans, blanch for 2 minutes. For French style beans, blanch for 1 minute.

If you dry the beans between towels after they have been drained, they may be packed in large, heavy plastic bags and will separate easily in the amounts needed for preparation. The taste is also superior if excess moisture has been removed. Or you may package them in family serving–size bags first and then in a larger, heavier bag to prevent freezer burn.

Drying Pod Beans

The Schweitzer (Swiss-German) Mennonites in the Freeman-Marion [South Dakota] area plant a Parisien or "Swiss" bean that is a mottled red and white. Others refer to them as "shellie" beans or "hay" beans. Some call them "leather britches" beans because they are sometimes threaded and hung, clothesline-fashion, in the home attic, where they dry in the summer heat. Others dry them on newspapers on the attic floor.

They should be picked after the bean is well developed in the pod but before the pod bursts and dies on the plant. *Getrokene Bohne* (Dried Beans) are served each spring at Freeman Academy at the *Schmeckfest* (tasting festival), which is sponsored by the Auxiliary as a fundraiser. The Auxiliary also publishes a booklet of recipes used. The recipe for *Getrokene Bohne* reads:

> Wash only if necessary since this will prolong the drying period; then remove stems and strings. . . . When sufficiently dry, store in paper or cloth sacks.
> When you get ready to cook them, soak beans (both pod and bean) overnight. Next morning pour off water, add fresh water, and cook 2 hours. Pour off water and add fresh again. Add a piece of pork, either fresh or smoked. Cook until tender. If ham or salt pork has been used, it may not need any more salt. Brown 1 tablespoon flour in 1 tablespoon lard and add to the beans.

Variation: After soaking, the beans may be parboiled for an hour with ½ t. baking soda, drained, and covered again with fresh water to cook. Also, a pod of red pepper may be added during the cooking process and removed before serving.

Beet Greens

Not often do dinner guests in our home decline to eat the vegetables served. But a Catholic priest who had been reared in an orphanage refused to take any pickled beets because he was forced to weed and then to eat so many beets in his youth that he could not stomach them in adulthood.

Most people do not abhor beets so much as avoid them. However, beets deserve to be added to our menus not only for their color but for their interesting texture and earthy flavor.

In the summer you will first want to enjoy the beet greens or the small beet roots with greens that you pull to thin the row, making it possible for some of the beets to grow to normal size for harvesting in autumn. (See Part III, Autumn, for recipes for full-grown beets.)

Beet greens may be cut from the beet root as it grows in the garden. When they are still tender and young, beet leaves may be added to a green salad or sautéed with spinach and/or chard leaves to make a "mess" to feed a family. When beet greens (including stems) are added to vegetable soup, they impart a nice pink or red color.

Sautéd Beet Greens

2 T. butter
$^1/_4$ c. chopped onion
$^1/_2$ lb. beet greens (including stems, chopped)
salt, pepper, and lemon juice to taste
sour cream and/or yogurt (optional)

Melt butter in skillet over moderate heat. Sauté onion until tender. Add chopped beet greens and stems. Sauté until tender. Remove from heat and add seasonings. Serve with sour cream or yogurt, if desired, passing it in a separate dish.

Since both my maternal and paternal grandparents migrated to America from South Russia in the 1870s, I grew up in a family that often had a pot of borscht (called Vorsch by the Hutterites) simmering at the back of the wood-burning cook stove. Even in the summer my folks made borscht or Vorsch, in the early days in the summer kitchen, a separate small building where cooking was done so as not to heat up the house. However, in the summer the borscht consisted primarily of garden-fresh vegetables. The contribution from the beet plant was primarily from the leaves, leaving the roots to mature in the soil for autumn and winter use.

Summer Borscht (Hot)

Meat or fowl should be cooked the day before so that bone, fat, and gristle may be removed and pieces of meat returned to the stock before reheating.

4 qts. beef, ham, or chicken stock (defatted)
1 onion
1 clove garlic, minced
1 carrot
2 stalks celery or chard
2 c. beet leaves and stems
1 head dill or bay leaf (dried dillweed or seed may be substituted)

1 large potato
2 large tomatoes
2 sprigs parsley
1 small head cabbage (or other cruciferous vegetable, such as chard leaves or broccoli)
salt and pepper to taste
sour cream and/or plain yogurt

Return stock to boiling point. Add chopped vegetables and cook gently until all are tender. Remove head of dill or bay leaf. Adjust seasonings. Serve with sour cream or yogurt. (This soup is better the second day or when reheated. If you desire more liquid, add tomato juice or vegetable juice cocktail.)

Summer Borscht (Cold)

4–6 small beets thinned from garden, including leaves, stems and roots intact. (Do not cut into any portion of beets or they will bleed.)
1 c. cold water
1 c. beef stock, fat removed, or bouillon
1 small onion
1 t. dillweed (fresh preferred)
¹/₂ t. chives
salt, pepper, and lemon juice to taste
sour cream and/or yogurt to pass

Wash beets, leaves, and stems thoroughly and cook gently, beginning with cold water. When all are tender, cool the mixture. Do not throw away the water in which beets were cooked. When cooled, purée in blender. Add beef stock or bouillon, onion, dill, and chives. Blend again until all is of the same consistency. If you wish to add more liquid, do so with ice cubes. Season with salt, pepper, or lemon juice. Chill until icy cold. If it is not cold enough at serving time, you may add an ice cube to the bowl. Ladle into chilled bowls. Pass sour cream and/or yogurt.

Beet Greens as Vegetable

¹/₂ lb. freshly cut new beet greens
¹/₄ c. water
¹/₄ t. salt
1 T. butter
1 T. lemon juice

Cut greens sparingly from beet root as it is growing in the garden, being careful not to pull out the root or to cut too much from each plant. Wash carefully and place in microwave-safe casserole with salted water. Microwave on high for 4 minutes. Drain excess water, saving it for soup to be cooked at a later time, and dress with butter and lemon juice.

Piquant Beets and Beet Greens

10 small to medium-size beets, including greens
$^1/_2$ c. cold water
4 T. butter, divided in half
3 T. minced onion

1 T. prepared horseradish
1 T. Dijon-style mustard
salt and pepper to taste
$^1/_2$ c. sour cream or yogurt

Trim beets, scrubbed, leaving roots and $^1/_2$ inch of the stems attached. Reserve beet greens. Place beets in microwave-safe casserole. Add cold water and microwave on high for approximately 10 minutes or until tender. Cool and drain the beets, reserving juice for later use in soup. Cover drained beets in casserole with cold water. Slip off the skins and cut the beets into $^1/_4$-inch slices. In a small skillet cook the beets in 2 T. of the butter over low heat for approximately 2 minutes. Set aside and keep warm.

In rinsed microwave-safe casserole, cook beet greens using recipe above for Beet Greens as Vegetable. Drain the greens, reserving liquid for soup. Chop coarsely.

In large skillet cook minced onion in remaining 2 T. butter over moderate heat until translucent. Add the chopped greens, horseradish, mustard, salt, and pepper. Reduce heat to low, stir in sour cream or yogurt, and cook just to warm and blend.

Transfer greens mixture to center of heated serving dish and arrange beet slices, overlapping, around it. Serves 6.

Svekolnik
A Russian favorite.

3 lbs. young beets with greens
12 c. water
small amount olive oil
2 c. chopped onions
2 cloves garlic, minced
$^1/_2$ c. white vinegar
salt and pepper to taste
2 c. diced cucumber
2 c. peeled, seeded, and diced tomato

4 hard-cooked eggs, peeled and diced
$^1/_2$ c. fresh dillweed sprigs, chopped fine
$^1/_2$ c. cilantro or parsley, chopped fine
1 c. green onions, diced fine, or $^1/_2$ c.
   sweet Bermuda or red onion, diced
   fine
1 c. sour cream or plain yogurt
vinegar to pass, if desired

Remove greens and stems from beet root by cutting at $^1/_2$ inch above beet root. Place scrubbed beets in large pot and cover with cold water, bringing water to boil slowly and simmering until beets are tender, approximately 45 minutes. (Beginning with cold water helps to retain red color.) Drain and reserve water for later use. Plunge into cold water to aid in slipping skins from beets.

While beets are cooking, combine onion, garlic, and chopped beet greens and stems and cook slowly in small amount of olive oil. Cool when softened. Add vinegar and salt and pepper to taste.

Combine mixture with chopped beets and chill.

To serve, pour mixture into large bowl or covered tureen. Sprinkle with cucumber, tomato, eggs, dill, cilantro or parsley, and green onions. Serve with sour cream or yogurt and additional vinegar (if desired) on the side. Serves 12.

Dried Beet Greens for Soup

Dry beet greens by spreading them on old window screens out of doors in sun. When greens have dried completely, chop in food processor. Store in plastic bag in pantry. When used in soups they add color and zest.

Blackberries

Our friend George Guthrie exclaimed upon seeing blackberry vines along the fence at the rear of our urban yard, "I can't believe you actually planted blackberries! Do you know how hard they are to get rid of?"

No, I did not when I planted them. Yes, they are very invasive, and you will want to be aware of that before planting. But, fortunately, that is why children can often find blackberries along the roadside and why we consider them one of the joys of summer, unless, of course, they have been sprayed with herbicides.

Blackberries may be used interchangeably with other bramble berries or mixed with other berries, particularly raspberries. Some people prefer the tiny "black cap" variety of blackberries to raspberries, for they are sweeter, particularly when dotting the cereal and milk bowl at breakfast.

Blackberry Summer Pudding

7 or 8 very thin slices dense white bread (such as Pepperidge Farm), crusts removed
4 c. sorted blackberries
1/2 c. sugar
2 T. sweet red wine
1 t. lemon juice

Line bottom and sides of 1-qt. deep glass bowl with bread slices, cutting slices to fit snugly.

In stainless steel saucepan combine blackberries, sugar, 1 T. wine, and lemon juice. Simmer mixture, stirring gently, for 5 to 7 minutes, or until sugar is dissolved.

Pour mixture gently over bread-lined bowl and top with remaining 2 thin slices white bread. Sprinkle the top with remaining tablespoon wine.

Invert a small flat plate just large enough to fit inside the bowl over bread; weight it down; and chill pudding for 8 hours in refrigerator or overnight.

Remove weight and plate, invert a platter over the pudding, and invert the pudding onto platter. Serve with whipped cream. Serves 6.

Blackberry Roly-Poly
An old-fashioned dessert.

2 c. sorted blackberries
$^1/_3$ c. sugar
1 c. all-purpose flour
2 t. baking powder
$1^1/_2$ t. sugar
2 T. cold butter
3 to 4 T. cold milk
2 T. soft butter

Combine blackberries with $^1/_3$ c. sugar and stir gently until sugar is dissolved. Set aside.

In another bowl sift together the flour, baking powder, $1^1/_2$ t. sugar, and salt. Blend in cold butter until mixture resembles coarse meal. Stir in cold milk, enough to make a ball of dough. Knead dough lightly with palm to distribute butter evenly. Roll out into a rectangle on large sheet of waxed paper dusted with flour. Brush top with 2 T. softened butter.

Spread blackberry mixture over the dough, leaving a 1-inch border. Carefully roll up dough lengthwise. Transfer the roll, seam side down, to a buttered jelly-roll pan and bake in preheated 425° oven for 30 minutes, or until golden brown.

Carefully transfer the roll to a platter and serve with sweetened whipped cream, garnishing with fresh blackberries, if desired. Serves 6.

Of course, blackberries may be frozen or canned. When cooking with frozen or canned berries, treat them as if they were fresh. Roly Poly may also be made with canned blackberries and prepared biscuit mix. Follow recipe for a sweet biscuit dough and proceed with recipe above, except that you will want to drain at least 1 c. of blackberry juice to make the following sauce:

Hot Blackberry Sauce

1 T. sugar
1 T. cornstarch
$^1/_4$ t. salt
1 c. blackberry juice (drained from canned berries)
1 T. butter
2 T. lemon juice

Mix sugar, cornstarch, and salt in stainless steel saucepan. Blend in the blackberry juice. Bring to a boil, stirring constantly. Boil 1 minute. Remove from heat and stir in the butter and lemon juice.

Serve over ice cream or Roly Poly (above).

Blackberry Cobbler

2 c. sorted blackberries
$^1/_3$ c. sugar
1 c. all-purpose flour
$1^1/_2$ T. sugar
$1^1/_2$ t. baking powder
$^1/_4$ t. ground cinnamon
$^1/_4$ t. salt
1 beaten egg
4 to 5 T. milk

Combine blackberries with $^1/_3$ c. sugar and stir gently until sugar is dissolved. Place blackberry mixture in glass baking dish.

Stir together flour, $1^1/_2$ T. sugar, baking powder, and cinnamon. Combine egg and milk. Stir into dry ingredients until just moistened.

Spoon 6 dollops of cobbler topping over fruit mixture, spacing them evenly across the baking dish. Bake at 400° for 15 to 20 minutes or until golden brown. Serve warm with ice cream or whipped cream. Serves 6.

Blackberry Cordial

2 c. sorted blackberries
1 c. white vinegar
1 c. sugar
$^1/_3$ c. honey

In a crock combine blackberries and vinegar and let the mixture stand, covered, in a cool, dark place, stirring it 3 times a day, for 1 week.

Strain the mixture through a fine sieve into a stainless steel saucepan, pressing hard on the solids. Add sugar and honey.

Bring liquid to a boil over moderate heat, stirring and washing down any sugar crystals clinging to the sides of the pan until the sugar is dissolved.

Simmer mixture, undisturbed, for 5 minutes.

Let mixture cool, pour into a clean dark-colored wine bottle with a cork. Cork the bottle. Makes 3 cups. Serve over ice cream or crushed ice.

Blackberry jam is a favorite way to use fresh or frozen blackberries. Simply follow the recipe on a commercial box of fruit pectin.

Blueberries

Blueberry bushes are relatively easy to grow in sandy, acidic soil. In some areas, such as South Dakota, small bushes, called huckleberries, are grown. Huckleberries may be substituted for blueberries in most recipes.

Blueberries are best eaten fresh or frozen. Because they are high in sugar content, no additional sugar need be added for flavoring. Blueberries contain only 84 calories per cup, but when fresh cream or sour cream is added as topping, the calorie count rises appreciably. You may wish to flavor the cream with ground mace, nutmeg, or ginger.

Blueberries may be frozen by simply spreading them on cookie sheets in the freezer and then storing the frozen berries in plastic bags. Some cooks advise freezing them in an unwashed state, but I have an aversion to frozen dirt. So I prefer to wash them under running water or in water baths, draining (or drying) them well in the warm air before placing them on cookie sheets to freeze.

The authoritative recipe for Blueberry Pancakes comes from Dr. Edwin L. Becker, chef extraordinaire and professor emeritus of the sociology of religion of Christian Theological Seminary, Indianapolis. I quote it in full:

> First, find an empty 3-pound coffee can and a full can of Cutter insect repellent. Go to a timber patch in northern Minnesota [where his family vacations] which has a good stand of poison ivy and an active mosquito population. Pick with care at least half a can of blueberries. Keep in the refrigerator until pancake time.
>
> Second, find a good pancake recipe in a standard made-in-USA cookbook and buy a box of Aunt Jemima pancake mix. Follow the directions on the box until you have a mix ready for the skillet. Wash a cupful of blueberries and set it by the skillet. Each time you pour the batter on the skillet, scatter a handful of blueberries across the top of the cakes. When the cakes begin to bubble on the top, take a peek under the edges and if the color on the bottom side is pleasing, e.g., is the proper color for a well-done pancake, turn the cake with a quick twist of the wrist. Most of the time the blueberries will follow the cake in flight and remain embedded and gradually become covered with the batter, exuding their lovely blue color throughout the surrounding batter. When done, serve with Land-O-Lakes butter and Vermont maple syrup.

Children enjoy making faces in the pancake as it is baking. Provide a chair next to the range so they can provide the eyes, nose and mouth after the batter has been poured onto the griddle.

Frozen blueberries may be substituted for fresh blueberries in any recipe such as blueberry pancakes, blueberry muffins, or blueberry buckle. When frozen in a large bag, simply remove from the bag the amount of berries needed.

A tasty winter treat is a compote made from equal portions of frozen blueberries, frozen cantaloupe balls (or chunks, if you don't want to waste food or time), and frozen sliced peaches. Remove the compote from the freezer in time for the fruit to thaw slightly, but serve in stemmed glasses while some ice crystals still remain. Garnish with mint leaves and serve with a simple sugar cookie.

Fresh Blueberries in Cantaloupe

How could one find a more beautiful, delicious, inexpensive, and nutritious breakfast when blueberries and cantaloupes are in season? And remain on a low-calorie diet at the same time? A $^3/_4$-cup serving of fresh, unsugared blueberries is only 64 calories. Half of a $4^1/_2$-inch cantaloupe is only 30 calories!

While we are thinking of breakfasts, let us consider some other wonderful reasons to get up in the morning:

Blueberry Yogurt Delight

$2^1/_2$ c. blueberries, cleaned and chilled
1 c. plain yogurt
1 packet sugar substitute (if desired)

Crush $^1/_4$ c. berries. Combine crushed berries with yogurt and sugar substitute. Spoon berries into dessert bowls and top with berry-yogurt mixture. Serves 4.

Blueberry Pancake Sauce

$^3/_4$ c. apple jelly
2 T. water
1 c. fresh blueberries

Stir apple jelly with water over medium heat until mixture is smooth. Add fresh blueberries and heat until berries are tender but do not let them burst. Serve warm on waffles, pancakes, individual shortcakes, or pound cake slices. Or serve on ice cream, custard, or puddings.

Microwaved Warm Blueberry Sauce

2 c. fresh or frozen unsweetened blueberries
2 T. orange juice
1 T. lemon juice

Combine berries and juices in 4-cup glass measuring cup. Microwave, uncovered, on full power until heated through, 4 to 5 minutes if the berries are fresh and 7 to 9 minutes for frozen berries. Stir once if you do not have a rotating tray.

Blueberry Muffins

2 eggs	1 T. baking powder
1/4 c. butter, melted	1/2 t. baking soda
1 c. milk	1/2 t. salt
2 c. flour	1 c. blueberries
3/4 c. sugar	

In a large bowl combine eggs, butter, and milk. In another bowl combine all dry ingredients. Add dry ingredients all at once to wet ingredients. Stir or fold mixture just until all dry ingredients are moistened.

Stir in blueberries. Spoon batter into greased or paper-lined muffin tins. Bake in 400° oven for 25 minutes or until nicely browned. Remove from pan and cool on rack. Serve with butter or softened cream cheese.

Huckleberry Buckle

Children will enjoy making and eating this recipe. I have served it at innumerable committee meetings and morning coffees.

3/4 c. sugar	2 t. baking powder
1/4 c. soft shortening	1/2 t. salt
1 egg	1 pint (2 c.) fresh or frozen huckle-
1/2 c. milk	berries or blueberries
2 c. flour	Crumb Topping (recipe follows)

Preheat oven to 375°. Mix thoroughly sugar, shortening, and egg with a rotary beater. Mix dry ingredients. Stir in. Blend in berries. Spread in greased 9-inch square pan. Sprinkle with Crumb Topping. Bake for 45–50 minutes or until toothpick comes out clean. Serve warm. Makes 9 3-oz. squares.

Crumb Topping

1/2 c. sugar	1/2 t. cinnamon
1/2 c. flour	1/4 c. soft butter

Mix above ingredients together and spread evenly over Huckleberry Buckle batter.

Blueberry Upside Down Cake

1/2 c. (1 stick) butter	2 t. grated lemon peel
1 c. brown sugar, loosely packed	1 package white cake mix
2 c. fresh or frozen blueberries	(2-layer size)

Melt butter in 9 x 13-inch glass cake baking pan as you preheat oven to 375°. Sprinkle brown sugar over butter. Mix berries and lemon peel. Place over sugar in pan.

Prepare cake mix according to directions on package. Spread over berries. Bake for 30–35 minutes. Let stand 10 minutes before turning out on serving platter, or serve from cake pan. Serves 12–16.

Do not overlook the potential for blueberries in salads. Fresh blueberries over cottage cheese on a lettuce leaf are always good. Another possibility is Patriotic Salad.

Patriotic Salad

1 t. grated orange rind
juice of 1 orange
1/3 c. salad oil
2 T. minced parsley
salt and freshly ground pepper
6 c. mixed greens (mesclun, if you want to be "fancy")
1 1/2 c. sliced red and white radishes
1 c. fresh blueberries

Combine and mix well the first 4 ingredients. Season with salt and pepper. Put greens in bowl. Top with radishes. Sprinkle with blueberries. Just before serving, add dressing and toss. Serves 6.

Variation: In winter, frozen blueberries and sliced oranges make a good combination with salad greens.

Blueberry Triangle Pastries

pastry for double crust pie or 1 package of two 9-inch deep dish frozen pie crust
*   shells*
1 c. fresh blueberries, washed and drained
1/4 c. sugar
1 T. cornstarch
1/4 t. nutmeg
1 egg, beaten

Roll out pastry dough or loosen pie shells from rim of pans. Place each shell on waxed paper. With kitchen shears, cut each shell into quarters.

Toss blueberries with sugar, cornstarch, and nutmeg. Divide blueberry mixture among pastry quarters. For each quarter, dampen with water along cut edges and rim. Fold one cut edge of crust over blueberries, lining up the two cut edges. Seal edges and rim tightly. Prick tops with fork. Brush with beaten egg wash.

Bake on cookie sheet in 400° oven for 15 minutes or until golden brown. Serves 8.

Blueberry Cheesecake

16 graham crackers, crushed with rolling pin
¹/₂ c. sugar
¹/₂ c. butter
2 8-oz. packages cream cheese
1 t. vanilla
2 eggs
1 c. sugar

Mix together the graham cracker crumbs, sugar, and butter. Spread in a pan and press up the sides as for pie.

Mix together cream cheese, vanilla, eggs, and sugar. Pour on top of crumbs. Bake for 15 minutes in 325° oven. Cool.

Combine 1 qt. of fresh blueberries with 1 T. cornstarch dissolved in ¹/₂ c. water and cook slowly over moderate heat until thickened. When cool, pour on top of cream cheese filling. Chill in refrigerator and serve. This is a rich recipe, so it will serve 8–12. (From Ruth Frick, Elmhurst, Illinois.)

Blueberries are very versatile and lend themselves to combining with ingredients in such staples as cornbread, oatmeal muffins, or nut breads. It is hard to go wrong when experimenting with blueberries.

Cantaloupe

Cantaloupe and muskmelon seem to be interchangeable as names for the small, rough-skinned, orange-colored melons grown in warm, sandy soil. Technically, cantaloupe is the melon with the ribbed rind. The area around Decker in southwest Indiana is well known for these melons, but home gardeners who have room for the vines to spread will enjoy growing them too. My father, John P. Kleinsasser, used to plant them near the fence line in his South Dakota cornfield (see my *Bread of Life: Diaries and Memories of a Dakota Family, 1936–1945*). When the corn got too tall to cultivate, the melon vines would spread between the rows and we children would be able to watch the progress of the melons from the road and pick them easily when they were ripe—unless some mischievous neighbor boys discovered them first!

Like blueberries, cantaloupe are low in calories. They are very satisfying, too, for persons on a low-calorie and a low-salt diet. (Don't spoil this benefit by using the salt shaker on them!)

When melons are plentiful at the local Farmers' Market, Butler University professor Louis Chenette has been known to buy them by the bushel. Louis finds them a refreshing treat when in season, particularly when he is sailing. But he knows they may also be frozen, canned, or pickled. More about that later. First let us consider the wonderful ways in which to use them fresh.

Of course, you will want to serve cantaloupe halves or quarters fresh for breakfast when they are in season. And a large melon slice with a dip of vanilla ice cream in the center is hard to beat for a healthful and easy dessert. The watermelon boat with honeydew and cantaloupe balls added to the watermelon is an elegant buffet centerpiece in summer, but I have difficulty justifying the time spent "balling" the melons and wasting the melon pulp. One solution to the waste is to turn it into Cantaloupe Ice, the recipe to follow below.

"Bayou Bill" Scifres, *Indianapolis Star* columnist, got rhapsodic about cantaloupe possibilities in his column on July 29, 1994. He suggested the following recipe for using overripe melons:

Cantaloupe Milk Shake

1 *c. cantaloupe pulp*
$^1/_2$ *c. milk*
$^1/_2$ *c. vanilla ice cream*
2 *T. finely chopped hickory nut meats*
2 *T. honey*

Cut from the rind of overripe cantaloupe enough pieces that when blended in a food blender they will yield 1 cup pulp. Add milk, ice cream, nuts, and honey. Blend a few more seconds. If desired, more chunks of cantaloupe may be added to the drink.

As a teenage "cherub" at Northwestern University's High School Institute of Speech, living at a sorority house on Rogers Place and being served by young men working their way through college, I was introduced to a fruit cup of melon balls with sparkling ginger ale poured over them. Now I serve the same fruit cup by simply cutting the melon into bite-size chunks and adding a sprig of mint after the ginger ale has been poured. Serving the fruit cup in a stemmed parfait glass adds a touch of class. Blueberries may also be added.

Dom De Luise's Salad

Arrange on a lettuce leaf equal portions of thin, peeled cantaloupe, tomato, and avocado slices. Sprinkle lemon juice over all, particularly the avocado. Shake salt and grind fresh pepper to taste. (De Luise shared this decades ago over a television talk show, maybe Merv Griffin's, but who can remember? The recipe, however, was memorable!)

Sweet and Sour Cantaloupe Salad

1 medium-size cantaloupe
$1/2$ c. sugar
1 T. mixed pickling spices
$1/2$ c. vinegar
$1/2$ c. water
salad greens

Pare and slice cantaloupe. Place in shallow dish or pie plate.

Combine sugar, pickling spices, vinegar, and water in a small steel saucepan. Heat to boiling, then simmer 5 minutes. Strain over cantaloupe, toss lightly to mix, and cover. Chill several hours or overnight to season and blend flavors. Serve on individual salad plates over mixed greens.

Cantaloupe Ice

$1 1/2$ c. sugar
$1 1/2$ c. water
1 medium cantaloupe
$1/4$ c. orange juice
$1/3$ c. lemon juice

In medium saucepan, combine sugar with water. Stir over low heat to dissolve sugar. Bring to boil and cook, uncovered, without stirring to 230° on a candy thermometer or until syrup spins 2-inch thread from top of spoon.

Cut melon in half, zigzag fashion. Discard seeds, scoop out pulp, and save the shell. Purée pulp in blender. Place in large bowl and stir in hot sugar syrup, mixing well. Let cool for 15 minutes. Stir in orange and lemon juice and turn into a 13 x 9-inch pan.

Place pan in the freezer for 3 hours or until edges are frozen. Turn into bowl and beat with electric beater until mushy. Place in a covered 1-quart plastic container. Refreeze for several hours. To serve, mound scoops of ice in melon shell and garnish with mint if desired. Let stand 5 minutes before serving.

(This also is a good way to use surplus, overripe melons, particularly if you must discard some portions. In that case, do not save the shell; use enough cantaloupe pulp equivalent to a complete melon. Throw the shells on the compost pile!)

Frozen Cantaloupe Chunks

As indicated under our discussion of blueberries, I enjoy serving a winter compote of frozen cantaloupe, blueberries, and sliced peaches. All three fruits may be frozen together in large-mouth, tapered jars (to make removal easier) or plastic containers in a light syrup (1 part sugar to 3 parts water) or separately, as the fruits become available. Hard-ripe cantaloupes, not mushy ones, work best for freezing.

Canned Cantaloupe Chunks (or Balls)

Select hard-ripe cantaloupes. Make a syrup by boiling 2 c. sugar with 5 c. water until the sugar dissolves. Keep hot but do not let boil. Cut cantaloupe into cubes or balls and drop them into salt-vinegar-water solution (1 T. each of salt and vinegar to 1 quart cold water).

When all have been prepared, fill jar about ¼ full with hot canning syrup. Then add lemon juice (1½ T. for pints and 3 T. for quarts.) Fill jars to within ½ inch of top with the melon. Add more syrup if needed to cover the melon. Put dome lid on jar. Screw band tight. Process pints and quarts for 20 minutes in boiling water bath, counting after water has come to boil.

It is best to let melons ripen on the vine, because they gain little sweetness after picking if they are harvested green. However, nearly ripe ones that must be picked when frost threatens may be buried in a bin of oats or other grain in a cool outbuilding. They will last 4 to 6 weeks in this environment. (As a child I did not understand why my sister Ruth and I would find melons in the oat bin when we fed the horses. Aunt Katherine Hofer, who was unusually generous with her melons, probably put them there to protect them from the cold weather—and the hungry children!)

Cherries

Many home gardeners have a sour cherry tree or two in their yards. The new dwarf varieties make picking the fruit before the birds do a much easier job. Black netting may be purchased to cover the tree when the cherries reach ripening stage in order to prevent birds from taking the entire crop. Hanging used aluminum baking tins also helps to scare birds away. However, the spring of 1994 posed a problem we had not had previously: an overpopulation of chipmunks, who scale the tree heights with little impediment, and devour the entire crop.

Normally, I have a compulsion to freeze at least enough cherries to bake a pie on February 22, honoring not only Washington's but my father's birthday. I invite you to try it! Remove the pits with the tip (and scoop) of a potato peeler. Freeze the pitted cherries whole in their own juice or mixed with sugar and cornstarch for thickening, ready to dump into an unbaked pastry shell. Add almond flavoring, if desired.

If your cherry tree produces only a few cherries each year, or if the birds beat you to it, pick them as they ripen and cook with sugar and cornstarch until the filling is clear (after removing the pits). This makes a fine sauce for vanilla ice cream and may be served either hot or cold. Store in the refrigerator in a beautiful covered glass dish and bring to the table for diners to build their own cherry sundaes. A sprinkling of cinnamon adds flavor.

Tart Cherry Sauce for Pancakes

1 c. maple or maple-flavored syrup
1¹/₂ c. fresh red sour pitted cherries or frozen cherries, thawed and drained

Bring syrup to a boil over medium heat and boil 5 minutes. Remove from heat. Add cherries. Cool slightly. Serve warm over pancakes. Makes 1¹/₂ cups sauce.

Hot Cherry-Walnut Sauce for Ham

2 T. cornstarch
¹/₃ c. sugar
¹/₈ t. salt
2 c. canned or cooked red sour cherries (pitted)
2 T. lemon juice
¹/₃ c. broken walnut meats

In saucepan combine cornstarch, sugar, and salt. Stir in liquid from cherries and lemon juice to make a smooth sauce. Add nuts and cook over medium heat until thick and clear. Add cherries and bring to a boil. Remove from heat. Serve hot with hot or cold baked ham. Yields about 2 cups or enough for 8–10 servings.

Cherry Moos (Fruit Soup)
This is a traditional Hutterite Mennonite dish. In the Hutterische dialect, Moos is pronounced as two syllables, i.e., moo-us.

1 qt. water
1 c. sugar
2 c. pitted cherries
¹/₂ c. sweet cream or half and half
1 T. (heaping) flour

Bring water and sugar to a boil. Add pitted cherries. Cook until soft. Combine sweet cream and flour. Add to first mixture slowly, adding a small portion of hot cherry juice to the thickening agent first. Cook a few minutes longer. Serve warm or cold as a dessert.

All of the previous recipes have utilized sour red cherries because they are what most home gardeners have in the Midwest. However, if you live in the states of Washington, Michigan, or New York, you might grow dark sweet cherries or have access to them through farm markets.

I grew up in a family that canned at least two "lugs" (12-pound wooden boxes) of Washington Bing cherries each summer. There was always a struggle between the forces of "eat and enjoy now" and the advocates of "put up for the winter when you'll really appreciate them." Our elder sister, Pearl, has never been allowed to forget the summer when she rationed to her younger sisters three fresh cherries *each* during the stemming and washing process! We were definitely of the "eat and enjoy now" persuasion.

Sweet cherries may be frozen three different ways: whole with stem (to enjoy by eating out of hand), in a heavy syrup pack (1 part sugar to 2 parts water, boiled), or in a dry sugar pack (about 1/3 c. sugar sprinkled over each pint of cherries, pitted or unpitted). For more information about preparing and preserving sweet cherries, see Resources.

Microwave Cherry Preserves

3 c. pitted sweet cherries, chopped
1 c. water
1/4 c. powdered pectin
2 t. lemon juice
3 c. sugar
1/2 t. almond extract

Combine cherries, water, pectin, and lemon juice in microwave-safe casserole. Cover with plastic wrap and microwave on high until mixture reaches a boil, 6 to 8 minutes. Stir in sugar and almond extract. Cover, return to a boil, and cook 3 minutes after boil is reached. Stir and return to microwave, uncovered. Cook until preserves sheet from spoon, about 3 minutes. Remove from microvave and remove foam from top. Pour hot preserves into hot, sterilized jars, leaving 1/4 inch head space. Process 10 minutes in boiling water bath, counting from time water comes to a boil. Or store in refrigerator or freezer.

Black Cherry Pudding

4 c. fresh sweet cherries, pitted
1/3 c. sugar
1 t. grated lemon peel
1 T. lemon juice
1 package Jiffy yellow cake mix (1-layer size) or 1/2 yellow cake mix (2-layer size)
1/3 c. melted butter

Put cherries in glass casserole dish. Sprinkle with sugar, lemon peel, and juice, stirring until evenly mixed. Sprinkle dry cake mix evenly over cherries. Drizzle melted butter over the top. Bake, uncovered, in a 375° oven about 45 minutes, until topping is bubbly and brown. Cool. Serve with ice cream or whipped cream. Serves 8.

A comparatively new item on the market is dried cherries. In 1990 the Cherry Central Cooperative of Traverse City, Michigan, test-marketed them under the Traverse Bay Fruit Company brand, using the Montmorency variety. Since it takes eight pounds of fresh cherries to make a pound of dried fruit, they are costly. If you have a cherry tree and a microwave oven, you might try drying them by placing no more than ¼ c. of diced fresh pitted cherries between paper towels and zapping them for 2–3 minutes. If not dried enough, zap for 30 seconds more. Store the dried cherries in an airtight glass jar. If condensation appears on the inside of the jar, dry the cherries longer.

Since dried cherries are so "dear," I suggest using them only for color and flavor, as in the recipe below:

Cherry Vinaigrette

1 t. Dijon-style mustard
4 T. lemon juice or red wine vinegar
³/₄ c. olive oil
salt and pepper to taste
1 T. walnuts, chopped fine
2 T. chopped dried cherries

Shake all together and serve over mixed salad greens. (Adapted from a recipe by Chef Drew Goss of Something Different in the *Indianapolis Star* Food Section, Donna Segal, ed.)

Chokecherries

The chokecherry tree is small, seldom taller than 20 feet. Its leaves are thin and oval, about 3 inches long. The cherries are small, like small peas, which ripen in clusters at the tip of branches during July and August. As the name suggests, the fruit is astringent and puckery when fresh, but when cooked becomes quite delightful. The jam or jelly made from it is also beautifully red.

When drought prevailed in South Dakota during my early childhood, our family could almost always fall back on the chokecherry tree as a source of juice for jelly.

Chokecherry Jelly (Modern Method)
This makes a wonderful Christmas gift when paired with a jar of mint jelly.

2¹/₂ quarts ripe chokecherries
7 c. sugar
1 box powdered pectin
2 c. apple mush (crab apples cooked and rubbed through colander)

Wash cherries and discard any green ones. Place in large kettle and cover with water. Cook until cherries are soft and have split. Rub through colander and measure out 6 c. chokecherry juice.

Pour juice into *large* stainless steel or enameled kettle. Stir in apple mush and powdered pectin. Bring to a hard boil. Add sugar all at once and stir. Bring to a boil again and boil rapidly for 12 to 15 minutes, stirring constantly. Skim off foam with spoon and pour quickly into hot sterilized jars. Seal with lids and bands. Yields 5 pints of jelly.

Other uses for chokecherries: Use chokecherries as a substitute for blueberries in recipes for muffins, buckle, etc. Simply simmer chokecherries in water for 20 minutes. Drain the juice and pit the cherries by gently squeezing them until pits pop out. Discard the pits.

Chokecherry juice drained from the cherries may be added to lemonade for interesting color and taste. Adjust for taste by adding sugar, if needed.

Chokecherry and Gooseberry Jam
This is an adaptation of an old prairie Hutterite recipe.

4 c. chokecherries
2 c. gooseberries
sugar to equal amount of juice derived
1 bottle Certo

Clean and wash fruit. Mash gooseberries. Place both fruits in stainless steel saucepan and add enough water to cover. Bring to a boil. Reduce heat and simmer until chokecherries pop and flesh comes off pits very easily. Strain though sieve to obtain juice. Measure juice and add the same volume amount of sugar.

Boil hard for 10 minutes and add Certo. Boil for 1 minute more. Pour into hot sterilized jars. Seal with paraffin. Store in cool, dark, dry place.

Collards

Collards are among those "cruciferous" vegetables (so called because of the four-leafed flowers on their plants), all of which are members of the cabbage family. They are highly recommended by the American Cancer Society for our diets because they have powerful enzymes called "phenols" and "indoles" which may help to prevent some types of cancer. Studies show a decreased risk of bladder, colo-rectal, stomach, and respiratory cancers among people who eat more cruciferous vegetables.

In addition to the favorable enzymes, collards are beneficial because they contain Vitamins A and C. They also provide necessary dietary fiber. For these reasons, dietitians recommend we eat several servings of cruciferous vegetables each week.

Simple Collards

1 T. chopped onion
2 T. shortening
1¹/₂ lbs. collard greens, finely shredded
salt

Sauté onion in shortening until brown shows. Add collards and salt. Cook over low heat, stirring frequently, until tender, about 15 minutes. Serves 6.

Red Hot Collards

2¹/₂ lbs. fresh collard greens
1 T. cooking oil
¹/₂ lb. ham pieces cut from ham bone
¹/₄ c. chopped onion
2 cloves garlic, minced
1 pod red chili pepper, minced
¹/₂ c. bouillon (chicken-flavored), ham broth, or water
2 medium tomatoes, chopped

Remove leaves from tough large stems. Wash leaves thoroughly and chop into large pieces. In cast-iron skillet, heat oil, add onions and garlic and sauté until translucent. Add ham pieces and fry until all ingredients begin to brown. Add red hot pepper and ¹/₂ c. bouillon, ham broth, or water and cook slowly.

Add half of the chopped tomato and remove from heat. Do not overcook; collards should retain their green color. Arrange on platter and garnish with remaining chopped tomato. Serves 8.

Brazilian Collards

1¹/₂ lbs. young collard leaves
3 T. olive oil
salt and pepper to taste
¹/₃ c. lemon juice or vinegar

Wash leaves thoroughly and pat dry with paper towels. Chop the leaves coarsely. Heat skillet or wok over high heat until smoking. Add oil to skillet and let stand for a few seconds.

Toss in the greens. Cook over high heat, stirring constantly, until they wilt (3 to 5 minutes). Season with salt and pepper. Add lemon juice or vinegar. Taste and adjust seasonings. Serve immediately. Serve Brazilian style, with beans, rice, and pork roast. Serves 4.

Corn

If you have grown your own sweet corn or picked it fresh from a farmer's field, you will never want to purchase it from a supermarket where corn has been lingering in illness following a lengthy journey from distant, chemical-laden corporate farms. The received wisdom about cooking corn on the cob is to start heating the water before picking the corn.

I can remember farm meals consisting entirely of sweet corn, probably not a good idea for young children or elders. Elders usually know when to quit eating, however. A better idea, if one must go to excess in enjoying summer vegetables, is to reduce the number of ears of corn and add fresh sliced tomatoes and fresh sliced cucumbers in cream or dilled vinegar to the menu.

People who insist on worm-free sweet corn will insist on pesticides being added to their corn. However, if you are able to husk an ear of corn and not faint dead away upon sight of a little worm enjoying the delicacy as well, you will simply cut away the worm-damaged spot and proceed with the cooking.

Corn silks are easily removed if you will divide the silks and husks neatly at the tip of the ear and pull down both silks and husks in one movement to the stalk end with each hand.

Once the kettle of water is boiling, drop the corn into the water carefully, ear by ear, slowly enough so as not to disturb the boiling. Cover the kettle and boil the corn rapidly until tender, 4 to 10 minutes, depending upon maturity of the ears. Carefully remove each ear with tongs and place on a serving platter. Serve with butter, margarine, or salt, as desired. (Do not add salt to the cooking water because it lengthens cooking time and toughens the kernels.)

Unhusked corn on the cob may be microwaved. Lay up to 6 ears on the rotating tray and zap 2–3 minutes for one ear, 3–4 minutes for two ears, etc. Silks will come away easily with the husks if they are grasped together at the tip (the silk end) of the ear.

Or, to prevent zapping worms in organically grown corn, husk the corn first, cut away worm-infested parts, break or cut cob in half, rinse the ears and stand them upright in a microwave-safe plastic steamer with a cover. Add a few tablespoons of water and cover, cooking on full power for $1^{1}/_{2}$ to 2 minutes per ear.

Any leftover ears of corn should not be discarded, regardless of how bountiful your harvest. Cut the kernels from the cob with a sharp knife, resting the ear on a plate or cutting board at the stalk end and cutting down the ear. Be careful not to cut into the cob, or you may have more fiber than you desire. Corn kernels may then be warmed in milk or butter, used in soup, salad, or relish, or frozen in a plastic container for later use as a vegetable dish.

Corn may be frozen on the cob for a winter treat, but cobs take up an inordinate amount of freezer space. It really doesn't make sense to use electricity to freeze cobs. If you have nothing else to put in your freezer, however, and wish to freeze corn on the cob, it must be blanched first (6 minutes for small, 8 minutes for medium, and 10 minutes for large ears). Then it must be cooled rapidly in cold running or icy water, drained, and "sharp" frozen quickly, if your freezer has such a compartment.

Frozen corn on the cob may be microwaved satisfactorily. Microwave two large frozen ears for 7–9 minutes on high power after arranging them in the plastic covered baking dish and adding 2 T. of water. Turn ears and rearrange once. Let stand for 3–5 minutes. For two small frozen ears, cook for 5–6 minutes on high.

Corn for canning or freezing should be more mature than for eating fresh from the ear. When the "milk" from the kernel is "paste-y" but the kernel is not dented, it is ready for freezing.

When freezing corn cut from the cob, blanch, cook, and drain before cutting from the cob as described above. Cut corn may be frozen in sturdy plastic bags. Be sure to remove air from the bags and tie securely. If you have drained the corn well, you should be able to remove from the bag the desired amount of corn for meal preparation. Another method is to freeze the cut corn in small bags appropriate for the size of your family or in sandwich bags, tying securely. When the smaller bags have been "sharp" frozen, transfer them to a heavier plastic bag for permanent storage.

Roasted Corn

A wonderful treat at picnics or cookouts is corn roasted over hot coals.
It may also be used as a fundraiser at fairs.

1 dozen ears of "perfect" corn　　　　　*1 clean bucket of clean water*

Pull back husks just enough to remove majority of silks from ear and to examine ear for worm infestation. A few remaining silks are all right and can be removed later. Reclose husks tightly around the ears. Stand the ears, stalk side up, in bucket of water, and let soak for one-half hour to 2 hours. When coals are white hot, remove corn from water, and shake ears thoroughly to remove excess water. Place ears on grill. Do not stack ears.

To keep the ears from drying out, thoroughly wet a large terrycloth towel. Wring out completely. Place towel over corn so ears are completely covered. Be careful that towel does not come in contact with the grill. Cook corn on one side for 5–8 minutes. Remove towel and rewet it. Turn ears. Wring out towel again and replace on corn. Cook on other side until ears are done. Corn is ready when husks are charred and silks come away easily from corn. Serve with dipping container of melted butter or margarine. (Teenagers will enjoy munching their ears of corn as they "check out" who else is at the fair.)

Corn—fresh, frozen, canned, or dried—may be used in a myriad of ways. Combining corn with beans, as native Americans have always known, affords a complete protein meal. While "succotash" grown during the thirties and forties on our South Dakota farm consisted of oats and barley used for poultry feed, now "succotash" in human cookbooks refers to beans and corn combined not only for improved nutrition but for aesthetic enjoyment.

Succotash

1 chopped onion
¹/₂ c. chopped green pepper
2 T. bacon drippings
1 c. cooked fresh corn
1 c. cooked fresh lima beans or cut green beans
¹/₂ c. bits of leftover ham
2 T. chopped fresh parsley
salt and pepper to taste

Sauté the onion and green pepper in bacon drippings. Add remaining ingredients and heat through.

Corn Scramble

¹/₂ c. bits of leftover ham
small amount of oil
2 c. leftover corn kernels cut from cob
¹/₂ c. milk
3 eggs (beaten)

Brown ham bits in oil in skillet. Blend together corn kernels and milk to consistency of creamed corn. Add eggs. Place mixture in skillet and cook over moderate heat, stirring, until eggs are set. (Adapted from recipe contributed by Miriam Fay, Fairview Presbyterian Church, Indianapolis.)

Curried Succotash Salad

2 c. cooked whole kernel corn

2 c. cooked baby lima beans

1 medium onion, chopped

1/2 c. chopped celery

1/4 c. chopped green pepper

1/4 c. diced pimiento

1/2 c. firmly packed brown sugar

1 T. curry powder

2 3-inch pieces stick cinnamon, broken

1 t. whole cloves

1 t. celery seed

1 t. salt

1 c. cider vinegar

Drain liquids from corn and beans into 2-cup measure. Combine corn, beans, onion, celery, green pepper, and pimiento in a bowl.

Combine 1/2 c. of the reserved vegetable liquid, brown sugar, curry powder, cinnamon, cloves, celery seed, salt, and vinegar in steel saucepan. Heat, stirring constantly, to boiling. Simmer 10 minutes. Strain over vegetable mixture. Cool, then chill overnight to season. Serves 8.

Deutsch Vegetable Salad

2 c. cooked whole kernel corn, drained

2 c. cooked green beans, drained

1 medium sweet onion, diced

1 small green pepper, diced

1 c. celery, chopped

1/2 c. cider vinegar

1/2 c. sugar

1/4 t. dry mustard

Place vegetables in a serving bowl. In a saucepan combine and bring to a boil the vinegar, sugar, and mustard. Pour dressing over vegetables and refrigerate overnight. (Salad improves as flavors blend.) Leftover kernels of white or yellow corn cut from the cob or canned shoepeg corn may be used. (Adapted from a recipe of Betty Wiest, who served it to us while we were on sabbatical at Pittsburgh Theological Seminary in 1988–89. Betty is a volunteer at Pittsburgh's Food Bank and an avid gardener and recycler.)

Fresh Corn Pancakes

1/2 c. flour

2 1/2 t. baking powder

1 t. salt

1 T. sugar

1/4 t. pepper

2 eggs, separated

1 1/2 c. fresh corn, cut from cob

3/4 c. milk

3 T. melted butter

Mix flour with baking powder, salt, sugar, and pepper in mixing bowl. Beat egg yolks and mix with corn and milk. Stir into dry ingredients. Add melted butter.

Wash beaters and beat egg whites until they stand in soft peaks. Fold into batter. Drop from a tablespoon onto hot greased griddle to make 2½-inch pancakes. Cook until golden brown, turning once. Serve as vegetable course with a dollop of sour cream. Makes 3 dozen small pancakes.

Corn Fritters

1 egg
¼ c. milk
1 c. pancake mix
1½ c. cooked whole kernel corn, drained, or cut from leftover cooked ear
cooking oil to depth of 1 inch in stainless steel saucepan

Blend egg and milk. Add pancake mix, stirring until just mixed (batter will be stiff). Fold in corn. Drop by teaspoonfuls into hot oil, a few at a time. Cook quickly until golden brown, turning once. Makes 24. Serve with maple or maple-flavored syrup.

New England Corn Chowder

4 slices bacon, diced
1 medium onion, chopped
4 c. diced potatoes (peeled or unpeeled, depending on preference and condition)
1 c. water
3 c. milk
2 c. fresh corn, cut from cob
¾ t. salt
freshly ground pepper
2 T. chopped fresh parsley

Fry bacon for 2 minutes. Add onion and continue to fry until onion is soft but not browned. Add potatoes and water. Simmer, covered, about 20 minutes or until potatoes are tender. Add milk, corn, salt, and pepper and continue cooking over low heat for 10 minutes. Serve sprinkled with fresh parsley.

Quick Corn Luncheon Dish for Two

4 large eggs
²/₃ c. leftover cooked corn cut from cob
salt and pepper to taste
2 T. butter

Beat eggs just enough to blend yolks and whites. Add corn, salt, and pepper. Melt butter in an 8-inch skillet over medium heat. Pour in egg and corn mixture. Cook gently, lifting egg mixture from bottom of skillet as egg sets. Serve at once.

Quick Corn Relish

1¹/₃ c. cooked whole kernel corn
¹/₂ c. finely diced celery
1 T. chopped green pepper
3 T. vinegar
2 T. brown sugar
¹/₂ t. salt
¹/₈ t. pepper
¹/₈ t. turmeric
1 T. chopped canned pimiento (optional)

Combine all ingredients, except pimiento, in saucepan and mix well. Heat thoroughly. Add pimiento. Cool and refrigerate. Makes 2 cups.

Corn Relish to Can

16 ears corn (8 c. whole kernel corn) *1 c. chopped green bell peppers*
4 c. cabbage, chopped *1 c. chopped onion*
1 quart vinegar *2 T. dry mustard*
1¹/₂ c. sugar *1 T. salt*
1 c. water *1 T. celery seed*
1 c. chopped red bell peppers *1 T. yellow mustard seed*
  1 T. turmeric

Place ears of corn in boiling water and boil 5 minutes. Cut corn from cob and measure. Combine corn with remaining ingredients. Simmer 20 minutes. Then bring to boil, stirring constantly. Ladle into sterilized jars, leaving ¹/₄ inch head space. Adjust lids and process in boiling water bath for 15 minutes.* (Start counting processing time when water returns to a boil.) Remove jars and cool. Yields 6 pints.

*1989 USDA recommendations are 10 pounds of pressure for 20 minutes for pints.

Dried Corn

This is a popular Pennsylvania Dutch or Amish method for preserving corn. Obviously, it is best used at the end of the season when cool days have returned and when you have exhausted all other ideas for using a bumper crop of corn.

Cut kernels from 12 ears of corn and spread them in one layer on a large baking sheet. Sprinkle corn with 2 t. sugar and dry it in a preheated very slow oven (150°) with the oven door ajar, stirring occasionally, for 6 to 8 hours, or until it is completely dry and brittle. Let corn cool, transfer it to a glass jar, and store it, sealed, in a cool, dark, dry place. Makes 1 quart.

Using Dried Corn

In a bowl soak 4 c. dried corn in water to cover overnight. Transfer corn and water to saucepan, bring water to a boil, and simmer the mixture, adding more water if necessary, for an hour or until corn is tender. Continue simmering the mixture until liquid has evaporated and add 2 T. butter, 1 T. sugar, 1 t. salt, and $1/8$ t. pepper. Serves 6 to 8. (A real delicacy!)

Cucumbers

Cucumbers are not pickles until they are pickled! Eaten fresh from the garden, cucumbers are very refreshing and low in calories because of their high water content. Twelve slices of cucumber will cost you only 10 calories. It is the sour cream and the sugar in the pickling brine which raise the calorie count. One large dill cucumber pickle, however, is only 15 calories.

When cucumbers are home grown or bought from a certified organic grower, you may eat the peel, but do not eat the peel of a highly waxed cucumber bought in a supermarket. The wax is used to lengthen shelf life but will not lengthen yours.

I find the simple dressings the most delicious and refreshing. Cultured sour cream and dillweed (fresh or dried) added to sliced cucumbers and onions make an unbeatable salad when it is chilled and served on a lettuce leaf on a chilled plate. Another simple but delicious dressing for cucumbers is vinegar sweetened with a touch of sugar and flavored with dill seeds.

In order to save calories, substitute plain yogurt for sour cream when preparing salads made with cucumbers. Yogurt also helps to make a wonderful cold summer soup.

Blender Cucumber Soup

This is a very refreshing soup which may be served as a first course or as an accompaniment to a hot, spicy dish such as curried chicken or lamb.

Peel and remove seeds from 2 large cucumbers that have been chilled in the refrigerator crisper. Slice or dice into the blender a little at a time the cucumber pieces until all have been puréed. Add 1/2 medium-size sweet onion and blend until smooth. Blend in 1 c. plain yogurt. Salt to taste. Serve chilled in colorful (preferably green) chilled bowls. If the soup is too thick in consistency, an ice cube may be added. Garnish with a slice of cucumber, unpeeled, and fresh dillweed.

Cucumber Raita

I was first introduced to raita by my stepmother, Marie Duerksen Kleinsasser, a former Mennonite missionary to India. It is delicious served with curry.

1 large cucumber (preferably English seedless type)
2 c. plain yogurt
1/2 t. roasted cumin seed, ground in mortar and pestle
salt, pepper, and cayenne pepper to taste
1 medium tomato, seeded and finely chopped
1 T. chopped fresh mint (optional)

Peel and grate cucumber. (Remove seeds from a regular cucumber before grating.) Squeeze out excess moisture. Empty yogurt into bowl and mix with fork until smooth. Add grated cucumber, cumin seed, and other seasonings. Finally add tomato and mint and mix well. Cover and refrigerate until serving time.

Scottish Frozen Cucumbers

6 c. peeled, thinly sliced cucumbers
1 c. sliced onions
2 c. sugar
1 c. vinegar
1 t. pickling salt (kosher)

Mix cucumbers and onions. Combine sugar, vinegar, and salt but do not heat. Pour dissolved liquid over vegetable mixture which has been transferred to plastic freezing containers. Do not fill to brim; leave room for expansion due to freezing. Crushed waxed paper may be added to the top before placing lid on container to help keep cucumber slices under the brine.

(South Dakota Hutterite communities use the same recipe except that they start with 10 gallons of cucumbers and use 20 onions! During the winter, when good cucumbers are rare and expensive in the supermarket, you may substitute these frozen cukes for fresh ones in a tossed salad. Just lay the slices with ice crystals on top of the individual salad bowl. As they thaw, the brine will flavor the greens nicely.)

Molded Cucumber Salad

1 package (3 oz.) lime-flavored gelatin
3/4 c. boiling water
1 c. cottage cheese
2 T. grated onion
3/4 c. grated peeled cucumber
dash of salt
1 c. mayonnaise

Dissolve gelatin in boiling water. When cool, stir in remaining ingredients and blend well. Pour into mold that holds 3 to 4 cups liquid. Refrigerate until firm and unmold. Serves 6.

Variation: 8 oz. cream cheese may be substituted for the cottage cheese and mayonnaise, and 1 c. diced celery added. I have also eliminated the mayonnaise with good results; in that case dissolve the gelatin in 1 c. boiling water.

Greek Salad

4 tomatoes, cut in wedges
2 cucumbers, peeled, halved lengthwise, and cut crosswise into 1/4-inch slices
1/4 lb. feta cheese, broken into chunks
16 Greek olives
1/3 c. Lemon and Garlic Dressing (recipe follows)
1 T. minced flat-leaf parsley
2 t. oregano

In large bowl combine tomatoes, cucumbers, cheese, and olives. Add dressing and toss. Sprinkle with parsley and oregano. Makes 4 main-dish salads.

Lemon and Garlic Dressing

1/4 c. olive oil
2 T. lemon juice
1 small garlic clove, minced
salt and pepper to taste

In a blender on high blend all ingredients until mixture is pale and smooth. Makes about 1/3 c. or enough for salad above.

Cucumber Salad

2 large cucumbers, peeled, sliced thin
2 T. sugar
¹/₂ t. garlic, minced
1 t. salt
¹/₄ t. freshly ground pepper
2 T. fresh dill, coarsely chopped
¹/₂ c. sherry vinegar

Combine cucumbers, sugar, garlic, salt, pepper, dill, and vinegar in a large bowl. Cover with plastic wrap. Refrigerate for 1 to 2 hours, stirring occasionally. Serve cold. These taste like pickles. Serves 6. (From Ellen Walsh. Courtesy of *Indianapolis Star* Food Section, Donna Segal, ed.)

There is much lore and competition associated with pickling cucumbers. The following recipe is one I learned to make from my sister Pearl, and I have made it almost every year for more than 40 years!

Bread and Butter Pickles

25–30 medium cucumbers
8 large white onions
2 large green bell peppers
¹/₂ c. salt
5 c. cider vinegar
5 c. sugar
2 T. yellow mustard seed
1 t. turmeric
¹/₂ t. cloves

Scrub cucumbers with vegetable brush and slice as thinly as possible. (A metal slicer such as one made by the Slawcutter Company [see Resources] may be used instead of a paring knife.) Slice onions and peppers and combine with cucumber slices and salt. Let stand, covered, for 3 hours in a large crockery bowl. Drain. Combine vinegar, sugar, and spices in a large enameled preserving kettle. Bring to boil. Add drained vegetables, heat through, but do not boil. Ladle into hot, sterilized pint jars and seal with lids and rings. To help ensure that the lids will seal, soften the rubber on the lids by separating and heating them in a small pan of hot water while the vegetables are heating in the brine.

If, during the winter, you run out of cucumber relish for hot dogs, a jar of Bread and Butter Pickles, drained and chopped in the food processor, will produce fine relish.

My sister Pearl is also famous for her sweet "Heinz" pickles. However, having smelled the pickles soaking in salt water for 7 days and pouring off the moldy brine for three successive mornings, rinsing them in cold water, preparing a sweet pickling solution which needed to be reheated 3 mornings before the pickles could be canned the third morning, I have left the monopoly on "Heinz" pickles to Pearl.

My father's diary records that after my mother died in 1937, Mrs. Jacob P. Maendl made a "batch" of pickles for our family. Here is the recipe:

Mrs. Maendl's Dill Pickles

Wash cucumbers, drain, and pack in sterilized jars. [Clean jars are placed on cookie sheets and heated in the oven.] Put dill head and folded stalks on bottom and top of cucumbers. A clove of garlic and hot red pepper pod may also be added.

Make a brine of 14 c. hard well water, 1 c. coarse pickling salt (kosher), and 1 c. cider vinegar. Boil 5 minutes and pour over cucumbers in jars.

After an hour or two [depending upon whether you are milking the cows at this time], pour the brine from the jars back into the kettle and reheat. Refill the jars and seal tight using rubbers and zinc caps. [Rubbers may be softened to aid the sealing by placing them in a small pan of hot water.]

Put the jars on a layer of newspaper [either the *Sioux Falls Argus Leader* or the *Freeman Courier*] and cover them with a rug [wool or cotton]. Let the jars stand covered for a day or two, depending upon whether the Hutchinson County Fair is in session. [The reason for covering jars is to prevent their cooling off too soon.]

Variation: Add mixed pickling spice to the jars before refilling with brine. (With apologies to Mrs. Maendl's spirit.)

It has been reported in the media that Iowa State University researchers have found that cucumber leaves contain a cholesterol-reducing enzyme. The scientists are trying to determine how to add this enzyme to meat and dairy products.

So, the lowly cucumber (known as *Kratsivitz* to immigrants from the Ukraine), already benefiting our diets by being 96% water, may shortly be minimizing the damage done by some of our other favorite foods. (It is well to remember that cucumbers lose 22% of their ascorbic acid just by slicing them. So the most beneficial way to eat them is whole, from the garden and out of hand—after dusting and shining them on your coveralls, of course.)

Currants

Don't be surprised if you find a currant bush in your back yard along the fence row. But do be surprised if you get to the clusters of bright red berries before the birds do!

Red Currant Cordial

*A large "mess" of currants from my friend Gerald Wilson
was the inspiration for this recipe.*

2 qts. currants
1 pt. cider vinegar combined with 1 pt. water
2 c. sugar for each pint of juice

Clean and wash currants. Drain and pour diluted vinegar over them in large crockery bowl. Let stand for 24 hours. Strain through a sieve or colander. Add sugar to juice and stir until dissolved. Boil for 30 minutes and seal in half-pint or pint jars using lids and rings. When serving as a drink dilute with water, sparkling water, or carbonated clear beverage to suit your taste.

Red Currant Jelly

4¹/₂ qts. fresh currants
1¹/₂ c. water
7 c. (3 lbs.) sugar
1 box powdered fruit pectin

Remove large stems from currant clusters. Crush berries one layer at a time and add water. Cover and simmer 10 minutes, stirring occasionally. To extract juice, place cooked currants in dampened jelly bag or several thicknesses of cheesecloth. Allow to drip. When dripping has almost ceased, gently press or squeeze bag. Measure amount of juice. If amount is less than 6 ¹/₂ cups, add water to make up difference. Pour into large saucepan. Measure sugar exactly and set aside. *Do not use less sugar or results will not be satisfactory.* Bring to full boil over high heat, stirring constantly. *At once* stir in sugar. Stir and bring to full rolling boil that cannot be stirred down. Boil hard 1 minute, stirring constantly. Remove from heat. Skim off foam with large metal spoon. Ladle into half-pint jelly jars and seal with lids and rings. (Rubber on lids may be softened by warming in small amount of water in a small saucepan.)

Variation: Before serving, 1 t. dried mint may be crumbled into each half pint of currant jelly which has been reheated in top of double boiler and returned to jelly glass.

Daikon Radish

Daikon has come into my consciousness only recently. I suspect it was introduced into American cookery by Japanese war brides or by men who had been stationed with occupation forces after World War II.

Our son Karl plants this gigantic vegetable each year and uses it in a variety of ways, including thinly sliced as a relish, shredded in salads, boiled as a vegetable, and pickled. It is low in calories and an excellent source of Vitamin C when eaten raw.

Tsukemono (Pickled Radishes)

Ready in about 6 hours, but holding for at least 2–3 days in the refrigerator, this pickle is enhanced with red food coloring, if desired, to add excitement to your dinner. Use the long white radish (8–10 inches long) now grown in home gardens. But beware—they can grow 3 feet long!

1 long Japanese white daikon radish (8–10 inches)
salt
1/2 c. sugar
1/2 c. vinegar
red food coloring, if desired

Peel the radish and cut into thin slices. Put in bowl in layers and coat liberally with salt as you build up layers. The slices will sweat and become limp. After an hour, drain and place in dish towel and squeeze out liquid (or squeeze in colander). If using the dish towel method, do not overdo it! Put back in dry bowl, add sugar and vinegar and stir to dissolve. Add red food coloring to desired intensity. They will end up deep pink, if you choose to use the coloring. (From Joe Bishop's *How to Cook a Porcupine and Other Culinary Delights*. Joe, my husband's College of Wooster roommate in the forties, loved to entertain his guests with exotic foods.)

Daikon Vichyssoise

1 lb. daikon radish
2 baking potatoes
1 quart chicken broth
1/4 c. whipping cream
white pepper and salt
1 green onion

Finely dice about 1/2 c. daikon for garnish, wrap, and chill. Slice the rest 1/2 inch thick. Peel and slice potatoes 1/4 inch thick and combine the vegetables with broth in saucepan. Simmer about 20 minutes. Purée in blender. Add cream, salt, and pepper. Chill, covered, at least 2 hours. Serve in chilled bowls, garnished with diced daikon and thin slices of green onion.

Variation: Turnips may be substituted for daikon in this and in most recipes calling for daikon.

Shredded Carrot and Daikon Salad

6 raw carrots, trimmed
1 medium daikon, trimmed and peeled
2 T. minced fresh ginger root
$^1/_3$ c. olive oil
2 T. fresh orange juice
1 T. lemon juice, or to taste
salt and pepper to taste

Shred carrots and daikon. Mix remaining ingredients and combine with shredded vegetables. Chill in covered bowl until ready to use. Serve on lettuce leaf. Serves 4.

Pickled Vegetables
A Vietnamese recipe.

2 c. white vinegar
1 c. water
$1^1/_2$ c. sugar
2 or 3 medium carrots, cut diagonally in paper-thin slices, then julienned
1 3-inch piece daikon radish, peeled, cut in paper-thin slices, then julienned
$^1/_2$ small green bell pepper, seeds and membrane removed, then julienned
$^1/_2$ small yellow or red pepper, seeds and membrane removed, then julienned

In medium saucepan combine vinegar, water, and sugar. Cook over medium heat until hot and sugar is dissolved. Remove from heat and cool completely. Pour mixture into clean large glass jar with tightly fitting lid. Add vegetables. Secure lid and refrigerate overnight or longer. As vegetables are used, others may be added to the marinade for later use. Makes 1 quart.

Mashed Daikon Radish

4 c. thinly shredded, loosely packed daikon radish
$2^1/_2$ T. oil
1 T. soy sauce
large pinch sugar
2 t. green onion, minced
$^1/_8$ t. salt

Heat pan over high heat. Add oil. When oil is hot, put in the vegetable and stir-fry for 2 minutes. Turn heat to medium and continue to fry 1 to 2 minutes, pressing frequently and firmly with spatula. Sprinkle on soy sauce, sugar, green onion, and salt. Mix and mash for another minute. Serve.

Daylilies

I could hardly contain my shock one summer day while strolling in our front yard with our son Jon to see him yank a daylily bud off its stem, pop it in his mouth, and proceed to chomp it down! It was a perfect opportunity for Jon to explain that the common orange daylily (sometimes called ditch lily) is not only edible, but nutritious and delicious.

Euell Gibbons, famous for *Stalking the Wild Asparagus,* has assured us that daylily buds, fresh or dried, may be boiled and seasoned like green beans or fried in an egg batter. The buds will be a bright green and will have the crunch of green beans if cooked sparingly—not in the Hoosier "mushy" style. The beautiful orange-colored blossoms may be fried as fritters without pangs of guilt because they last only one day.

Boiled Fresh Daylily Buds

1 lb. unopened daylily buds
8 c. salted boiling water
¹/₂ c. sour cream
1 t. lemon juice

Drop buds into boiling water and cook 4 minutes. Drain and dress with combination of sour cream and lemon juice.

Variation: Add uncooked buds to vegetable soup.

Daylily Tempura
To feed a party crowd.

1 can beer (the cheaper, the better)
1 c. all-purpose flour
salt to taste (a dash or two)
2 lbs. daylily buds
flour for dusting
2 c. vegetable oil

Combine beer, salt, and flour in a deep bowl and beat together until frothy. Let stand for 3 hours. Wash and drain the daylily buds. Just before frying, dust the buds with flour and dip them into the batter. Deep fry in oil (375°) until golden brown. Drain on insides of surplus brown paper bags. Serve immediately.

Guiltless Daylily Flower Fritters

1 c. all-purpose white flour
1 t. baking powder
dash of salt
1 well-beaten egg
¹/₂ c. milk
2 c. vegetable oil

Combine flour, baking powder, and salt. Fold in egg and milk. Batter should be just thick enough to coat flowers. (Adjust milk and flour to achieve desired thickness.) Dip flowers in batter and fry in deep fat fryer at 360° until golden brown. Drain on absorbent brown paper bags. Serve immediately.

Variation: This recipe works well with squash blossoms and pumpkin blossoms also.

Dill

One automatically thinks of pickles when thinking of dill, but that is a very limited use of this flavorful member of the parsley family.

Dill is an annual and must be planted from seed. Often a patch of dill will reseed itself, making one think it is a perennial. It may be grown indoors, of course, but needs full sun. If planted outdoors in the spring, the seeds will form in July, just in time for pickling. Growing it near tomatoes will ward off the tomato hornworm!

Fresh dillweed will keep in the refrigerator for several days if it is sealed in a plastic bag. To keep it longer, first wash it and then place it, stem side down, in a canning jar filled with 1 inch of tap water. Trim the stems, if necessary, to make it fit inside. Stored in the refrigerator, it will keep for several weeks if you change the water every 3 days or so.

Dill may be frozen or dried for future use. And both the seeds and the leaves (called dillweed or dill frond) may be used. Small amounts may be frozen in freezer or sandwich bags.

A teaspoon or two of crumbled dillweed is an excellent addition to chicken gravy, sour cream sauce, fish, and seafood sauces. A bowl of cottage cheese mixed with dill seed and allowed to stand for a few minutes is both flavorful and healthful. One teaspoon of dill seed is a perfect flavoring for vegetables such as green beans, cabbage, zucchini, and potatoes. Just sprinkle the dill seed over the vegetables during the last 10 minutes of cooking. Russians use it liberally in beet dishes, especially borscht.

Dill Sauce

¹/₂ c. (1 stick) butter
1 T. chopped fresh dill or 1 t. dried or frozen dill

Melt butter in small saucepan. Stir in dill. Serve over cooked potatoes, carrots, or turnips. Store any remaining sauce, covered, in refrigerator. Reheat on low heat for later use.

Dill Dressing

¹/₂ c. mayonnaise
¹/₂ c. sour cream
1 T. chopped fresh dillweed

1 t. lime juice
dash of onion salt
¹/₄ c. milk

Mix mayonnaise and sour cream. Add chopped dill, lime juice, and onion salt. Gradually stir in milk and blend. Chill for at least 2 hours.

Scandinavian-Style Potato Salad

1 lb. potatoes, boiled in skins about 20
  minutes
salt and pepper to taste
1 c. sour cream

3 hard-cooked eggs, chopped
¹/₄ c. chopped onion
3 T. chopped fresh dill or 1 T. dried dill

Drain boiled potatoes and remove skins. Cut into 1-inch chunks and place in mixing bowl. Season with salt and pepper and toss with sour cream. Add eggs, onion, and dill, and toss again. Cool and refrigerate several hours before serving. Serves 4.

Lemon-Dill Chicken

6 chicken breasts, skinned, boned,
  and halved
salt and pepper to taste
¹/₄ c. fresh chopped dill or 4 t. dried dill

¹/₄ c. chopped parsley
1 clove garlic, minced
1 lemon
butter

Press chicken breasts to flatten them and place each on a sheet of foil large enough for wrapping. Season with salt and pepper. Blend dill, parsley, and garlic and sprinkle over breasts. Slice lemon in thin rounds and place two rounds over each breast. Dot each breast well with butter and fold each piece of foil into a packet. Put packets on a baking sheet and place in a preheated 350° oven. Bake for 30 minutes. Serves 6. (This dish may also be grilled outdoors on a charcoal fire, grilling over hot coals for 10 minutes, turning often or until done, when juices run clear, not pink. Do not overcook, or chicken will be tough.)

Note: Remember to include a few dill sprigs with celery, carrots, and parsley when cooking chicken soup. With mustard and sour cream, dill makes a good sauce for seafood, especially shrimp.

Eggplant

Beautiful to look at, this deep purple or black vegetable is good for more than centerpieces. Because it is very watery, it is important to try to get rid of some of its moisture before cooking. To do so, slice and salt before draining on a rack. Slices may also be stacked and weighted down with a heavy plate to squeeze out some of the moisture. Because eggplant discolors quickly, rub the slices with lemon juice.

Basic Microwave Preparation of Eggplant

Using a knife, pierce three medium size eggplants in three places. Place on paper toweling. Turning each eggplant over midway through cooking, microwave on high for 10–12 minutes. When cooled, scoop eggplant flesh out of shell and chop coarsely.

Add to eggplant mixture the following which have been microwaved for 2 minutes in a 2-quart measure covered with plastic:

1/2 c. chopped onion
1 clove garlic, minced
2 T. olive oil
1 large tomato, seeded and coarsely chopped
salt and pepper to taste

To serve mixture hot, microwave the finished dish on high for 2 minutes. Dish may also be chilled and served cold.

Ratatouille

1/3 c. olive oil
3/4 c. sliced onions
2 cloves garlic
4 green bell peppers, sliced

2 1/2 c. peeled, diced eggplant
3 c. zucchini cut in half-inch slices
2 c. peeled and quartered tomatoes

In olive oil sauté onions and garlic. When golden in color, remove and combine in casserole with alternate layers of bell peppers, eggplant, zucchini, and tomatoes. Add to each layer salt and pepper. Sprinkle the top with olive oil. Bake, covered, at 300° for 35–45 minutes. Uncover and continue baking for 10 more minutes in order to reduce the liquid. May be served hot as a vegetarian entrée or cold as a salad with crusty French bread.

Fried Eggplant

1 lb. long, thin eggplants	1/2 t. salt
2 eggs	1 t. sugar
1/2 c. cornstarch	oil for frying

Wash eggplants and cut off stem ends. Slice eggplant diagonally 1/2-inch thick. Beat eggs slightly. Add cornstarch, salt, and sugar. Mix until smooth. Dip eggplant pieces into batter and fry in deep hot oil until golden brown and tender, turning to brown both sides.

Dessert Fried Eggplant

1 lb. eggplant, trimmed and cut into strips about 3 inches long
1 t. salt
1/4 c. flour for dredging
oil for deep frying
1/2 c. confectioners' sugar for dipping

In a bowl toss eggplant with salt. Cover with plate and place weight on plate so that plate is in direct contact with eggplant. Let stand for 1 hour. Drain and rinse. Pat strips dry with paper towels and dredge by shaking eggplant strips in flour in paper bag. Fry strips in oil a few at a time. Transfer to paper towels to drain. Serve hot with sugar for dipping. Serves 4 to 6.

Stuffed Eggplants

4 medium eggplants	2 lbs. lean ground beef
salt and pepper	1 T. chopped parsley
2 medium onions, chopped	1 T. mint leaves, minced
1/2 c. olive oil	4 c. tomatoes, solidly packed

Wash eggplants, cut off stems, and cut each eggplant in half lengthwise. Scoop out pulp, leaving a shell about 1/2 inch thick. Sprinkle with salt and pepper.

Chop pulp and sauté with onions in olive oil, stirring frequently, 15 minutes, or until soft. Set aside.

In oil remaining in pan, cook beef, stirring with fork until redness disappears. Mix vegetables and beef with parsley, mint, and tomatoes, broken up with fork. Season with salt and pepper.

Arrange eggplant halves in baking pan and fill each with meat-vegetable mixture. Pour any remaining mixture in pan around eggplant. Cover and bake at 350° for 45 minutes. Serves 8.

"Poor Man's Caviar"

2 lbs. eggplant
1¹/₂ lbs. fresh tomatoes
3 or 4 onions
3 or 4 large carrots, grated

¹/₄ c. olive oil
salt, pepper, and minced garlic to taste
1 T. sugar (optional)

Prick skin of eggplant and bake until tender in oven or microwave. Cool and peel.

In a meat grinder or by hand very finely chop the tomatoes, 2 medium or 1 large onion, and eggplant. Add grated carrots.

Place oil in saucepan. Slice 1 or 2 of the onions in thin rounds and sauté in oil until soft and golden. (A bit of minced garlic may be sautéed with onions if desired.)

Add all ingredients to the sautéed onions. Season to taste. Cook over low flame approximately 30 to 45 minutes or until tomatoes are cooked and the mixture has thickened. Add a little more oil if desired. Correct seasonings. If using fresh tomatoes, you may add extra salt and the tablespoon of sugar to cut down on tartness. (With canned tomatoes this may not be necessary.)

Serve chilled as a spread on crisp toast or Ry-Krisp or as a dip with tortilla chips. It may also be used as a sandwich spread or served as a side dish. Yield: approximately 1 quart.

Note: This recipe never comes out exactly the same, as the flavor depends on the flavors of the vegetables used and the ratio of eggplant to tomato, but it is always good. If you wish, you may add commercial seasoning salt for more bite. (Contributed by Natalie Ashanin, who has a Russian background and participates in food preparation at her St. George Syrian Orthodox Church.)

Elderberries

You may be harboring elderberries in your backyard without your knowledge, as we were for years. Never mind—the birds enjoyed them!

However, if you want to enjoy them too, there are many ways—in wine, jelly, muffins, pancakes, you name it. Bushes are very easy to start and require no maintenance. (Just order at least a pair from a nursery and set them out in any kind of soil.)

Within one to two years they will form a flowering, fruiting, property-barrier hedge. Berries are easy to pick and prepare. Pick the cluster, hold it under the faucet, and strip the berries from the stems with a fork. Use as desired, substituting elderberries for blueberries or currants in baking or jelly-making.

If you can't wait for the berries and want to make something with the blossoms, try Elderberry Blossom Wine or an Elderflower Cocktail.

The giant clusters or heads bear tiny, creamy white flowers and bloom in early to midsummer. Avoid using flowers that have been sprayed with chemicals. When all the flowers are in bloom, snip the heads and use immediately. Do not use the woody stems or leaves, because they are poisonous!

Elderflower Cocktail

8 oz. chilled carbonated water or white wine
2 T. Elderflower Syrup (recipe follows)
crushed ice
lemon slice

Mix carbonated water or wine with syrup in a stemmed glass. Add ice and lemon slice. Makes 1 8-oz. serving.

Elderflower Syrup

50 heads fresh elderflowers
12 c. water
7 1/2 c. sugar
1 t. powdered citric acid (bought in a drugstore or canning section of supermarket)
3 lemons

Rinse flower heads. Using a table fork, comb through flower heads over a large nonmetal bowl, removing individual flowers. (Do not use stems or leaves.) In saucepan bring water, sugar, and citric acid to boil. Pour sugar syrup over flowers. Squeeze juice from lemons and stir into the syrup mixture. Cover and chill for four days. Strain through cheesecloth. Chill up to 1 month.

Alternate method for preserving: Boil syrup in a saucepan. Pour the hot syrup into clean, hot pint or half-pint jars. Adjust lids. Process in boiling water bath for 15 minutes (counting from when water returns to boil). Yields 7 pints.

Elderberry Pie

pastry for 2 9-inch crusts
2 1/2 c. elderberries
3/4 c. sugar
2 T. flour
1/8 t. salt
3 T. lemon juice

Line pie pan with pastry. Stem and wash elderberries. Drain well. Fill pie shell with berries. Mix sugar, salt, and flour. Sprinkle over berries. Cover with top crust and fasten edges securely. Bake at 425° for 10 minutes, reduce to 350°, and bake 30 minutes more. Makes 1 9-inch pie. Serve warm or cold with vanilla ice cream.

Variation: If you do not have enough elderberries, make up the difference in amount of fruit by combining with peeled tart apples and adding 1/4 c. sugar.

Elderberry Jelly

Elderberry juice is made by covering berries with water, cooking slowly, and draining juice through muslin jelly bag or square securely tied.

2 c. elderberry juice
2 c. apple juice
3 c. sugar

Combine juices and bring to boil. Add sugar gradually and cook rapidly. Cook until jelly stage has been reached (when the last two drops on the spoon run together and "sheet off"). Pour into half-pint jelly jars and seal with lids and rings. (Or follow recipe on commercial pectin box or jar.)

Gooseberries

Many homes have a gooseberry bush in the backyard. If yours does, you should know that gooseberries are good for more than feeding the birds, though that is an admirable use itself.

I grew up knowing only about gooseberry pie baked early in the spring when the gooseberries were still green. (It must be due to that primal urge for a spring tonic.) However, gooseberries may be allowed to mature to a tawny red and canned. When combined with cooked whole cranberry sauce, they make a tasty accompaniment to the holiday ham or turkey. I learned this thanks to my daughter-in-law, Carol Courtney, who one Christmas brought me a jar of gooseberries that had been canned in Czechoslovakia.

Gooseberries also make elegant jam if they are allowed to mature and mixed with rhubarb. Before my stepmother removed her gooseberry bush, she favored us with a "batch" of gooseberry jam to take back to our home in Hyde Park, Chicago. (For recipe, see folder inside the powdered pectin box.)

There are still people interested in baking a gooseberry pie: a request for the recipe was published in the Food Section of the *Indianapolis Star* in July 1989. I answered the call by sending in the following:

Gooseberry Pie

pastry for 2 9-inch crusts
4 c. gooseberries, stems and stickers
   removed*
2 T. flour
²/₃ to 1 c. sugar, depending upon
   whether green or ripe berries are
   used

¹/₄ t. nutmeg
¹/₈ t. salt
¹/₄ t. cinnamon
1 t. lemon juice
2 t. butter

Lightly roll half of the pie crust pastry and fit into bottom of pie plate. Fill pie shell with gooseberries. Mix sugar, salt, spices and lemon juice and sprinkle over gooseberries. Dot with butter. Roll out remaining pie crust and place on top, making 3 slits for steam escape. Glaze by brushing top crust with milk and sprinkling with sugar. Bake for 40 minutes at 425° in preheated oven.

*The Pixwell variety is nearly thornless. The fruit is easily picked off 1-inch stems, well away from the small thorns.

Gooseberry Tarts

2 c. stemmed gooseberries
3/4 c. sugar
1 T. cornstarch
3 T. water
pastry dough, rolled out and cut to fit
    tart pans

Mix cornstarch and water until smooth, then combine with gooseberries and sugar. Heat slowly until berries burst, then cool. Line tart pans or muffin tin cups with pie pastry and bake in 425° oven for 15 minutes. Fill tarts with gooseberry mixture. Makes 6–12 tarts, depending on size of cups used. Serve warm or cold. (May be served with whipped cream or ice cream.)

Molded Gooseberry Salad

2 c. cooked green gooseberries
1/2 c. sugar
water
1 6-oz. package lemon-flavored gelatin
2 T. sugar
2 c. water

1 t. vinegar
1 c. chopped celery
1/2 c. shredded Cheddar cheese
1/2 c. chopped pecans
leaf lettuce

Cook gooseberries in small amount of water and sugar. Drain berries, reserving syrup. Add enough water to syrup to make 1 1/2 c. liquid. In saucepan combine syrup mixture, gelatin, and sugar. Heat and stir until gelatin is dissolved. Add water and vinegar. Chill until partially set. Fold in gooseberries, celery, cheese, and pecans. Turn into 6 1/2-cup mold. Chill until firm. Unmold onto lettuce-lined plate. Serves 10–12. (May also be made in 9 x 9-inch glass baking dish, cut into squares, and served on a lettuce leaf.)

Gooseberry Pickle
This is an old prairie Hutterite recipe.

2 qts. freshly picked green gooseberries
3¹/₂ c. sugar
1 c. cider vinegar
2 t. ground cloves
1 t. ground cinnamon
2 t. ground allspice

Combine all ingredients in a stainless steel saucepan and mix well. Boil over medium heat until thickened, approximately 7 minutes. Stir frequently. Pour into hot, sterilized jars. Adjust lids. Process in hot water bath for 10 minutes, counting time from when water returns to boil. Yields 2 pints. Excellent accompaniment to baked ham or cold cuts.

Gooseberry Moos (Gooseberry Fruit Soup)

2 c. fresh or frozen gooseberries
¹/₂ c. raisins
1¹/₂ c. water
1 c. sugar
¹/₂ c. half and half
4 t. flour
1 egg, well beaten

Cook gooseberries, raisins, water, and sugar over low heat for about 5 minutes. Combine cream, flour, and beaten egg. Add 1 T. hot gooseberry mixture to combined cream, flour, and egg to prevent lumps. Then add combined thickening mixture slowly to gooseberry mixture, stirring constantly. Cook for 1 minute. Serve hot or cold as dessert or as accompaniment to meat course. Serves 6.

Grape Leaves

The importance of organic growing has been highlighted for the nation in the second national boycott of California table grapes, organized by the United Farm Workers of America and supported by many organizations, including the National Farm Worker Ministry, related to the National Council of Churches.

Needless to say, my recipes will not include table grapes sold in supermarkets. Instead they will call for grapes grown in backyards without hazardous chemical applications, or grapes foraged from wild vines along creeks and streams where you may be confident no spraying has been done.

But, before the grape (see Part III, Autumn) comes the *grape leaf!* All grape leaves you find growing in your backyard or along your fences are edible. It's best to harvest grape leaves in early summer, when they are full size but still tender. The young tendrils may be eaten as a snack or in salads, and the young leaves, blanched in boiling water, may be used in making the Greek delicacy *dolmades* (stuffed grape leaves).

Blanched Grape Leaves for Stuffing

To prepare fresh grape leaves for stuffing with rice, meat, or cheese, pick 50 young leaves about the size of your palm. They may be found at the ends of your vine branches, and they'll be a bright, tender green.

Divide the fresh grape leaves into piles of 6 leaves and tie each pile together gently with thread. Plunge the piles, 3 at a time, into a large saucepan of rapidly boiling water and blanch for 2 minutes. Drain and let cool. Separate leaves and transfer them, dull side down, to paper towels to dry in one layer. While leaves are drying, prepare the stuffing.

Dolmades with Rice Stuffing

Blanched Grape Leaves (recipe precedes)	*1¹/₂ T. minced parsley*
1¹/₃ c. chopped onion	*1 t. dried mint*
1 large garlic clove, minced	*1 t. snipped dillweed*
¹/₂ c. olive oil	*¹/₄ t. cinnamon*
1 c. long grain rice	*¹/₄ t. sugar*
1¹/₂ t. tomato paste	*salt and pepper to taste*
¹/₂ c. water	

Cook onion and garlic in oil over moderate heat for 3 minutes or until onion is softened. Add rice, tomato paste, and water. Simmer mixture for 5 minutes. Remove skillet from heat and add remaining ingredients, combining well.

Stuff leaves as follows: Place scant tablespoon of stuffing on the dull side of one of the prepared leaves at the stem end. Trim the stem with a pair of kitchen shears and discard. Remove any heavy veins at the stem which would impair rolling the leaf into an envelope. Fold in the sides and roll up lightly, leaving room for rice to expand as it cooks.

Line a large, heavy saucepan with prepared grape leaves that have torn, and slices of tomato. Over them arrange the stuffed grape leaves close together, seam side down, in layers, sprinkling 3 large garlic cloves, slivered, among the layers. In a bowl combine 1 c. each of water and olive oil, ¹/₄ c. lemon juice, and 1 t. sugar. Pour mixture over stuffed grape leaves and weight them down with a heatproof plate to prevent them from unrolling. Bring the liquid to a boil over moderate heat and simmer, covered, adding water as necessary to prevent sticking, for 1 to 1¹/₂ hours or until tender. Serve chilled with hummus (garbanzo bean or chickpea paste) or warm with yogurt. Cooking liquid may be strained and poured over stuffed leaves.

Stuffed grape leaves may be frozen, uncovered, on a baking sheet until solid. Transfer to airtight plastic containers and store in freezer for up to 3 months.

Dolmades with Meat Stuffing

Blanched Grape Leaves (recipe above)
$^1/_2$ lb. ground lamb or beef
$^1/_2$ c. long grain rice
1 onion, minced
2 T. olive oil
2 T. tomato paste

1 T. minced parsley
2 t. salt
1 t. dried mint
1 t. snipped dillweed
1 t. pepper
$^1/_4$ t. cinnamon

Combine all ingredients and stuff fresh grape leaves. Cook as directed in previous recipe.

Cheese in Grape Leaves

Put pieces of feta cheese, 2 x $^1/_4$ inches, on the dull side of prepared fresh grape leaves and roll up as directed in recipe for Blanched Grape Leaves (above). Arrange rolls seam side down in buttered baking dish and bake in preheated 350° oven for 6 to 10 minutes, or until cheese is melted and tops of leaves are slightly brown. Serve warm with crusty French bread.

Canning Grape Leaves

Wash 5-inch leaves, remove stems, and arrange in piles of 10. Roll each pile tightly and tie with string. Boil 2 quarts water with $^1/_2$ c. salt. Add a few rolls at a time and cook until all leaves have changed color (about 2 minutes after last addition of leaves). Remove rolls from water and pack into sterilized canning jars. Fill jars with boiling salted water and seal at once. Six dozen leaves can be packed into a quart jar.

When using canned grape leaves to make dolmades, remove the required number of canned bundles from the jar with a slotted spoon. Soak in cold water to cover for 15 minutes. Do not try to separate leaves before soaking. Drain leaves in colander and transfer them, dull side down, to paper towels to dry in one layer. Proceed with stuffing as directed in previous recipes. Unused leaves may be stored in the brine, refrigerated, for future use.

Ground Cherries (Husk Tomatoes)

My maternal grandmother, Anna Kliewer Tieszen, grew delicious ground cherries (*Physalis* sp.) in her garden in Marion, South Dakota. Naturally, we grandchildren, when small, always found our way to the garden during a Sunday afternoon visit if the weather was warm.

When ground cherries ripen to plump golden globes, they fall off the low-lying bush and rest on the warm soil, ready to be picked up by tiny fingers. The cherries are protected by a paper-thin covering resembling a five-sided Japanese lantern. Very easily broken, the paper husk opens to luscious sweetness. Ground cherries ripen late and will continue to ripen in their husks after falling from the plant. Eat the fruit only after it turns orange yellow, indicating it is completely ripe.

Grandma Tieszen followed the Plattdeutsch custom of serving *Faspa* (a light tea or supper, derived from the word "Vespers"). Invariably we sat down to a dining room table laden with *Zwiebach,* butter, cheese, fresh or canned fruit, hot tea or weak coffee, and . . . ground cherry jam. Here's the recipe:

Ground Cherry Jam
This jam is a best seller at the Freeman [SD] Academy's Schmeckfest.

7 c. ground cherries
4 c. sugar
$^1/_2$ c. water

Boil the whole "batch" for 35 minutes. Avoid overcooking, for the jam has a tendency to crystalize. The process may be speeded by first freezing ground cherries, then puréeing them in a blender. Seal in hot sterilized pint or half-pint canning jars.

Variation: $^1/_4$ c. lemon juice may be substituted for half of the water called for. Ground cherries respond nicely to added tartness.

Crumb-Topped Ground Cherry Pie

pastry for 1 9-inch crust
$2^1/_2$ c. ripe ground cherries
$^1/_2$ c. brown sugar
1 T. flour
2 T. water
Crumb Topping (recipe follows)

Wash ground cherries and place in unbaked pie shell. Mix sugar and flour. Sprinkle over ground cherries. Sprinkle water over top. Add Crumb Topping.

Bake at 425° for 15 minutes. Reduce to 375° and continue baking for 25 minutes.

Crumb Topping

3 T. flour
3 T. sugar
2 T. soft butter

Combine and blend with a pastry blender all three ingredients. Sprinkle over ground cherries and sugar.

Kohlrabi

According to the *New World Dictionary* the derivation of the word kohlrabi is *cavolo rapa,* "cole rape, a kind of cabbage with an edible, bulbous stem that looks somewhat like a turnip." Kohlrabi is sometimes called cabbage turnip or turnip cabbage.

Kohlrabi are easy to grow and have many culinary uses. First is eating the vegetable raw. I can remember as a young child pulling the bulb from the soil, handing it to my father for peeling with his pocket jackknife, and both of us having a refreshing snack in the summer's heat.

For use on a raw vegetable tray, choose those no larger than a golf ball, cut off the leaves and root, peel off the fibrous bulb covering, and slice the pale green or white centers into rounds of uniform size.

For use as a hot vegetable, cut off the tops and roots. It is best to use the bulbs before they get too large, or they will become woody and lose flavor. Peel the bulbous stem. Slice or quarter the bulb, depending upon its size, and drop it into boiling water. Cook, uncovered, until crisp-tender. Drain and serve with white sauce or butter.

The tops, which taste similar to Swiss chard or kale, may also be cooked as a vegetable, chopped, and then combined with the bulbs in the white sauce. Kohlrabi may also be substituted for cabbage or turnips in soup or stew.

In our enthusiasm for canning as teenage 4-H club members, my sister Ruth and I even canned kohlrabi, but we recommend saving your jars for other garden goodies.

Kohlrabi have only 40 calories per cup, are high in fiber content, and are an excellent source of vitamin C and potassium.

Creamed Kohlrabi

6 kohlrabi
boiling water
1 t. salt
paprika
1 egg yolk
2 c. thin white sauce

Pare kohlrabi and cut into cubes or slices. Let stand in mixture of cold water and 2 T. vinegar for 1 hour. Rinse. Cook uncovered in boiling salted water for 20–35 minutes. (Makes 4 c. cooked.) Drain. Add paprika and egg yolk to white sauce and pour over kohlrabi. Serves 6.

Kohlrabi with Beef Stock

4 kohlrabi
1 t. salt
pinch of baking soda
2 T. butter
1 T. flour
1 c. beef stock
salt, pepper, and nutmeg to taste
1 T. chopped parsley
2 T. cream or evaporated milk

Remove tender leaves from stalks and cook in salted water with pinch of baking soda. Rinse in cold water, drain well, and chop fine. Pare and slice the tubers. Cook in lightly salted water until done, 25–30 minutes. Prepare a light sauce from butter, flour, beef stock, seasonings and cream. Add sliced kohlrabi and bring to a boil again. Either add chopped, cooked greens to this or serve separately, with the greens surrounding the tubers. Serves 4.

Browned Kohlrabi

1 T. butter
1 lb. kohlrabi, peeled and sliced
$^1/_2$ t. sugar
4 T. chopped parsley
$^1/_2$ c. chicken broth

In a nonstick skillet melt the butter and stir in kohlrabi, sugar, and parsley. Cover and cook over low heat for approximately 25 minutes or until tender. Add chicken stock if necessary to keep from burning. Serves 4.

Microwaving Kohlrabi

Peel and dice kohlrabi. Place in microwave-proof casserole with a few tablespoons of water. Cook on high power for 8 to 10 minutes or until tender. Drain well. Serve with butter or a white sauce or cheese sauce over them.

Creole Kohlrabi

Because kohlrabi are bland, they lend themselves well to stronger flavorings,
such as garlic, onions, green pepper, and tomatoes.

6 medium kohlrabi
1 clove garlic, minced
1 small onion, chopped
1 small green pepper, chopped
1/8 c. oil, heated
2 small tomatoes, peeled and diced
water, salt, and pepper to taste

Peel and dice kohlrabi and cook in hot water until tender or microwave 6 to 8 minutes. Drain water. Sauté garlic, onion, and green pepper in hot oil until tender. Add kohlrabi and tomatoes. Season to taste, adding water if necessary. Heat through.

Freezing Kohlrabi

Select tender, young kohlrabi. Scrub, peel, and cut into 1/2 inch cubes. Blanch in boiling water 1 minute. Cool, drain, and pack in plastic freezer containers. (May also be frozen mashed or puréed by simmering cubes in small amount of water until just fork tender, draining, and mashing.)

Mesclun (Mixed Greens)

We often use a variety of lettuce or greens in the spring when lettuce is just beginning to grow. However, a mixture of greens may be used year-round when an insufficient supply of one or the other is at hand. Besides lettuces, young and tender greens which may be combined include spinach, kale, chard, broccoli rabe, broccoli sprouts, endive, arugula, onion tops, chives, mustard and turnip greens, herbs such as basil or parsley—in short, any greens you have in limited supply alone. Flowers such as nasturtiums may be added to the salad greens.

Within recent years new varieties of greens have appeared at markets, and the home gardener can try growing a larger number of varieties too. They include the following:

Arugula (sometimes called rucola or roquette) has dark green and narrow lobed leaves with a peppery flavor. Young leaves (less than 3 inches long) are right for salads. Larger ones can be torn and used in stir-fried dishes.

Belgian or French endive is cream in color and has tightly formed, narrow leaves. As they mature, the heads grow more bitter.

Bibb lettuce, sometimes called butterhead, is popular for its nice, small rounded head with lighter leaves inside.

Buttercrunch has more texture and its leaves are more tightly formed.

Curly endive or chicory has frizzled edges with both yellow and green leaves, which tend to be quite bitter.

Escarole has large, broad dark green outer leaves with a small yellow center forming a flatter head. Less bitter than curly endive or chicory.

Mâche (also called corn or field salad) has a sweet, nutty flavor and a soft, creamy texture.

Radicchio (or red-leaf chicory) is dark green tinted with bright red in early summer and dark red in winter. Small golf-ball sized heads are crunchy and strong flavored.

Romaine (cos) has large dark green leaves moderately flavored.

Sorrel looks like spinach but has smoother and paler green leaves. With a sharp, lemony bite, it is delicious in small amounts in a fresh salad. It may also be cooked as a vegetable or added to cream sauces or soups when a tangy flavor is desired.

Chicken on the Green [Salad]

2 boneless, skinless chicken breast halves
3 c. mixed salad greens
$1/2$ c. bottled salad dressing

Broil chicken breasts 3 minutes on each side or until chicken no longer shows pink juices when pierced. Slice into strips.

Toss salad greens in a serving bowl. Arrange sliced chicken on top. Garnish with carrot and celery sticks, if desired. Serve with salad dressing. Serves 2 for luncheon.

Vegetable Broth

Use leftover greens with considerable "structural integrity," such as stems from collards, kale, turnips, chard, parsley, mustard, etc., chopped coarsely; onions, garlic, bay leaf for seasoning; and water to cover bottom of microwave-proof casserole.

Place all of above in microwaving casserole and microwave on high for 10 to 15 minutes. Allow to cool before draining. Throw solids on the compost pile. Use broth as base for clear soups.

Variation: Do not separate solids from broth. Instead, use both in vegetable soup or chowder. For cream soups the solids may be puréed in a blender.

Mustard Greens

The benefit of eating dark leafy greens has always been known by our forebears, but nutritionists have recently confirmed and publicized it. Cancer experts are touting the need to increase consumption of vegetables and fruits while cutting down fat. Greens, high in vitamin C, beta-carotene, antioxidants, folic acid, calcium and trace elements from the soil such as magnesium, zinc, selenium, manganese and copper, are a sure bet for giving us what we need. In addition, they are low cost, when compared to citrus fruits, as sources of vitamin C. And they are easy to grow, particularly in the fall. I usually plant greens in late summer for fall harvest. In the fall of 1994, I harvested mustard greens and chard on December 31, and stored them on the bottom shelf of the refrigerator for later use.

Unfortunately, we associate cooking greens with fatty pork, added for flavor. This tends to undo the cancer-fighting program. However, the amount of meat and fat can be significantly reduced while maintaining desired flavor. Greens like mustard may be added to other vegetables in soups and chowders, enhancing appearance and flavor.

Chicken Borscht with Mustard Greens

1 qt. defatted chicken broth
1 bunch fresh mustard greens
    (2 c. chopped)
$^1/_2$ medium onion
1 clove garlic, minced
3 carrots, sliced
2 c. coarsely chopped cabbage
$^1/_2$ c. chopped celery
1 small bell pepper

1 bay leaf
1 t. dillweed
$1^1/_2$ c. fresh diced or canned tomatoes
salt and pepper to taste
1 green tomato, diced (optional)
$^1/_4$ c. sour cream or yogurt (optional)
1 t. vinegar (if greater tartness desired)
2 c. diced cooked chicken

Place in large saucepan the chicken broth which has been refrigerated overnight to facilitate the removal of fat that has risen to the top. Add mustard greens. (If you are using tougher stems of the greens, cook them until tender in the broth. More tender leaves of the greens require less cooking and may be added along with other ingredients.) Add other vegetables in order, adding the diced chicken after the vegetables are tender. Flavor with sour cream, yogurt, or vinegar, if desired. (Adapted from a recipe of Marie Kleinsasser, Glendale, Arizona.)

Mustard Greens and Beans

1 quart navy beans
1 medium onion, diced
1 clove garlic, minced
1 bay leaf
$1^1/_2$ lbs. mustard greens, washed and chopped
salt and pepper to taste
vinegar to taste

Use canned white navy beans or cook dried beans after they have been soaked overnight or at least 4 hours. (The slow cooker or Crock-Pot is a good appliance for this.) Add onion, garlic, and bay leaf. Do not add salt when cooking beans as this will lengthen cooking time.

Add greens when beans and onion are tender. If stems of greens are thick and tough, cook for 20 minutes; if tender leaves are used, cook 10 minutes. Adjust with additional water, depending upon whether you want a "soupy" or thicker consistency.

Season with salt, pepper, and vinegar. Serve with hot slices of corn bread. (The combination makes a "complete" protein dish.)

Mustard Greens with Pork

4 slices cured bacon, diced (or use leftover ham bits, pork shoulder, or pork sausage)
1 onion, sliced
1 clove garlic, minced
2 c. water
1¹/₂ lbs. mustard greens
salt, black pepper, and red pepper, to taste
vinegar to pass

In a large saucepot fry the bacon or other pork product. Drain off excess fat. Add onion and garlic and sauté until translucent. Add water and cover pot, allowing ingredients to steam. Wash and chop the greens. Add tough stems first, allowing them to steam until tender. Add water if needed. Add leaves when stems are tender and cook for only 10 minutes or so. Season with salt and peppers. Serve with vinegar passed in cruet.

Variation: Chunks of potato may be added along with tough stems of greens.

Nasturtiums

Nasturtiums and tomatoes complement each other in the garden. Nasturtiums help the tomatoes grow better, and the tomatoes help ward off aphids common on nasturtiums.

Nasturtiums should be planted near cabbage, cucumbers, and squash because they help control pests such as cabbage worms, cucumber beetles, and squash bugs.

Nasturtiums, usually orange in color, also add contrasting brilliance and a watercress-type flavor to green salads. Add them last, after the greens have been dressed, as they are very fragile.

Although they are most commonly added to salads, they may also be used in butters for tiny tea sandwiches, stuffed, and as garnishes.

Okra

Okra is most often used in southern states for gumbo dishes. However, in recent years we have seen it on salad plates and pickled. When growing or buying organically grown okra, the most important thing to remember is to pick or buy it young, before the okra pods get woody or stringy—what Eric Limbach called "having too much structural integrity." Optimal size is 3 to 4 inches long.

Stewed Okra

Using small okra pods, drop the clean pods into a small amount of boiling water. Simmer, until tender, with the pot covered, about 5 minutes. Season with butter, salt, or hot pepper sauce, if desired.

Okra Salad

Drain the whole small okra pods prepared as above. Place in covered refrigerator dish and marinate in French or vinaigrette dressing. Chill and serve very cold on lettuce.

Gumbo

When cooking chicken, turkey, seafood, or sausage gumbo, add approximately 1 c. sliced okra to the other vegetables (2 c. tomatoes, and 1/2 c. each of corn, peppers, onions). Cut, okra will feel gummy or slimy. It acts as a thickening agent in the soup or stew. Do not discard okra simply because it is slippery. That is its very nature!

Okra on the Raw Vegetable Tray

Okra is delicious when young and eaten raw with a sprinkling of salt. To eat it, pick up the little pods and eat up to the stem end. Okra has practically every nutrient in any other vegetable plus flavor and ease of cooking. (You don't have to peel it either!)

Fried Okra

3 doz. young, tender okra pods
2 eggs, lightly beaten
2 T. milk

3/4 t. salt
1/2 c. fine bread crumbs
6 T. shortening

Boil okra pods in about 8 cups of water until almost tender, about 5 minutes. Drain. Mix eggs with milk and salt. Dip pods in crumbs, then egg mixture, then again in crumbs. Heat shortening in skillet, add okra, and sauté until brown. Serves 6.

Fresh Okra-Tomato Sauce

2 T. butter
$^1/_3$ c. chopped fresh onion
4 c. chopped peeled fresh tomatoes
$^1/_2$ t. salt
$^1/_8$ t. pepper
$^1/_4$ t. sugar
$^1/_4$ t. dried leaf thyme
1 t. fresh lemon juice
$^1/_4$ c. chopped parsley
2 c. sliced fresh okra

In medium saucepan melt butter. Add onion and cook until tender. Add remaining ingredients. Cover and simmer 30 minutes. (My sister, Ruth Pollman, freezes a "batch" of this every year. It is a good base for spaghetti sauce.)

Quick Chicken-Okra-Lentil Soup

$^1/_2$ c. uncooked lentils or split peas
5 c. chicken or turkey broth (or water and bouillon cubes)
3 c. cooked chicken or turkey, chopped
2 medium onions, chopped
salt and pepper to taste
2 ears fresh corn, cut from cob, or $1^1/_2$ c. whole kernel corn
1 c. chopped celery with leaves
8 fresh okra cut in rounds or 6–8 oz. frozen okra
chopped parsley for garnish

Cook lentils slowly in broth until tender, about 1 hour. Add remaining ingredients except parsley and continue to simmer for another 10 minutes, adding more water if needed. Serve at once garnished with parsley.

Creole Seafood Gumbo

¹/₄ c. butter

2 T. flour

1 large onion, chopped

2 c. cut okra

2 c. canned or fresh tomatoes, peeled and diced

1 small green pepper, chopped

¹/₄ t. hot red pepper sauce

¹/₈ t. thyme

1 bay leaf

2 c. liquid (water and juice from seafood, if possible)

2 c. shrimp, crabmeat, crayfish,* oysters, or a combination (fresh, frozen, or canned)

cooked rice

Melt butter in saucepan. Stir in flour and brown lightly. Add remaining ingredients except seafood and rice. Simmer 30 minutes. Stir occasionally. Add shrimp or other seafood and cook 10 to 15 minutes longer. Season with a final dash of pepper sauce. Serve in soup bowls with mounds of hot rice in the center. Serves 6.

---

*In South Dakota during the thirties and forties our farm family used the abundant natural supply of crayfish (what we called crabs), but heavy pesticide use in farming has done away with that food source. A recent ad in *The Freeman* [South Dakota] *Courier* revealed that entrepreneurs are now importing the delicacy from Texas and Louisiana. However, I was happy to learn from my cousin, John J. Kleinsasser, of Hoffman, Minnesota, a retired school superintendent, that he still goes crayfish trapping. Presumably he frequents the "sky-blue waters" of his adopted state.

Turkey Gumbo Soup

After I roast a turkey, I place the carcass, skin, and all the bones from which meat has been cut in a large pot, season it with salt and a dried red hot pepper pod, and cover it with water. Then I bring it to a boil and simmer it for several hours until all the meat drops from the bones. By this time all the flavor will be in the broth. I then strain the broth, retrieve any meat from the bones, and make this soup. My children when young called it "Gobble Gobble Soup."

3 T. butter or chicken fat

¹/₄ c. green pepper, diced

1¹/₂ c. sliced okra, fresh or frozen

¹/₄ c. onion, diced

4 c. turkey stock

2¹/₂ c. cooked tomatoes

1 small bay leaf

¹/₂ c. rice, uncooked

salt and pepper to taste

1 T. minced parsley

1 c. finely diced cooked turkey, picked from bones

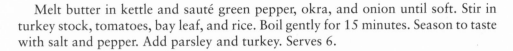

Melt butter in kettle and sauté green pepper, okra, and onion until soft. Stir in turkey stock, tomatoes, bay leaf, and rice. Boil gently for 15 minutes. Season to taste with salt and pepper. Add parsley and turkey. Serves 6.

Dilled Okra

3 lbs. young okra (4 inches long)
4 c. water
2 c. cider vinegar
1/2 c. pickling salt
3 t. celery seeds
6 cloves garlic
6 heads dill

Pierce each okra with fork. Do not stem or slice. Combine water, vinegar, and salt in 3-quart saucepan. Bring to a boil. Place 1/2 t. celery seeds, 1 clove garlic, and 1 head dill into each of 6 sterilized hot pint jars. Pack okra lengthwise into jars. Pour boiling brine over okra, filling to within 1/4 inch of the jar top. Wipe jar rim. Adjust lids. Process in boiling water bath for 20 minutes, counting processing time from when water in canner returns to boiling.* Remove jars from hot water and cool on wooden rack.

*1989 USDA recommendations are 10 pounds of pressure for 20 minutes for pints.

Freezing Okra

Select tender young pods less than 4 inches long. Remove stems without cutting into seed sections if leaving whole or cut into 1-inch lengths after blanching. Blanch in boiling water for 2 minutes. Plunge into ice water to cool and drain. Pack in small plastic bags. Tie securely and freeze. The pods, even when frozen, may be sliced crosswise quite easily for use in soups and stews.

Peaches

Peaches may be used in a myriad of ways when they are fresh, and they are one of the easiest fruits to can or freeze. They may also be dried at home. So if you have a peach tree, especially of the dwarf variety whose buds have not been eaten by a deer, or have access to organically grown peaches, you are indeed fortunate. If no late spring frost damages the buds, we can often get very fine peaches in Indiana from the southern part of the state. (How well I remember the Georgia Church Women United members who brought paper bags full of Georgia peaches to the Common Council meeting in Atlanta a few years ago. What a wonderful afternoon snack!)

During the late thirties and early forties it was possible to buy for little more than a dollar a 16-pound box of large Elberta peaches transported by train from California to South Dakota. This was especially the case when there was a "fruit war" going on among the local merchants who supplied the avid canners among the farm women. I can remember getting a "real good price" on several boxes of peaches late one Saturday night when a merchant had an oversupply and our family still had credit from the sale of our weekly surplus egg supply. Nowadays it seems impossible to buy a peach in a supermarket that will not rot from the inside before it ripens on the outside.

The phrase "peaches and cream complexion" did not arise for no reason. Fresh sliced peaches with cream or atop ice cream, with raspberry sauce to make a "melba," in cobblers or pies, canned for winter "sauce" (as all canned fruit was called in South Dakota), preserves for warm toast—all receive warm plaudits from most diners. Frozen with blueberries and cantaloupe pieces, peach slices make a wonderful winter compote.

When canning or freezing peaches, blanch the fruit in hot water for a few minutes, drain the hot water, and plunge the blanched peaches into cold water. The skins will then slip off easily. Never waste precious vitamins by peeling peaches with a knife.

Some canners like to place a peach pit (or leave it in one peach half) in each jar for a nutty flavor. The "syrup" covering the peaches in the jar need not be 1 part sugar to 2 parts water, as some recipes call for. Three or 4 parts water to 1 of sugar make a juice sweet enough. But be sure to arrange the halves neatly in the jar, overlapping them pit side down. That will reduce the amount of "syrup" needed also. Hands of small children are very useful at this point, as well as for washing the jars in advance. In fact, this is a good time to initiate youngsters to the pleasure of home preserving. They will also enjoy "snitching" some fresh fruit from time to time.

When freezing peaches, you may apply vitamin C in the form of Fruit Fresh or lemon juice to prevent discoloration. Work with small "batches" of fruit, covering with sugar and vitamin C in plastic containers as soon as possible to minimize exposure to the air. "Burp" the containers also to remove air pockets before closing permanently.

Peach Ice Cream Soda

2 medium peaches
2 T. sugar
4 scoops vanilla ice cream
club soda

Peel, pit, and crush peaches. Stir in sugar. Divide peach mixture among 4 tall glasses. Add ice cream and fill with club soda. Stir to blend. Garnish with mint sprigs. Serve with long spoons and straws. Serves 4.

Peach Soup, Hot or Cold

*I first tasted this soup hot, prepared by Bertha Kleinsasser and Sarah Hofer
for the Freeman [SD] Academy cooking class in 1950.*

2 c. water
$^1/_8$ t. cinnamon
2 cloves
2 c. sliced peaches
2 c. unfermented white grape juice
sugar to taste

Add spices to water. Add peaches. Cook until tender. Remove cloves. Purée with blender. Add grape juice and sugar to taste. Heat just to boiling point and serve in hot, shallow bowls. Garnish with a mint leaf.

For cold soup, follow above procedure and then chill for several hours. Serve in chilled bowls and garnish with mint leaf. Add an ice cube if desired. A mint leaf frozen in a mold adds a special touch!

Peach Yogurt Popsicles

1 pint plain yogurt
1 large ripe peach, mashed
1 T. honey

Freeze yogurt to a mushy consistency; then put in blender with peach and honey. Blend until smooth. (It will be the consistency of a milkshake.) Pour into popsicle molds and freeze until solid.

Peach Rummy

4 c. sliced peaches
$1^1/_2$ c. sugar
1 c. rum

In 2-quart jar or crock layer sliced peaches and sugar. Drizzle rum over each layer. Allow it to stand, lightly covered, in a cool, dry place for at least a week. The mixture may be maintained by adding more peaches, sugar, and rum as it is used. Serve as a topping for ice cream. Makes about 6 cups. Replenish fruit as some is used.

Fresh Peach Coffee Cake

2 c. sifted flour
1 T. baking powder
$1/2$ t. salt
1 t. cinnamon
1 egg

$1/4$ c. sugar
$1/3$ c. melted butter
$3/4$ c. milk
2 to 3 fresh peaches
Crumb Topping (recipe follows)

Sift together dry ingredients. Beat egg slightly. Add sugar and mix well. Stir in melted butter and milk. Add dry ingredients and mix just until moistened. Spread batter in greased 9-inch square cake pan. Now scald and peel peaches. Slice and arrange in rows over top of batter, overlapping if necessary. Sprinkle with Crumb Topping. Bake at 400° for 30–35 minutes. Serves 9.

Variation: A sprinkling of ground mace (the outer shell of nutmeg) over the peaches before adding the Crumb Topping adds a distinctive flavor.

Crumb Topping

$1/4$ c. brown sugar
$1/4$ c. butter
$1/4$ c. flour

Cream sugar and butter. Cut in flour with pastry blender. Sprinkle mixture on top of peaches.

Pickled Whole Small Peaches
If your home-grown peaches are small, this recipe is a good way to use some of them.

5 c. sugar
2 c. water
1 c. vinegar
12 inches stick cinnamon, broken
2 t. whole cloves
5 lbs. small peaches

In a large kettle combine sugar, water, vinegar, cinnamon, and cloves. Heat syrup to boiling. Keep hot but not boiling. Wash fruit. Peel and pit, if needed. To prevent discoloration of peaches, add the fruit to the syrup as soon as it is cut. Heat peaches in hot syrup for 5 minutes. Pack fruit and syrup into clean, hot pint or quart jars, leaving $1/2$ inch head space. Adjust lids. Process in boiling water bath for 20 minutes. Start counting time when water returns to boiling. Makes 5 or 6 pints.

Uncooked Fresh Peach Jam

1 t. citric acid or 3 T. lemon juice
2 c. mashed or thinly sliced peaches
4 c. sugar
1 package powdered pectin
1 c. water

In bowl, combine citric acid and peaches. Add sugar and let stand about 20 minutes, stirring occasionally.

Combine pectin and water in saucepan. Bring to boil and boil 1 minute, stirring constantly. Add pectin to peaches and sugar. Stir about 2 minutes. Pour into clean jars at once, allowing for expansion if freezing. Cover with clean lids or aluminum foil. Let stand at room temperature for 1 hour. Refrigerate until set.

Store in refrigerator up to 3 weeks or in freezer about 1 year. Uncooked jams will develop mold if kept at room temperature.

Peach Chutney

3½ c. sugar
2 c. vinegar
1 quart chopped, peeled, firm peaches
1½ c. raisins
1 clove garlic, minced
4 pieces whole dried ginger or candied ginger, chopped

Heat sugar and vinegar to boiling in large kettle. Add peaches, raisins, and garlic. Add whole ginger, tied in cheesecloth bag, or add chopped ginger. Bring to boil and cook slowly, uncovered, for 2 hours or until thick, stirring occasionally. Remove whole ginger if used. Ladle into hot sterilized half-pint jars and seal.

Dried Peaches

Obviously, drying peaches is best done on a cool day near the end of the season when you are looking for ways to use up the remainder of an abundant supply. Of course, if you own a commercial food dryer, that equipment is preferred. But it will raise the electricity bill! Best of all is drying fruit in a hot, dry climate such as Glendale, Arizona, where Marie Kleinsasser does it. But you will have to cover fruit with netting and watch for predators!

6 lbs. fresh, ripe, firm peaches
3½ T. sodium sulfite (supplied by pharmacist)
1 gallon water

Wash and drain peaches. Cut into halves and remove pits. To prevent discoloration, soak fruit for 14 minutes in sodium sulfite solution. Drain. (If you are allergic to sulfites, omit this procedure. The fruit will be dark but wholesome.)

Drain and arrange fruit on trays and place in 150° oven with the bottom tray 3 inches from oven floor. Do not use top unit in electric oven. Prop open the door of an electric oven 1/2 inch. A gas oven door should be propped open 8 inches. (This helps control heat and lets moist air out.)

Alternate trays every 1 or 2 hours. Fruit is dry when pliable and leathery, usually in 6 hours or more. Pieces around the edges will dry first. Remove these as soon as they are dry.

Cool and package at once. Pack dried fruit in glass jars, using a tightly fitting lid. Dried fruit will keep a year or so when stored in a cool, dry, dark place. (From *Freeman* [South Dakota] *Courier.)*

Raspberries

Members of the bramble family, raspberries (both red and black) are good fruits for the home gardener to grow, even in the city. They require a minimum of care and, after the first year, will produce delicious fruit for eating fresh, canning, freezing, or drying. They also may be found in the wild state and, like blackberries and dewberries, are interchangeable in most recipes.

I maintain that the best use of raspberries is eating them fresh off the canes. If you can get them into the kitchen, serve them on cold cereal, in pancakes, as topping for ice cream, or freeze them whole in plastic containers for later similar use.

Flavored vinegars are very popular, and raspberries make some of the best vinegars. The following Raspberry Vinegar is particularly good on delicate greens or on fruit salads in which peaches and pears predominate.

Raspberry Vinegar

3 quarts raspberries (or other berries)
1 pint white wine vinegar
sugar

Rinse fruit and drain well. Crush to release juices. In stainless steel or crockery bowl, cover raspberries with vinegar. Let stand about 20 hours in a cool area. Strain through cheesecloth or fine mesh. Measure liquid, then mix with equal amount of sugar. Place in saucepan and bring to boil. Reduce heat and simmer 10 minutes. Let stand, covered, overnight.

Slowly decant vinegar into sterilized bottles, discarding sediment in the bottom of the container. Cap and store in cool, dark place. Makes about 1 1/2 pints. Makes a nice Christmas kitchen gift.

To Make Quick Raspberry Vinegar in Microwave

Place 2 c. of frozen sugared raspberries on glass pie plate and microwave on defrost setting 2 minutes. Let stand 5 minutes to fully defrost. Drain raspberry juice (about ¼ cup) into 1-cup glass measure or small bowl and reserve raspberries for another use. Add white vinegar to taste to raspberry juice and stir.

Mixed Greens with Raspberry Vinaigrette

2 T. raspberry vinegar
1 T. olive oil
1 T. chopped fresh basil
1 T. chopped fresh parsley
1 t. sugar

dash salt and pepper
8 cups mesclun (mixed salad greens such as lettuce, young chard leaves, spinach, green onions with tops)
1 c. fresh raspberries

To make dressing: combine vinegar, oil, herbs, and seasonings. In salad bowl toss the greens. Pour on the dressing and toss again. Sprinkle fresh raspberries over top and serve. Serves 6.

Melba Sauce

2 c. frozen raspberries
½ c. currant or apple jelly
½ c. sugar

Combine all ingredients in saucepan and bring to boil. Simmer 20 minutes or until of desired thickness. Pour into jar to store. Makes about 1 cup or half a pint. Serve in stemmed glassware over half of poached peach filled with vanilla ice cream.

Raspberry Pie

Crust

18 graham crackers rolled fine
½ c. butter, melted
¼ c. sugar

Add sugar to crumbs and mix thoroughly. Add melted butter and blend well. Press into 9-inch pie pan. Let cool in refrigerator for 30 minutes. Bake at 350° for 10–12 minutes.

Filling

1 qt. raspberries
$^1/_2$ c. sugar
$2^1/_2$ T. cornstarch

    Mash berries with fork lightly. Strain juice into pan. Add cornstarch and cook over low heat until thick and transparent. Cool, then add sugared berries. Blend until mixture is smooth.
    Pour into crumb crust. Place in refrigerator for at least $^1/_2$ hour before serving. Top with whipped or ice cream, or serve plain.

Red Raspberry Jam (Quick Method)

7 c. sugar
5 $^3/_4$ c. crushed berries
1 box powdered fruit pectin

    Measure and set aside the sugar. Rinse, drain, crush, and measure berries into large (4–6-quart) stainless steel kettle. Add pectin. Stir to dissolve pectin while bringing mixture to a hard boil. Then add sugar all at once. Keep stirring. When mixture reaches a fast rolling boil, begin counting time. Boil for just 1 minute.
    Remove from heat, quickly skim off foam and pour jam to $^1/_8$-inch of top of half-pint jars. Wipe off any jam on top or threads of jar. Screw band on tight. Invert jar as it is closed. When all have been sealed, set them upright to cool.

Raspberry Jam Cake

$1^1/_2$ c. fine dry bread crumbs
2 t. baking powder
$^1/_4$ t. salt
6 eggs, separated
$^1/_4$ c. sugar
$^3/_4$ c. raspberry jam
$^1/_2$ c. corn oil
1 t. vanilla

    Grease the bottom of a tube pan (9 x $3^1/_2$ inches). On waxed paper, thoroughly stir together the bread crumbs, baking powder, and salt.
    In a large mixing bowl, beat egg whites until foamy. Gradually beat in the sugar. Continue to beat until soft peaks form.
    In a medium mixing bowl, beat egg yolks until thickened and lemon colored. Gradually beat in jam, then corn oil and vanilla. Blend in bread crumb mixture. Fold into beaten egg white mixture.

Turn into prepared tube pan. Bake in a preheated 325° oven until cake springs back when touched or when toothpick tester comes out clean. Remove from pan after allowing it to cool for 10 minutes.

The Sherman House in Batesville, Indiana, holds a Raspberry Festival in late July, serving dinner entrées such as Broiled Lamb Chops with Fresh Raspberry-Orange Glaze, Grilled Rainbow Trout topped with Raspberry-Walnut Sauce, and Boneless Breast of Duck served with Wild Rice and topped with Raspberry Glaze. A chilled raspberry soup is also on the menu. This adaptation of a recipe for Fresh Berry Soup from a flyer advertising Alpine Berry Farm on Pocket Road near Batesville will give you the raspberry experience at home:

Fresh Berry Soup

1 qt. fresh orange juice
4 c. plain yogurt
1 T. honey (more or less, to taste)
2 T. lemon juice
dash each of cinnamon and nutmeg
1¹/₂ pts. fresh raspberries

Whisk together everything except the berries. Chill thoroughly.
Wash and drain berries, leaving them whole.
When ready to serve, divide berries into individual serving bowls and ladle soup on top. Garnish with fresh mint sprigs.
Note: This soup is more suited to serving for dessert than as a first course.

Summer Savory

Because of its affinity for fresh green and yellow beans or dried beans of various kinds, this herb is commonly known as the "bean herb." Among Mennonites with a German background it is called *Pepar Krut* (to purists, *Bohnenkraut*), but in Bible times it was known as hyssop. It has a sharp, spicy flavor, must be planted each year, and grows to be twelve inches high. It is commonly used dried, but may be used fresh as well. It is particularly good combined with other herbs in poultry dressings.

Savory Green Bean Soup

1 leftover ham bone with bits of ham attached
1 medium onion
2 qts. water
4 large potatoes
1 small carrot (optional)
1 qt. fresh cut green or yellow wax beans (or mixed)
$^1/_2$ t. parsley
1 t. dried summer savory
$^1/_2$ c. sour cream or yogurt

Cook ham bone and onion (cut up) in water for about an hour. Add potatoes (diced), carrot, and fresh beans and herbs. Cook until vegetables are tender but not mushy. Remove ham bone and cut from the bone any remaining bits of ham. Return ham bits to soup. Just before serving, stir in sour cream or yogurt or add dollop of cream to individual bowls. (Or pass cream.) Serves 6.

Savory Tomato Sauce for Summer Grills

1 lb. ripe tomatoes
1 onion, finely chopped
2 t. dried savory or 3 t. fresh savory
1 c. water
salt and pepper to taste
2 oz. butter
1 T. (heaping) flour

Peel and chop tomatoes. Simmer in stainless steel saucepan with chopped onion, savory, and water. Add salt and pepper to taste.

When cooked, purée in blender. Melt butter and blend in flour. Add some of the tomato sauce to the flour mixture, and gradually add remaining sauce. Stir until thickened. Refrigerate any remaining sauce for later use.

Summer Savoried Rice Stuffing

ground giblets (including heart, gizzard, and liver) from chicken, turkey, duck, or
    other fowl
2 c. cooked rice
2 T. chopped summer savory
2 T. chopped fresh parsley
bits of meat picked from cooked neck of fowl
salt and pepper to taste
excess broth in which giblets and neck have been cooked

Simmer raw giblets and neck in small amount of water until tender. (Liver should be added last since it requires less time and will get tough and bitter if cooked too long.)

Add herbs to the cooked rice. When giblets and neck meat are tender, put all through grinder. Mix with excess broth and combine with rice and herb mixture. Stuff bird cavity or cavities with mixture and bake at 325° until browned and juices run clear.

Summer Squash

We refer here to any light-colored, thin-skinned squash that matures rapidly and which must be prepared with a minimum of water and heat. Sometimes I have returned from vacation to find that yellow summer squash had turned to warted, heavy-skinned, crook-necked winter squash, in which case I treated them as such, halving and baking or peeling them and parboiling the cubed squash for a casserole with cheese and sunflower seed topping.

Yellow squash rings or strips may be added to a fresh vegetable plate or cut in rounds for salads when very young. They need not be seeded, for the seeds are very soft and highly digestible.

Sautéd briefly in butter and flavored with dried basil or summer savory, a few yellow summer squash make a quick, delicious vegetable dish to accompany most meats and may be considered a substitute for a starch such as potato, rice, or pasta. Since they are high in water content, no water need be added to the skillet in which they are prepared. Because they are bland in flavor, they take on the flavor of whatever is added, such as grated Parmesan cheese, olive oil, onion, herbs, tomato sauce, etc.

Yellow Summer Squash with Parmesan and Herbs

3 patty pan or yellow crookneck squash
2 T. melted butter
salt and pepper (optional)
2 T. Parmesan cheese
herbs (parsley, chives, basil, or sage)

Cut patty pan into quarters or wedges. Slice crookneck. Steam over boiling water until crisp tender. Drain. Rinse under cold water to stop the cooking. Place squash in a buttered, shallow ovenproof dish. Drizzle top with melted butter. Sprinkle with salt, pepper, and Parmesan cheese. Place dish under preheated broiler, about 5 inches from heat, for 3 minutes or until tops are lightly browned. Sprinkle herbs over squash before serving. Serves 3 or 4.

Yellow Squash Sauté

1 t. chopped onion

1 t. chopped garlic

2 T. butter

2 small or 1 medium yellow squash, cut into quarter-inch slices

1 medium tomato, coarsely chopped

dried marjoram, salt, and pepper

dash hot pepper sauce

Parmesan cheese

In a large skillet, sauté onion and chopped garlic in butter until onion is soft and translucent. Add squash slices, tomato, and 1 or 2 pinches marjoram, salt, pepper, and hot pepper sauce. Sauté, stirring frequently, about 5 minutes. Sprinkle with Parmesan cheese and stir for just a few seconds more. Makes 2 servings.

Stuffed Yellow Squash

6 small yellow straight-neck squash

1 c. fine soft bread crumbs

1 c. finely chopped cooked ham

$1/4$ t. crushed rosemary leaves

$1/2$ t. salt

$1/8$ t. pepper

8 T. melted butter

Wash squash, split in half lengthwise, and remove seeds. Set aside. Combine bread crumbs, ham, rosemary, salt, and pepper, and half of butter. Spoon into cavities of squash halves. Put halves together and tie with a string to keep in stuffing or hold in place with toothpicks. Brown lightly in remaining butter. Reduce heat, cover, and cook 20 minutes, or until squash is tender, turning to cook both sides.

Grilled Squash Parmesan
While meat, fish, or fowl is cooking on the grill, cook your vegetable as well.

3 small yellow squash

10 cherry tomatoes, halved

$1/2$ t. oregano

2 T. Parmesan cheese

$1/4$ t. salt

dash pepper

2 T. butter

Slice squash $1/4$-inch thick. Stir together all ingredients except butter. Place in center of an 18-inch square of heavy-duty foil. Dot with butter. Bring four foil corners up to form pyramid. Fold opening together loosely to allow for heat circulation and expansion. Seal by folding over ends and pressing to the package. Grill over medium hot coals 20–30 minutes or until squash is tender.

Cheddar-Squash Bake

2 lbs. yellow summer squash
2 eggs, separated
1 c. sour cream
2 T. flour
1½ c. (6 oz.) Cheddar cheese
4 slices bacon, crisp-fried, drained, and crumbled
⅓ c. fine dry bread crumbs
1 T. butter, melted

Scrub squash and trim off ends. Do not peel. Cook whole, covered, in boiling salted water for 15–20 minutes or until just tender. Drain thoroughly. Cut into thin slices. Sprinkle with salt. (There should be about 6 c. sliced squash.) Reserve a few slices of squash for garnish.

In a small bowl, beat egg whites until stiff peaks form. Set aside. In a larger bowl, lightly beat egg yolks, then beat in sour cream and flour. Fold in beaten egg whites.

Layer half the squash, half the egg mixture, and half the cheese in greased 12 x 8-inch baking dish. Sprinkle bacon over top. Repeat layers. Combine crumbs and butter and sprinkle around edge. Arrange reserved squash atop. Bake in 350° oven for 20–25 minutes. Garnish with bacon curls and parsley sprig, if desired. Serves 8–10.

Yellow squash combines nicely with other summer vegetables such as zucchini, green beans, corn, and tomatoes.

Squash-Tomato Pasta Supper

1 large onion
1 clove garlic
¼ c. oil
4 medium ripe tomatoes
3 c. diced yellow summer squash
3 c. diced zucchini
pepper
½ t. dried basil
½ t. oregano
½ t. thyme
½ lb. spaghetti
2 quarts water
2 t. salt
grated Parmesan cheese

Chop onion and garlic. Heat oil in skillet and sauté onion and garlic until tender, not browned. Peel and dice tomatoes. Add tomatoes, squash, pepper, basil, oregano, and thyme to skillet. Bring to a boil, reduce heat, and simmer, covered, about 20 minutes. Uncover and simmer 5 minutes longer.

Cook spaghetti in boiling water with salt for 8 to 10 minutes while sauce is simmering. Drain. Serve with sauce and Parmesan cheese. Serves 4–6.

Summer Squash Medley

1/4 c. butter
3 c. sliced yellow squash
3 c. sliced zucchini
1 T. brown sugar
1/8 t. powdered nutmeg or 1 t. fresh basil

Melt butter in large skillet. Stir in squash and zucchini, brown sugar, and nutmeg or basil. Cook and stir until vegetables are crisply tender, 8–10 minutes. Serves 4–6 as side dish.

Yellow Squash and Corn Baked in Custard

6 medium yellow squash
salt and pepper to taste
1/4 c. butter, melted
1 large onion, minced
1 clove garlic, minced
1 small green pepper, seeded and diced

1/2 t. oregano
1 1/2 c. cooked and drained whole kernel corn
1/2 c. grated Cheddar cheese
5 eggs, well beaten
1/2 c. light cream or half and half

Preheat oven to 325°. Slice squash into 1/2-inch slices. Steam for 5 minutes in vegetable steamer. Drain and sprinkle with salt and pepper.

Melt half the butter in a skillet. Sauté onion, garlic, and green pepper until soft. Add more salt, pepper, and oregano. Let cool.

Add squash, corn, and cheese to onion mixture. Add well-beaten eggs, cream, and remaining melted butter. Mix. Pour into greased casserole. Place casserole in a pan of hot water and bake for 40 minutes or until custard is set. Serves 6–8.

Squash and Green Bean Combo to Can

2 lbs. (2 qts.) yellow summer squash
2 lbs. (2 qts.) young green beans
4 c. coarsely chopped onion
4 t. salt
2 t. chili powder
1 c. water

Scrub unpared squash well with nylon netting. Slice crosswise into 1/2-inch slices. Wash beans, remove stem ends, and cut in inch-long pieces.

In large saucepan combine squash and beans with onion, salt, and chili powder. Add water. Cover and steam 5 minutes.

Pack into clean hot pint jars leaving half-inch head space. Add boiling water if more liquid is needed. Run spatula around inside of jar to work out air bubbles. Adjust lids. Process pints for 30 minutes at 10 pounds of pressure in a pressure canner. Yields 8 pints.

At serving time, add 1 T. butter to 1 pint vegetables. Boil gently for 10 minutes. Or combine 1 c. whole kernel corn with 1 pint vegetables.

Yellow Summer Squash for Twenty-Five

This makes a good main dish for a women's church luncheon, or any group that is ecologically conscious and has been studying eating lower on the food chain. It freezes well, so you may prepare family-size portions and freeze for winter use.

15 medium squash, sliced
2 c. diced onion
³/₄ c. butter
2 t. salt
1 t. black pepper
3 c. grated Cheddar cheese

6 eggs
1 can (12 oz.) evaporated milk
*3 c. saltine cracker crumbs or bread
    crumbs seasoned with herbs such as
    parsley, basil, marjoram, etc.*

Sauté squash and onion in butter. When soft, add to all other ingredients except crumbs. If mixture seems dry, add more milk. Turn into greased baking pans and top with crumbs. Bake at 350° for 45 minutes. Serves 25. (Adapted from *Simply Delicious*; see Resources for reference.)

Tomatoes

Costumed interpreters at Conner Prairie Pioneer Village on Allisonville Road northeast of Indianapolis talk about a Dr. Campbell coming from Kentucky to Indiana with tomatoes in 1836 and trying to convince Hoosiers that tomatoes were not poisonous. How grateful we are to Dr. Campbell and his clan for their efforts in popularizing the tomato. Can you imagine a summer without fresh, sun-drenched tomatoes? If a city dweller has room and time to grow any vegetable (or fruit?), she will try to grow tomatoes, for there is no comparison between home-grown tomatoes and the poor imitations bred to be harvested green by machine and encased in plastic after being "coated with food-grade vegetable-, petroleum-, beeswax-, and/or shellac-based wax or resin," which actually appears on the label of some "fresh" red-ripe tomatoes.

My adult sons joke about the daily "Tomato Surprise" I was able to concoct in order to utilize the generous output of vines after sliced tomatoes had waned in popularity. There were tomatoes stuffed with tuna or cottage cheese, broiled tomatoes, gazpacho, chili sauce, spaghetti sauce, and finally, green tomato chutney and green tomato mince pie.

Tomatoes lend themselves to serving fresh, canning, freezing and drying, the latter to be mixed with other dried vegetables such as celery leaves and herbs to be added to soups for flavoring.

I never peel tomatoes when serving them fresh because tomato skins are high in vitamin content. However, they tend to be troublesome in cooked tomatoes unless they are puréed in the blender—skins, pulp, seeds and all.

So, unless you want cold-packed canned whole tomatoes or large pieces of tomato in a dish you are preparing, why not go to puréeing in a blender and freezing the results in plastic containers without cooking? However, open kettle cooking will reduce the volume somewhat because some of the considerable water content of tomatoes will evaporate. But for spaghetti sauce, soup or chili to be prepared during the winter, frozen puréed tomatoes serve beautifully.

Tomatoes also lend themselves to ethnic cooking, particularly to what we North Americans call Italian or Mexican cooking. So, whether your family's preference is chili con carne, spaghetti and meatballs, or tacos, you will need a ready supply of tomato products.

Most experienced cooks are creative when it comes to cooking with tomatoes, adapting recipes to suit the tastes of their family members. Gazpacho, for example, comes in many variations. The following is a favorite easy recipe made in the blender:

Blender Gazpacho

1 large cucumber, peeled and seeded if very mature
1 sweet medium onion, such as Vidalia
1 small clove garlic, if desired
1 small hot green pepper, such as jalapeño, seeds removed
6 large ripe tomatoes
1 T. olive oil
1/2 t. salt

Blend together for 2 to 3 minutes, making sure that garlic and pepper, especially, are well blended. (Use rubber gloves when working with hot peppers to avoid burning hands and, worse, burning eyes!) Chill in refrigerator. Serve over several ice cubes in a bowl. Garnish with crisp, seasoned croutons.

Fresh Tomato Juice

Put cut-up ripe tomatoes in blender. (If tomatoes are pulpy and not juicy, add a few tablespoons water.) Whirl until smooth and put through strainer to remove seeds. Season to taste with salt. Freeze in plastic containers, allowing room for expansion.

When serving juice that has been frozen, thaw in refrigerator overnight. The next morning add pepper, Worcestershire sauce, or herbs to taste.

When serving tomato juice hot as an appetizer on a cold day, spice the tomato juice while you heat it with a few whole cloves, a pinch of oregano, prepared horseradish or hot pepper sauce.

Salsa I

2 medium tomatoes, diced

1 small red bell pepper, seeded and diced

2 T. chopped red onion

3 T. fresh chopped cilantro or parsley

1/4 t. dried oregano leaves, crumbled

1 t. red wine vinegar

2 t. olive oil

1/2 t. minced garlic

1/4 t. sugar

salt and pepper to taste

Combine all ingredients in a non-metallic bowl. Cover and refrigerate. This can be prepared up to two days in advance. Serve as appetizer with large tortilla chips.

Salsa II

4 medium tomatoes, chopped

1/2 c. finely chopped onion

1/2 c. finely chopped celery

1/2 c. finely chopped green bell pepper

1/4 c. olive oil

2 to 3 T. finely chopped jalapeño
    peppers, seeds and membranes
    removed (wear rubber gloves!)

2 T. red wine vinegar

1 t. mustard seed

1 t. coriander seed, crushed

1 t. salt

dash pepper

Combine all ingredients, cover, and chill several hours or overnight. Stir occasionally. Serve with large tortilla chips.

Tomato Ketchup

8 qts. red-ripe tomatoes

1 pt. cider vinegar

2 T. salt

1 1/2 t. pepper

2 T. ground cinnamon

1 1/2 t. ground cloves

1 T. allspice

1 t. cayenne pepper

1 c. sugar (optional)*

Coarsely chop tomatoes. Cook in a large kettle, uncovered, until soft, about 30 minutes. Strain through fine sieve or food mill. Press through as much pulp as possible.

Return juice to kettle. Add remaining ingredients and cook at a medium boil until thick and smooth. Ketchup will reduce to about half. Immediately ladle the mixture into sterilized jars, allowing 1/2 inch head space. Screw on lids and rings. Process in boiling hot water bath for 10 minutes after water has come to a rolling boil.** Makes 6–7 pints.

*Adding sugar makes ketchup taste more like commercial version.

**1989 USDA recommendations are 10 pounds of pressure for 20 minutes for pints.

Fresh Tomato Barbecue Sauce

¹/₄ c. oil	*1 t. dry mustard*
2 c. chopped onion	*1 t. paprika*
1 clove garlic, minced	*2 T. Worcestershire sauce*
4 lbs. tomatoes	*1 t. dried basil*
¹/₄ c. chopped parsley	*1 c. dark corn syrup*
4 t. salt	*¹/₄ c. vinegar*
¹/₂ t. pepper	

Heat oil in 5-quart Dutch oven. Add onion and garlic. Cook 5 minutes or until tender but not brown. Cut tomatoes into wedges. There should be about 10 cups. Add tomatoes, parsley, salt, pepper, mustard, paprika, Worcestershire sauce, and basil. Bring to a boil. Cover and simmer 30 minutes.

Uncover and simmer, stirring frequently, for 1 hour or until slightly thickened. Purée in blender until smooth. Return to Dutch oven. Add corn syrup and vinegar. Simmer, uncovered, for 30 minutes more or until thickened. Makes 6 cups. (May be frozen, canned, or stored in tightly covered container in refrigerator. When using, brush the sauce on meat during the last 15 minutes of cooking.)

About Freezing and Drying Tomatoes

Tomatoes may be frozen whole to be used in salads, soups, and stews year-round. To freeze, choose fully ripe and cosmetically perfect tomatoes. Wrap the tomato in clear plastic wrap or aluminum foil and tuck into available space in the freezer. Or enclose the individually wrapped tomatoes in a heavy plastic bag. When using, rinse the frozen tomato under *cold* water and the skin will pop. Then, on a wooden board, with a *sharp* knife, cut into wedges for the salad bowl. As the tomatoes thaw, they will chill the greens and become defrosted. Or you may skin the frozen tomato and use it to flavor soups or stews when only a small amount of tomato flavoring is desired.

Tomatoes may also be dried and added to soups with dried parsley, celery leaves, etc. To prepare tomatoes for drying, cut them into small wedges and let each wedge rest on its skin side to dry. This keeps the juice in so the flavor and nutrition are enhanced. Place wedges to dry on a cookie sheet lined with plastic wrap or parchment paper. Dry in gas oven with pilot light if you do not have a dehydrator. When dry, store in small plastic bags or mix with other dried herbs or mixed vegetables.

The U.S. Department of Agriculture suggests another method of drying tomatoes, using the meaty varieties only and dipping the tomatoes in boiling water for 1 minute to remove the peeling, stem, and end. Slice ¹/₈ inch thick. The dried product will be a leathery dull red.

Watermelons

Dr. David Livingstone is reported to have discovered these melons growing wild in the desert and semiarid regions of Africa. His find was published in 1858. Later the melons were cultivated in semidesert areas as an important water source during dry spells. If you grow watermelons, you know they will do best in sandy soil.

Though a slice of icy cold watermelon is as good a dessert as anyone can get on a hot summer day, there are other delectable dishes that watermelon may be turned into.

Watermelon Slushy

watermelon
lemon juice
mint or lemon balm leaves

Cut a slice of watermelon. Cut it off the rind. Start slushing it with a big spoon. Then add lemon juice (as much as you would like). Roll the mint or lemon balm. Then start tearing and dipping it in the slush. Now you have a delicious freshener. (Contributed by my granddaughter, Ariana Kaufman, at age 10.)

Frozen Watermelon Pops

extra-ripe watermelon
lemon-lime carbonated beverage (optional)

Purée the fruit in blender. Add small amount of beverage to make smoother pop. Spoon into molds or paper cups. Freeze partially. Add wooden sticks and return to freezer until firm. When frozen, remove paper cup or mold and serve with generous supply of paper napkins. When serving children, ask them to step outside and eat pops under a shade tree.

Triple Melon Soup with Mint

2 ice cubes
1 T. lemon juice
1 t. chopped fresh mint plus extra for garnish
$^1/_2$ c. plain yogurt
1 c. combined leftover cantaloupe, honeydew, and watermelon chunks

Place ingredients in blender and purée until smooth. Garnish with fresh mint. Makes 1 serving.

Frozen Watermelon Balls

2 c. sugar
4^1/$_2$ c. water
"heart" of watermelon
lemon juice

Boil sugar and water until thoroughly dissolved. Cool to ice cold. Allow ^{3}/$_4$ c. syrup for each 1^1/$_2$-pint tapered jar. (Tapered jars are used because they are wider at the top than bottom and have no shoulders. As a result, food can be removed before it is defrosted, preventing breakage.) Pour ^{1}/$_3$ c. cold syrup and 1^1/$_2$ T. lemon juice into a 1^1/$_2$-pint jar. As you cut a ball from the melon, drop it into the jar. Fill jar to within ^{3}/$_4$ inch of top. Shake jar to settle balls close together. Add more syrup if needed to cover balls. Place a wad of waxed paper in top of jar to keep melon under syrup. The lid will push it down. Put dome lid on jar and screw band tight. Put jar in freezer as promptly as possible.

This recipe may be used for other melons as well—cantaloupe, honeydew, etc. If you wish not to waste any melon, cut the heart into chunks instead of balls. Or use remainder from cutting balls for Melon Soup or Frozen Watermelon Pops, above.

Spiced Watermelon Pickle
This makes a nice Christmas kitchen gift.

rind from half of large watermelon
    (about 2 lbs.)
8 c. water (for brine)
^{1}/$_2$ c. salt
4 c. sugar
1 lemon, thinly sliced

1 T. whole cloves
1 T. whole allspice
6 one-inch sticks cinnamon
2 c. cider vinegar
2 c. water (for syrup)

Pare green skin from watermelon. Cut rind into 1-inch cubes. (There should be about 8 c.) Keep watermelon rind fresh in plastic bag in refrigerator until you are ready to pickle it. Soak overnight in brine of 8 c. water and salt in large crockery bowl.

Drain, place in kettle, and cover with fresh water. Heat to boiling, then simmer 10 minutes or just until cubes are tender but still firm. Drain.

While rind drains, combine sugar, lemon, cloves, allspice, cinnamon, vinegar, and 2 c. water in same kettle. Heat to boiling. Stir in drained rind. Simmer, stirring often from bottom of pan for 1 hour or until rind is clear and syrup is thick.

Ladle rind and spice evenly into hot sterilized half-pint jars. Fill to within ^{1}/$_4$ inch of brim with remaining hot syrup. Cover with dome lids and rings. Process in hot water bath for 10 minutes after water has come to a full rolling boil. Remove from bath and cool on wooden rack. You will know lids have sealed when you hear them pop. Any that do not pop should be stored in refrigerator and used first.

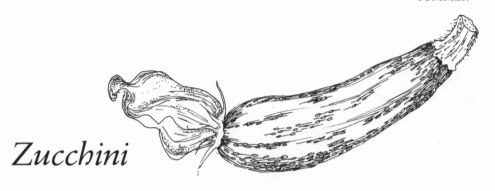

Zucchini

Zucchini is in a class by itself and has a lore of its own. (Have you heard the story of the giant zucchini that grew on the front seat of an automobile whose door had remained ajar one night?) Fortunately, recipes for zucchini abound because the vines produce so prolifically. One of my favorites is the recipe contributed by my late friend, Jane Smith:

Chopped Zucchini

Wash carefully 1 mature zucchini. Place it on cutting board. Slice diagonally. Do not sprinkle with salt. Do not douse with oil. Do not coat with flour or herbs. Throw on the compost pile and mix vigorously.

Because zucchini is so bland, it requires flavoring, just as yellow squash does. Therefore it is a perfect neutral base for whatever flavoring you wish to predominate—Cajun, chocolate, or Italian.

Zucchini is best picked when it is 8 to 9 inches long, at the stage when the skin is soft and the seeds highly edible. Like yellow squash, zucchini may be sliced or diced raw for salads, or cut in strips for a fresh vegetable plate. Because of its blandness, it will complement strongly flavored dressings and dips. An easy vegetable dip suitable for zucchini was suggested by Barbara Williamson:

Curry and Mayonnaise Dip

$^1/_2$ t. curry powder (or mix your own with turmeric, chili powder, cumin, and garlic salt)
$^1/_2$ c. mayonnaise or lower calorie salad dressing

Mix vigorously and place in an attractive stemmed glass or pottery bowl in the center of a plate of zucchini rounds or strips.

Creole Zucchini

2 strips bacon, cut in pieces
1 medium onion
1 medium green pepper
1 clove garlic
2 c. fresh peeled and quartered tomatoes
2 medium zucchini, unpeeled but halved lengthwise and cut in 1-inch pieces
1 bay leaf
$^1/_4$ t. basil
salt and pepper to taste
1 t. sugar

Sauté bacon pieces in skillet. When bacon is cooked, add onion, diced, and green pepper, cut in strips. Mince garlic and add to vegetables sautéing. Add tomatoes, bay leaf, and other seasonings. Cook only a few minutes, just until zucchini is crisply tender. (Leaving the skin on the zucchini helps to retain its shape.)

Variations: Creole Zucchini may be prepared without the bacon, sautéing the vegetables in oil instead. If the recipe is canned or frozen for winter use, serving it brings back a feeling of summer, especially during a blizzard. It may be added to Italian sausages which have been fully cooked and drained of excess fat. A good casserole is made by adding a jar of canned Creole Zucchini to cooked sausages, topping all with mozzarella cheese, and heating thoroughly in the oven. Accompanied by crusty French bread or toasted Italian garlic bread, it makes a sumptuous meal, warding off most winter blahs.

Zucchini-Cheese Casserole

During the 1970s a large gathering of Presbyterian women was served a zucchini casserole by the Purdue University food service. The dish proved so popular that the recipe was later printed in the Gathering's daily newspaper. A few months later I prepared it for the women of Fairview Presbyterian Church, the only difference being that I, instead of Purdue Farms, had grown the vegetables. This is a scaled-down version.

$^1/_2$ c. chopped onions
2 T. butter
1 lb. (1 qt.) sliced zucchini
salt to taste
$^3/_4$ c. Cheddar cheese, grated
$^1/_4$ c. American cheese, grated
$^1/_2$ t. Worcestershire sauce
1 drop red pepper sauce mixed with 6 T. butter, melted

Sauté onions in small amount of butter. Boil zucchini in salted water until barely tender. Drain zucchini, add other ingredients, and mix well. Top with ½ c. buttered bread crumbs and 2 T. sesame seeds or sunflower seeds. Bake in uncovered shallow baking dish for 10–15 minutes at 350°. Serves 6. (From Purdue University kitchens.)

Zucchini Omelet

1 c. zucchini, thinly sliced
¼ c. onion, finely sliced
⅓ c. celery, thinly sliced
3 T. oil
3 eggs

2 T. water
1 T. powdered milk
½ t. salt
½ t. pepper
1 T. grated Parmesan or Romano cheese

Sauté vegetables gently in 2 T. of the oil for 6–8 minutes. Beat eggs with water, powdered milk, salt, pepper, and cheese. Add remaining oil to vegetables. Pour egg mixture over hot vegetables and oil. Free the sides of the omelet as it cooks so that uncooked egg can run underneath. Fold in half when set. Serves 2.

Tossed Zucchini Green Salad

2 medium zucchini, thinly sliced
⅓ c. minced red onion
1 t. chopped fresh dill or ¼ t. dried dillweed
6 c. torn mixed greens
bottled Italian or blue cheese dressing

Put first 4 ingredients in salad bowl and chill until serving time. Pour ½ c. dressing on top, toss, and serve. Good accompaniment for pasta. Serves 6.

Zucchini Salad

2 lbs. small zucchini, thinly sliced
½ c. snipped fresh dill
1 T. lemon juice
1 T. red wine vinegar
1½ t. salt
pepper to taste
1½ c. sour cream (or half plain yogurt)

Combine all ingredients well. Be sure that zucchini slices are well coated. Chill, covered, for at least 2 hours. Serves 4–6.

Dilled Zucchini and Carrots

²/₃ c. oil
1 c. lemon juice
1 T. salt
1 T. onion powder
2 t. dillweed

¹/₂ t. pepper
2 qts. sliced zucchini
2¹/₂ c. shredded carrots
1 c. sliced ripe olives
1 small pimiento, diced

Combine oil, lemon juice, salt, onion powder, dillweed, and pepper in jar with lid. Cover and shake well. Combine zucchini, carrots, olives, and pimiento in large bowl. Add enough dressing to coat vegetables and toss gently. Reserve remaining dressing for another use. Makes 10 servings.

Zucchini and Tomato Salad

3 to 4 zucchini, thinly sliced (3 c.)
2 c. cherry tomatoes, cut in half
¹/₂ c. minced green onions
¹/₂ c. chopped fresh basil leaves
¹/₄ c. chopped parsley
salt and pepper
³/₄ c. vinaigrette dressing

Mix vegetables together. Season with salt and pepper to taste. Just before serving, add dressing and toss.

Zucchini Soup

1 T. butter
1 T. oil
1 small onion, chopped
6 c. chicken broth
6 medium zucchini, sliced
1 sprig fresh parsley or summer savory
salt and pepper to taste
yogurt and/or sour cream

Heat butter and oil in saucepan. Sauté onion until soft. Add broth, zucchini and herbs. Simmer 10 minutes.

Purée small amount at a time in blender. Season with salt and pepper and chill thoroughly for cold soup or reheat for warm soup. Garnish with dollop of yogurt and/or sour cream.

Sautéd Zucchini and Sausage

1 lb. bulk pork sausage
4 small zucchini, sliced
¹/₂ c. chopped onion
2 c. peeled and chopped fresh tomatoes
¹/₄ c. grated Parmesan cheese

Cook sausage in small skillet until browned, stirring to crumble. Drain off drippings, reserving 1 T. in skillet. Place cooked sausage on paper towel. Sauté zucchini and onion in skillet until tender, stirring frequently. Stir in tomatoes and cooked sausage. Cook until heated through. Place mixture in serving dish and sprinkle with Parmesan cheese. Serves 8.

Frittata of Zucchini

1¹/₂ lbs. young zucchini (about 4¹/₂ c. chopped)
1 medium onion
3 T. olive oil
6 eggs
salt and pepper
basil, crushed

Dice zucchini and chop onion. Heat olive oil in 10-inch skillet and add onions and zucchini. Sauté vegetables, stirring often, until onions are golden and zucchini tender. Beat eggs lightly with salt, pepper, and sprinkling of basil.

When zucchini is just tender, spread vegetables around the pan evenly and pour eggs over them. Lower the heat and cover the pan. Cook until eggs are completely set, about 15–20 minutes. (If it puffs up in a bubble, pierce it with a sharp knife.)

When eggs are firm on top, loosen frittata carefully by sliding spatula under it. Then place a plate upside down over the top of the pan like a lid and invert it, dropping the frittata out onto plate. Slide it carefully back into the pan with the top side down to brown the top. Then turn it out onto serving plate.

Serve frittata cut in wedges. May be served hot or at room temperature.

Tuna-Zucchini Burgers

1 large zucchini, shredded and drained (about 4 c.)
$^1/_2$ t. salt, divided
2 cans (6 $^1/_2$ oz. each) tuna
$^1/_2$ c. finely chopped onion
2 eggs, lightly beaten
$^1/_4$ c. flour
1 t. lemon juice
$^1/_4$ t. pepper

Shred zucchini and place in colander. Sprinkle with $^1/_4$ t. salt and toss to mix. Let drain 15 minutes. Press dry between paper towels.

Drain excess oil or water from tuna. In large bowl, flake tuna with fork. Mix in shredded and drained zucchini, onion, beaten eggs, flour, lemon juice, remaining $^1/_4$ t. salt, and pepper.

Use about $^1/_2$ c. mixture to make each burger. Shape into patties and place on a lightly greased baking sheet. Bake in a 350° oven 15 minutes. Turn and bake 15 minutes longer or until patties are brown. Serve plain or in a bun.

Deep-Fried Zucchini Sticks

1$^1/_2$ lbs. zucchini
salt and pepper
$^1/_4$ c. flour
2 eggs, beaten with $^1/_4$ c. milk or water
$^1/_4$ c. fine dry bread crumbs
fat for deep frying

Wash and dry zucchini and cut in sticks about $^1/_2$ inch thick and 4 inches long. Sprinkle with salt and pepper and roll in flour. Dip in egg mixture, then roll in crumbs and put on wax paper–lined sheet pan. Chill until shortly before serving time. Fry in deep fat heated to 380° on frying thermometer until golden brown. Drain on absorbent paper and serve at once. Serves 4.

Stuffed Zucchini à la Parmigiana

2 large zucchini (8–10 inches long)	*$^1/_4$ c. cottage cheese*
2 t. chopped green onions	*1 egg yolk*
1 T. melted butter	*salt and pepper to taste*
1 c. cooked ground beef (4 oz. uncooked)	*1 can (15 oz.) tomato sauce*
1 T. chopped parsley	*$^1/_2$ t. dried basil*
1 T. grated Parmesan cheese	*2 slices Monterey Jack cheese*

Cut zucchini in half lengthwise, scoop out centers, and discard (they will be mostly seeds). Steam zucchini until just crisply tender. Set aside to cool and drain (turned upside down).

Meanwhile, make stuffing by sautéing onions in butter and combining with ground beef, parsley, cheeses, egg yolk, and seasonings. Stuff each zucchini half with mixture. Pour tomato sauce in shallow baking dish. Place zucchini side by side in sauce. Sprinkle basil over top. Slice cheese into four strips and place on top of each zucchini half. Bake in 450° oven for 10 minutes or until zucchini are heated through.

Pasta with Creamy Zucchini Sauce

1 lb. pasta (e.g., rotini or shells)
1/3 c. oil
1 large clove garlic, minced
8 oz. mozzarella cheese, shredded
1/2 c. grated Parmesan cheese
1 lb. fresh zucchini, scrubbed and coarsely grated (about 3 c.)
1/2 c. chopped fresh parsley
1/2 t. salt
1/4 t. pepper

Cook pasta in boiling, salted water and drain. Then heat oil in pasta kettle over moderate heat, add garlic, and cook 1/2 minute. Return pasta to kettle and toss to coat with oil and garlic. Add cheeses and toss again. Add remaining ingredients and continue to toss over moderate heat until cheese and moisture from zucchini coat pasta with a light sauce. Serve immediately with additional cheese, if desired.

Pasta Primavera

1 clove garlic, minced fine
1 T. olive oil
1 small onion, diced
2 tomatoes, chopped
salt and pepper
1/2 t. basil
1/2 t. oregano
2 medium zucchini, coarsely grated
1 egg, beaten
1/4 c. grated Parmesan or Romano cheese
1 lb. pasta, cooked

In a large skillet, sauté garlic until lightly brown in oil. Add onion and sauté until clear. Add tomatoes, seasonings and herbs. Simmer a few minutes. Add zucchini. Cook for 5 minutes on high heat or until moisture is almost evaporated. Add egg and cheese. Serve mixture over pasta.

Zucchini-Parmesan Bread

1¹/₂ c. shredded unpeeled zucchini
3 c. flour
5 t. baking powder
¹/₂ t. baking soda
1¹/₂ t. salt
4 T. sugar
4 T. grated Parmesan cheese

1 c. buttermilk, yogurt, or sour milk
  (made by adding ¹/₂ t. lemon juice to
  sweet milk)
6 T. butter, melted
2 eggs, lightly beaten
3 T. grated onion

Preheat oven to 350°. Lightly grease two 8 x 4-inch loaf pans. Mix together shredded zucchini, flour, baking powder, baking soda, salt, sugar, and cheese. In another bowl mix buttermilk, melted butter, eggs and onion.

Add milk mixture to dry ingredients all at once. Mix until just blended. Spread in pans and bake 45–60 minutes or until toothpick comes out clean. Cool on rack before slicing.

Zucchini Corn Bread

1 lb. zucchini, grated
1¹/₂ t. salt
1 c. flour
³/₄ c. cornmeal
1 T. baking powder
2 t. salt
1 c. buttermilk, yogurt, or sour milk
  (made by adding ¹/₂ t. lemon juice to
  sweet milk)

1 egg, lightly beaten
¹/₄ c. butter, melted and cooled
¹/₂ c. grated Cheddar cheese
2 T. minced onion
1 T. minced fresh red and/or green bell
  pepper

Spread grated zucchini in colander and sprinkle with salt. Toss and allow to drain for half hour. Transfer zucchini to dish towel and squeeze out moisture. Into large bowl sift together dry ingredients. In small bowl combine wet ingredients and stir mixture into flour mixture. Stir in zucchini, cheese, onion, and fresh pepper. Transfer batter to greased 9-inch square baking pan. Bake in preheated 425° oven for 30–40 minutes or until top is golden and toothpick inserted in middle comes out clean.

Zucchini Cake

1 package (2-layer size) yellow cake mix
  with pudding
4 eggs
¹/₄ c. oil
3 c. grated zucchini

¹/₂ t. salt
1 t. cinnamon
1 c. chopped nuts

Put all ingredients in bowl and beat to blend. Beat for 4 minutes. Pour into 2 greased and floured 9 x 5-inch loaf pans. Bake at 350° 50–55 minutes or until cake tests done when toothpick is inserted in center. Do not underbake! Cool in pans 15 minutes. Remove from pans and cool on racks. Sprinkle top with confectioners' sugar, if desired.

Zucchini-Chocolate Cake

$^1/_2$ c. butter

$^1/_2$ c. oil

1 $^3/_4$ c. sugar

2 eggs

1 t. vanilla

$^1/_2$ c. sour milk (made by adding $^1/_2$ t. lemon juice to sweet milk)

4 T. cocoa

2$^1/_2$ c. flour

$^1/_2$ t. baking powder

1 t. soda

1 t. salt

2 c. grated zucchini

sugar, chocolate chips, and chopped nuts to sprinkle

Cream butter, oil, and sugar well. Add remaining ingredients through zucchini and pour into greased and floured 9 x 13-inch cake pan. Sprinkle with sugar, chocolate chips, and nuts. Bake at 325° for 40–45 minutes. (Contributed by Mrs. Joe Matt Hofer to *Freeman* [South Dakota] *Courier.*)

Variation: Coconut may be substituted for nuts.

Lemony Zucchini Refrigerator Pickles

6 zucchini

1 medium green pepper, finely chopped

1 medium onion, finely chopped

1 T. salt

2 t. celery seed

$^3/_4$ c. sugar

$^1/_2$ c. lemon juice

1 lemon, thinly sliced and halved

Cut zucchini into slices $^1/_{16}$-inch thick. Combine with green pepper, onion, salt, and celery seed in large bowl. Mix gently. Let stand 1 hour at room temperature.

Combine sugar with lemon juice. Stir to dissolve sugar. Pour over vegetables. Add lemon slices and stir to blend. Cover and refrigerate 24 hours.

These pickles will keep 3 weeks when stored, covered, in refrigerator.

Canned Zucchini Pickles

2 lbs. small zucchini	1 t. celery seed
2 medium onions	1 t. turmeric
$^1/_4$ c. salt	$^1/_2$ t. dry mustard
1 pint white vinegar	1 t. yellow mustard seed
1 c. sugar	

Wash and cut unpeeled zucchini and peeled onions in very thin slices into crock or bowl. Cover with water and add salt. Let stand 1 hour. Drain. Mix remaining ingredients and bring to boil. Pour over zucchini and onion. Let stand 1 hour. Bring to boil and cook 3 minutes.* Pack in 3 hot, sterilized pint jars and adjust lids.

*1989 USDA recommendations are 10 pounds of pressure for 20 minutes for pints.

Zucchini Marmalade

2 lbs. young zucchini	1 (1 $^3/_4$ oz.) package powdered pectin
juice of 2 lemons	5 c. sugar
1 t. grated lemon peel	2 T. finely chopped crystallized ginger
1 (13$^1/_2$ oz.) can crushed pineapple, drained	

Peel squash and cut in thin slices. Measure 6 c. sliced zucchini into large enameled or stainless steel kettle. Do not use aluminum!

Add lemon juice, peel, and crushed pineapple. Bring to a boil. Lower heat and simmer, uncovered, until squash is tender but holds its shape, about 15 minutes.

Add fruit pectin. Place over high heat and bring to boil. Stir in sugar and ginger. Bring to full rolling boil and boil hard 1 minute, stirring constantly.

Remove from heat. Skim off any foam. Stir and skim 5 minutes to cool slightly and prevent fruit from floating.

Ladle into hot sterilized jars. Cover with lids and rings to seal. Yields 5 half pints. (If a jar does not seal, store in refrigerator and use first.)

Recently our youngest son, Stephen (now a young father), reminded me that in his youth I had sometimes served zucchini three times a day. I disputed the statement, but now that I have shared just a few of my zucchini recipes, from soup to pickles to marmalade, I believe him!

Please remember, dear reader, that zucchini and yellow squash are interchangeable in recipes and may be mixed. Remember, too, that grated zucchini may be frozen for winter use in breads and casseroles. Just drain it well before adding it to recipes. Also, I have frozen with good success large slices of zucchini (sliced lengthwise) as a substitute for lasagna noodles. Even the baseball bat–size zucchini may be frozen with the stuffing of your preference, provided that one does not parboil the squash to death, it is not too woody to begin with, and it is securely double-wrapped for the freezer.

PART THREE

Apples

Beets

Broccoflower

Broccoli

Broccoli Rabe

Brussels Sprouts

Cabbage, Green

Cabbage, Red

Carrots

Cauliflower

Celery

Garlic

Grapes

Horseradish

Kiwi Fruit

Lima Beans

Onions

Pawpaws

Pears

Peppers

Persimmons

Plums

Popcorn

Potatoes

Pumpkins

Tomatoes, Green

Turnips

Winter Squash

Yams

Apples

Fortunate the family that has an apple tree in its backyard! Or the families, such as our own, that can pick apples at any number of orchards in the counties surrounding our city and use them in a variety of ways all autumn long. Then, at least, we won't have to bite into the distasteful commercial apple that has been waxed to lengthen shelf life after its long trip half way across country.

My husband grew up in Chautauqua County, New York, where his relatives, the Woodburys, were engaged in fruit farming. (Chautauqua County is on the western border; my husband considers himself a midwesterner.) During World War II, when older cousins and uncles went off to war, he helped younger cousins run the farm. So the Townes are very respectful of those who labor in the orchards and vineyards to bring us good, wholesome produce.

I grew up in South Dakota, where the Wealthy variety was most common. In addition to the raw apple eaten out of hand, apples may be eaten raw in salads, cooked with meats and vegetables, baked whole or in quick breads, cakes, and pies for dessert. And, of course, they may be canned and frozen as apple sauce and used as a favorite food for children and elders, as well as an accompaniment to meats such as pork. In some of the following recipes, I specify an ideal variety of apple, but of course another variety may be substituted.

Waldorf Salad

1 c. diced, unpeeled apples (McIntosh, Winesap, Rome Beauty)
1 c. diced celery
1/2 c. walnut meats
1/4 c. mayonnaise or boiled salad dressing

Mix above ingredients. A teaspoon of lemon juice may be sprinkled over the apples to prevent discoloration and to add tartness if the apple is not of a tart variety. Serve on a lettuce leaf. Serves 4.

Apple and Cabbage Slaw

2 c. shredded green cabbage
1 c. diced, unpeeled apples such as Jonathans
1/4 c. mayonnaise or boiled salad dressing
1/4 t. salt
1/8 t. celery seed

Mix above ingredients and serve on lettuce leaf or alone. A good accompaniment to pork or roast beef.

Apple in Chicken Salad

2 c. cooked chicken
1 c. diced celery
1 c. diced apple, such as Yellow Transparent, unpeeled
¹/₂ c. mayonnaise or boiled salad dressing

Mix above ingredients and serve as a main luncheon course on a lettuce leaf. Serve with hot whole wheat rolls. Serves 3–4.

Apple in Tuna Salad

1 can (6¹/₈-oz.) water-packed tuna, drained
¹/₂ c. diced celery
¹/₂ c. diced apple, unpeeled
¹/₄ c. mayonnaise or boiled salad dressing

Mix above ingredients and serve on a lettuce leaf for luncheon salad, or spread between slices of dark, whole wheat, zucchini, or date-nut bread. If served as a spread, dice the celery and apple more finely.

Japanese Apple-Vegetable Salad

1 medium apple, cored and thinly sliced
* (about 1 c.)*
¹/₂ c. sliced cucumber (sliced diagonally)
¹/₄ c. sliced carrot (sliced diagonally)

2 T. salad oil
2 T. white vinegar
onion powder, salt, and pepper to taste

Slice apple into cold salted water and let stand while slicing cucumber and carrot. Drain apple slices. Combine all ingredients and mix carefully. Serves 2.

Apple-Coconut Salad

2 large tart apples, such as Winesap
2 T. orange or lemon juice
2 T. raisins
2 T. coconut
1 T. peanuts, chopped

Chop apples and sprinkle with juice. In a bowl, combine all ingredients until they are well mixed. Use as accompaniment to ham or pork roast.

Apple Dressing for Pork

2 slices bacon
¹/₂ c. chopped celery
¹/₂ c. chopped onion
3 c. chopped apples, such as McIntosh
1 c. saltine cracker crumbs

¹/₄ c. chopped parsley
3 T. sugar
salt and pepper to taste
2 racks spareribs (about 3 lbs.)

Fry bacon until crisp. Drain and crumble. Cook celery and onion in bacon drippings until tender. Combine with bacon and remaining ingredients. Place stuffing between racks of seasoned spareribs. Bake in 350° oven for 1¹/₂ hours.

Sautéd Apple in Red Cabbage
Rome Beauty and Winesap are good here.

4 slices bacon, diced
1 medium onion, sliced
1 medium head red cabbage, shredded
2 apples, unpeeled and sliced

¹/₈ t. caraway seeds
¹/₄ t. salt
¹/₄ c. vinegar
2 T. brown sugar

Cook bacon in skillet until done. Pour off excess fat. Add onion slices and sauté until golden in color. Add shredded red cabbage and sliced apples. Stir until cabbage is crisply tender. Add remaining ingredients and stir carefully until all flavors are blended, being sure that mixture does not scorch. If there is too much liquid, cook it, uncovered, until most liquid is absorbed. A good accompaniment to roast pork.

Apple and Cheese Bread
This is especially delicious when served slightly warm.

2 c. flour
1 T. baking powder
¹/₂ t. salt
¹/₂ c. sugar
2 eggs, slightly beaten

¹/₂ c. oil
1¹/₂ c. finely chopped apples
¹/₂ c. shredded sharp Cheddar cheese
¹/₂ c. chopped nuts

Mix flour and sugar in large bowl. Combine remaining ingredients and add all at once to flour mixture. Stir only until flour is all moistened. Batter will be thick and lumpy. Spoon into greased loaf pan. Bake at 350° for 1 hour or until toothpick comes out clean. If top of loaf gets too brown, cover with foil during last 15 minutes of baking.

Apple Coffee Cake

Because this cake is so inexpensive to prepare, I have served it to many large groups, including committee meetings and a food co-op that used to distribute out of our family room. Mace, which is the outer covering of a nutmeg, gives it a distinctive flavor.

$^1/_3$ c. shortening	$^1/_2$ t. salt
$^1/_2$ c. sugar	$^1/_4$ t. mace
1 egg	2 medium apples, such as McIntosh,
$^1/_2$ c. milk	peeled and sliced
1$^1/_2$ c. sifted flour	2 T. sugar
1$^1/_2$ t. baking powder	$^1/_4$ t. cinnamon

Grease 8-inch square pan. Preheat oven to 400°. Cream shortening and sugar. Add unbeaten egg. Mix thoroughly. Add milk. Fold in sifted dry ingredients. Spread batter evenly in pan. Place apple slices on top of batter, pressing narrow edge into batter in straight rows, covering top. Sprinkle with 2 T. sugar mixed with cinnamon. Bake in preheated oven for 20–25 minutes. Serves 6 to 9.

Fresh Apple Fritters

These fritters are best when served warm.

1 c. flour
2 T. sugar
1 t. baking powder
dash salt
2 eggs, slightly beaten
$^2/_3$ c. milk
1 t. cooking oil
4–6 tart cooking apples, pared, cored and sliced crosswise
   (Winesap are good here)
fat for frying
granulated sugar

Stir together flour, the 2 T. sugar, baking powder, and salt. Combine eggs, milk, and 1 t. cooking oil. Add to dry mixture and beat until smooth.

Dip apple slices, one at a time, in batter to coat well. Fry in shallow hot fat (375°) about 2$^1/_2$ to 3 minutes or until brown and crisp on edges, turning once. Drain on paper toweling or surplus brown paper bags, torn open. Sprinkle with granulated sugar. Makes 18–24 fritters.

Apple Bundt Cake

This cake needs no frosting, but it may be glazed with a bit of warmed apple jelly or dusted with confectioners' sugar.

2 c. sugar

³/₄ c. oil

3 eggs

1 t. vanilla

2 c. flour

2 t. baking powder

1 t. soda

1 t. cinnamon

5 thinly sliced pared apples

1 c. chopped nuts

Grease and flour bundt pan. Cream together sugar, oil, eggs, and vanilla. Add flour, baking powder, soda, and cinnamon. Blend well and fold in apples and nuts. Bake 1 hour at 375°.

Dutch Apple Tart

1 unbaked 9-inch pastry shell

7 medium tart cooking apples (such as Winesap)

1 c. sugar

2 T. flour

¹/₂ t. cinnamon

¹/₄ c. cream

2 T. butter

Pare, halve, and core apples. Slice 4 halves into prepared pastry shell, making an even layer.

Mix sugar, flour, and cinnamon. Sprinkle half over sliced apples. Arrange remaining apple halves, cut side down, in single layer on top of sliced apples. Sprinkle with remaining sugar mixture. Pour cream in slowly, near center. Dot with butter.

Bake in 400° oven for 1 hour or until apples are tender but still hold their shape. The syrupy juices will thicken as the pie cools.

English Apple Pie

So called because it looks like a cake and lacks a crust.

2 eggs

¹/₂ t. salt

1 t. vanilla

1 c. sugar

1 c. flour

2 t. baking powder

2 c. chopped raw apples

¹/₂ c. finely chopped walnuts

Beat eggs. Add salt, vanilla, and sugar. Sift together dry ingredients and add to wet ingredients. Fold in apples and walnuts. Bake in greased 10-inch glass pie plate at 325° for 30–35 minutes. Cut into wedges and serve with vanilla ice cream.

Easy Applesauce

6 medium cooking apples, such as Yellow Transparent
$^1/_2$ c. water
$^1/_3$ c. sugar
$^1/_4$ t. cinnamon
dash nutmeg

Wash, quarter, pare, and core apples. Place in stainless steel or enameled saucepan. Add water and simmer, covered, over low heat until tender, 15 to 20 minutes. Mash with potato masher or press through sieve.

Stir in sugar, cinnamon, and nutmeg. Serve hot or cold. Or store in sealed container in the refrigerator.

To freeze, fill plastic containers, leaving $^1/_2$ inch head space to allow for expansion. Seal tightly and freeze immediately. After thawing for serving, add more spices, if desired.

Variation: For a change of flavor, mix a little peppermint extract or a few cinnamon candies into applesauce before serving.

Applesauce Cake

1 $^3/_4$ c. sifted flour	1 t. baking soda
1$^1/_2$ t. ground cinnamon	$^1/_2$ c. shortening
1 t. ground allspice	1 c. sugar
1 t. ground nutmeg	1 egg, well beaten
$^1/_4$ t. ground cloves	1 c. unsweetened applesauce
$^1/_2$ t. salt	

Sift together flour, spices, salt, and baking soda. Cream shortening. Add sugar gradually and continue beating until light and fluffy. Add egg. Beat well. Stir in applesauce. Add sifted dry ingredients. Stir only enough to blend. Pour into greased and floured loaf pan. Bake at 350° for 50–60 minutes or until cake springs back when lightly touched with fingertip. Cool in pan 5 minutes. Remove and cool on rack.

Moist Oatmeal-Applesauce Cookies

1 $^3/_4$ c. flour	1 t. cinnamon
$^1/_2$ t. baking powder	$^1/_2$ t. cloves
1 t. soda	$^1/_2$ t. nutmeg
$^1/_2$ t. salt	1 c. applesauce
$^3/_4$ c. shortening	$^1/_2$ c. raisins
1 c. sugar	1 c. oatmeal
1 egg	

Sift flour, baking powder, soda, and spices together. Cream shortening, add sugar, and cream together well. Add egg and beat. Add sifted dry ingredients alternately with applesauce. Mix well, add raisins and oatmeal. Combine thoroughly. Drop by teaspoons on a greased baking sheet. Bake at 350° for 10 minutes.

Apples with Butterscotch Sauce for Dipping

This is a popular item on buffet tables. Children especially enjoy dipping fruit in the sauce. You may give each child his/her own custard cup of dipping sauce. The sauce is also very good on vanilla ice cream, topped with dry roasted peanuts.

4 red apples, quartered, cored, and cut into wedge-shaped slices

2 T. lemon juice

$^1/_3$ c. white corn syrup

$^5/_8$ c. brown sugar, packed ($^1/_2$ c. + 2 T.)

2 T. butter

a few grains salt

$^1/_3$ c. evaporated milk

Prepare apples and store in plastic bag with lemon juice sprinkled over apples to prevent discoloration. (Move or shake apple slices within tightly closed bag so all slices come in contact with lemon juice.)

For butterscotch sauce, combine the syrup, brown sugar, butter, and salt in a saucepan. Bring to boil and boil to consistency of a heavy syrup, stirring constantly. Cool. When cooled, add evaporated milk and continue beating until thick. Makes $^3/_4$ c. sauce. Reheat it in microwave oven or in top of double boiler. May be served warm or cold.

When serving, place dipping bowl in center of large platter and arrange apple slices around it.

Apple Butter (Oven Method)

This is a strong-flavored apple butter from the Mennonite tradition.

7 lbs. apples to make 16 c. sauce (1 gallon)

3 lbs. brown sugar

1 c. cider vinegar or apple cider

2 T. ground cinnamon

Cook pared and cored apples until soft and press through sieve or colander. Add remaining ingredients and put in oven in a large roasting pan. Bake covered for 3 hours at 350°, stirring occasionally. (If consistency is too "runny" for your taste, remove cover for a few minutes and allow steam to evaporate in oven.) Pour or ladle into hot sterilized pint jars. Cover with lids and rings. Process in hot water bath for 10 minutes after water has come to a boil. Remove from water bath and place on wooden rack to cool.

Tangy Apple Chutney
This chutney is good served with roast beef or lamb.

16 medium tart apples, chopped	1 qt. vinegar
1 c. onions, chopped	2 hot red pepper pods
1 clove garlic, crushed	3 T. mustard seed
1 c. red bell peppers, chopped	2 T. ground ginger
2 lbs. raisins	2 t. salt
4 c. brown sugar	2 t. ground allspice

Prepare apples by paring and chopping. (Should measure 2 quarts.) Combine all ingredients and simmer until thick, about 1¼ hours. As mixture thickens, stir frequently. Fill pint canning jars with hot chutney, leaving ¼ inch head space. Adjust lids and bands. Process in boiling hot water bath canner for 10 minutes. Yields 10 pints.

Freezing Apples for Pies

Slice pared apples into cold salted water (½ t. salt per quart of water). Drain, place in freezer containers, and freeze. Salt water prevents apples from darkening. When ready to use for pie or other purposes, simply thaw, drain, and use.

Canning Apples for Pies

Slice approximately 10 c. peeled apples, such as Winesap, into 5 quart jars. Cover with following sauce:

4½ c. sugar
1 c. cornstarch
2 t. cinnamon
1 t. nutmeg
10 c. water

Mix together and cook until thick. Remove from heat and add 3 T. lemon juice. Seal and process in hot water bath canner for 20 minutes, counting from time water returns to a boil.

Note: Don't forget old-fashioned fried apples, apples baked in a Crock-Pot, or new-fangled apples baked in a microwave-safe casserole in the microwave oven.

Beets

Having already discussed using beet greens in salad, soup, or as a cooked vegetable, we shall now turn to using the beet proper, also called beet root.

Beets should be planted next to bush beans, any members of the cabbage family, lettuce, and onions. Beets are best harvested when they are about 2 inches in diameter. Pull larger ones gradually during the summer to allow room for others to expand. If allowed to get too large, they could crack or become woody. Do not be alarmed if beet roots pop up above the soil line. This is natural and will not harm the beet. They should be stored cold and very moist, at 32–40° and 90–95% humidity.

To minimize loss of dark red color, do not peel beets before cooking. Wash thoroughly and leave 1 inch of the stem and the entire tap root on. Start them cooking in cold water. Allow $1/2$ to 1 hour for cooking small, young beets, and 1 to 2 hours for cooking large, older beets. When they are tender, drain any remaining water and plunge directly into cold water. When they are cool enough to handle, slip off the skins and trim the tops and bottoms. Quarter, slice, or dice larger beets. Leave small beets whole.

Beets may be baked in their skins, as potatoes are, in a 325° oven. Place on a pan and bake until done, half an hour for young beets and an hour for older beets. Slide off the skins and season with butter and salt, if desired. Or they may be roasted in hot coals by wrapping them in aluminum foil first. They may also be microwaved in a covered casserole or steamer with a small amount of water, as one would potatoes.

Shredded Raw Beet and Lettuce Salad
This is good with fish.

$1/4$ c. vinegar

$1/3$ c. oil

1 t. sugar

salt and freshly ground black pepper

2 c. coarsely shredded raw beets

6 c. shredded firm greens (romaine or iceberg lettuce, Napa cabbage, etc.)

1 T. finely chopped chives

Combine first 3 ingredients and mix well. Season with salt and pepper. Put beets in salad bowl, add dressing, and mix well. Marinate at least $1/2$ hour. Just before serving, add greens, toss, and sprinkle with chives. Serves 6.

Molded Beet Salad

1 3-oz. package lemon-flavored gelatin
$1^1/_2$ t. vinegar
$^1/_2$ c. boiling water
$^1/_4$ c. chopped celery
beet juice plus enough cold water to
make 1 c.
$^1/_4$ c. chopped green pepper
$^1/_4$ medium onion, minced
$^1/_2$ c. sour cream and/or yogurt
$1^1/_2$ t. salt
2 c. diced cooked beets

Dissolve gelatin in boiling water. Add beet juice and cold water. Chill until slightly thickened. Combine remaining ingredients and blend into jellied mixture. Turn into 1-qt. ring mold. Chill until firm. To serve, unmold on bed of greens. Place bowl of sour cream or yogurt in center of ring to serve as a dressing.

Calico Potato Salad

If you planted radish seeds in late summer, you'll have fresh radishes in autumn for this salad.

5 medium potatoes, cooked and sliced (about 5 c.)
2 c. cooked cut green beans, drained
1 c. cooked whole tiny beets, drained (or diced beets)
$^1/_2$ c. sliced celery
$^1/_2$ c. sliced green onions
$^1/_2$ c. sliced fall radishes
1 t. salt
$^1/_2$ t. black pepper
1 c. chilled Horseradish Dressing (recipe follows)

Chill vegetables thoroughly. Combine and season with salt and pepper. Just before serving, toss vegetable mixture with dressing.

Horseradish Dressing

$^1/_2$ c. mayonnaise
$^1/_4$ c. sour cream and/or yogurt
3 T. prepared horseradish
1 c. vinaigrette dressing

Combine all ingredients and stir until smooth. Chill. Makes $1^3/_4$ c.

Russian Pink Potato Salad

3 lbs. potatoes
1 onion
pinch oregano
2 qts. canned beets or equivalent of microwaved or boiled beets, peeled
1 c. frozen peas, thawed
5 dill pickles, chopped
salt, pepper, and minced garlic to taste
3/4 c. mayonnaise or less

Peel potatoes and cut in chunks. Cook with onion (quartered) and pinch of oregano until soft. Drain. Discard the onion.

Dice potatoes. Drain beets and dice. Add to potatoes and stir. Add peas and chopped pickles.

Season with salt, pepper, and minced garlic. Add mayonnaise to taste, starting with just enough to bind other ingredients. Do not overwhelm other ingredients with mayonnaise.

Chill. Best if allowed to chill several hours or overnight so flavors can meld. (From Natalie Ashanin, who learned it from her Russian mother.)

Festive Mashed Potatoes with Beets

Use 1/3 c. cooked beets for every cup of cooked potatoes. Leftover beets, already cooked and seasoned, can be used to good advantage, if the original seasoning wasn't too sweet.

Mash the vegetables or purée them in a blender. For every cup of potato-beet purée, work in 1 egg and 1 T. cream. Salt lightly, if necessary, and flavor with dill, parsley, horseradish, or whatever will complement the main dish.

Mound in a ring around a heatproof serving platter whose middle will support a beef roast, leg of lamb, or ham. Reheat and brown the pink potatoes in the upper third of a 400° oven. Place entrée in the center and serve.

No-Salt Flavorings for Beets

If you are on a no-salt diet and have been told to substitute herbs and spices to season food, the nutritionists recommend allspice, bay leaf, caraway seeds, cloves, dill, ginger, or thyme on beets.

Harvard Beets (Sweet-Sour)

$^1/_2$ c. sugar
1 T. cornstarch
$^1/_2$ t. salt
2 whole cloves
$^1/_2$ c. cider vinegar
3 c. sliced or diced cooked beets

Combine sugar, cornstarch, salt, whole cloves, and vinegar in top of double boiler and cook until clear. Add beets. Place over hot water and warm for approximately $^1/_2$ hour, stirring occasionally. Butter may be added before serving.

Chinese Beets

6 c. cooked, sliced beets	24 cloves
$1^1/_2$ c. reserved liquid from beet cooking	3 T. catsup
1 c. sugar	3 T. oil (optional)
1 c. vinegar	1 t. vanilla
2 T. cornstarch	dash salt

Mix all ingredients in a saucepan, including the beets. Cook for 3 minutes over medium heat or until mixture thickens. Let cool. Store in refrigerator.

Beet Relish

1 qt. chopped cooked beets	1 T. prepared horseradish
1 qt. chopped cabbage (1 head)	$1^1/_2$ c. granulated sugar
1 c. chopped onions	3 c. cider vinegar
1 T. salt	1 c. chopped red bell peppers

Combine all ingredients in a 6-qt. stainless steel or enameled kettle. Simmer for 10 minutes and bring to boil. Pack boiling hot relish into hot sterilized canning jars, leaving a $^1/_4$ inch head space. Adjust lids and bands. Process in hot water bath canner, whether pints or half pints, for 15 minutes after water comes to a boil.

Pickled Beets

1 part water and/or beet juice from cooking beets
1 part cider vinegar
1 part sugar

Cook together to make the brine and add whole cloves or allspice as desired. Pour over sliced, diced, quartered, or whole cooked beets in jars or refrigerator dish. If canning beets, process for 15 minutes in hot water bath, counting time after water has come to a boil to ensure sealing.

If you are storing in refrigerator for a few weeks, sliced onions and hard boiled peeled eggs may be added to the brine. The onions and eggs will be beautifully colored, making a good salad for Easter. Salad may be served from the bowl or individually on a lettuce leaf.

The brine may be reheated and poured over more cooked beets when all the pickled beets have been eaten. Obviously, you can make pickled beets any time of year using canned beets. (From my late aunt, Katherine Kleinsasser Hofer, who shared much garden produce, hospitality, and expertise with our family after my mother died.)

Crunchy Beet Dip

1 pt. jar (2 c.) pickled beets (recipe above)
8 oz. cream cheese
6 T. chopped cucumber
1/4 c. chopped green pepper
1/4 c. chopped celery

1/4 c. chopped onion
1/8 t. salt
1/8 t. summer savory
1/8 t. thyme
chopped fresh parsley

Blend beets with cream cheese in processor until smooth. Stir in remaining ingredients. Chill well. Garnish with chopped fresh parsley. Serve with assorted crackers and raw vegetables. Makes 3 1/2 c.

Beet Spice Cake

1/2 c. butter
1 c. sugar
2 eggs
2 c. (1 pt.) pickled beets, drained
2 1/4 c. sifted flour
1 1/2 t. allspice

1 t. cinnamon
1/4 t. cloves
4 t. baking powder
1 t. soda
1 c. coarsely chopped walnuts
confectioners' sugar

Beat butter with sugar until light and fluffy. Add eggs and beat well. Purée beets in blender or processor until smooth. Add sifted dry ingredients alternately with puréed beets to sugar mixture, mixing well after each addition. Fold in walnuts. Turn batter into greased, lightly floured 9-c. bundt pan. Bake at 350° for 55 minutes or until cake tests done. Cool on rack for 30 minutes before removing from pan. Sift confectioners' sugar over top of baked cake.

Broccoflower

In 1990 a light green cauliflower appeared on the produce shelves in Indianapolis. It had first occurred as a cross between broccoli and cauliflower twelve years before in the Castroville, California, area, where Italian-Americans named it *broccoline*.

Broccoflower may be used as you would either cauliflower or broccoli. It is especially attractive on a vegetable tray. Preliminary tests at California Polytechnic State University report that it has even higher vitamin C content than broccoli or cauliflower. It also is easier to grow than cauliflower and can be refrigerated for a month without developing black spots.

Romanesque Broccoflower

1 head broccoflower
1/3 c. olive oil
2 cloves garlic, minced
salt and pepper to taste

Remove outer leaves and separate head into florets. Steam 2 to 3 minutes and set aside. Heat olive oil in pan. Add garlic and sauté until slightly golden in color. Reduce heat, add steamed florets, and turn gently to coat with oil. Cover and let simmer for 5 to 10 minutes, turning occasionally. Serve immediately.

Broccoflower-Pasta Salad

1 lb. pasta shells or rotini
1 c. broccoflorets
1 c. sliced zucchini or yellow summer
  squash
1/2 c. sliced celery
1 medium green bell pepper, chopped

1 medium red bell pepper, chopped
1/2 c. red onion, chopped
2 c. drained red or kidney beans
Parmesan cheese (optional)
bottled Italian dressing

Prepare pasta according to package directions, cooking it *al dente*. Drain well. Place broccoflorets in saucepan with 2 inches water and steam for 2 minutes, until crisply tender. Drain and rinse under cold running water. Combine florets and all other vegetables in large bowl. Add cooked pasta and beans to vegetables. Pour dressing over all. Mix gently and refrigerate several hours to meld flavors. Sprinkle Parmesan cheese on top and serve. Pass additional cheese and dressing, if desired. Serve with crusty French bread.

Variation: Other vegetables in season may be substituted. Adding diced tuna, ham, or leftover chicken creates a hearty main dish salad.

Marinated Italian Vegetables

3 c. each *florets of broccoflower, cauliflower, and broccoli*
3 *cloves garlic, minced*
$^1/_2$ c. *corn oil*
$^1/_2$ c. *cider vinegar*
$^1/_2$ c. *water*
1 t. *salt*
1 t. *dried oregano, basil, or Italian seasoning*
$^1/_2$ t. *freshly ground black pepper*
1 c. *drained pitted ripe olives (optional)*

In large skillet combine all ingredients but olives. Bring to boil. Reduce heat, cover, and simmer for 5 minutes or until vegetables are crisply tender. Cool. Add olives. Chill overnight. Makes about 9 cups. Serves 12–16.

Variation: Other vegetables such as pepper strips, carrot and celery sticks, onions, green beans, etc., may be substituted for some of the 9 cups of florets.

Broccoflower Tray

Around a large round platter, arrange alternately florets of broccoli, cauliflower, and broccoflower. Divide sections with strips of red bell pepper. Place bowl of dip made of 1 c. sour cream and 1 t. dillweed in center of tray.

Broccoli

Broccoli should be harvested or purchased when it is dark green. If any yellow is present, the broccoli is aging and beyond optimal freshness.

Broccoli florets may be served raw in tossed salads or on a fresh vegetable platter. If cooked, broccoli should be steamed just until crisply tender to preserve good color and flavor. Research by the U.S. Department of Agriculture recommends two methods of cooking that keep 65 to 80% of the vitamin C as well as good color, texture, and flavor: (1) add broccoli to boiling water and cook, uncovered, for 10–12 minutes; or (2) place broccoli in colander over boiling water, cover, and steam for 10 minutes. Broccoli may also be microwaved for a few minutes in a covered casserole or steamer with a small amount of water in the bottom.

Simple flavorings include a sprinkling of Parmesan cheese over buttered broccoli, sour cream sauce, or Cheddar cheese sauce. If any plain cooked broccoli remains, pour vinaigrette dressing over it and use later as a salad to be served on a lettuce leaf or on a cold vegetable plate.

Hot Broccoli Dip

Recently we have been seeing a lot of hot spinach dip served from hollowed-out rounds of rye bread. Here is a recipe for a similar dip made from broccoli.

1 lb. round rye bread loaf (unsliced)
$^1/_2$ c. finely chopped celery
$^1/_2$ c. finely chopped onion
2 T. butter
1 lb. cubed processed cheese, such as Velveeta
2 c. cooked, drained chopped broccoli
$^1/_4$ t. dried rosemary leaves, crushed

Cut slice from top of bread loaf. Remove center, leaving 1-inch shell. Cut removed bread into bite-size pieces. Sauté celery and onions in butter until tender. Add cheese. Stir over low heat until cheese is melted. Stir in remaining ingredients. Heat thoroughly, stirring constantly. Spoon sauce into bread loaf. Serve with vegetable dippers and the bite-size pieces of bread, which may be toasted in low-temperature oven or under broiler.

Cream of Broccoli Soup

1 c. minced onion
$^1/_2$ c. thinly sliced celery
$^1/_2$ c. sliced leek or green onion tops
1 clove garlic, minced
2 T. butter
$1^1/_2$ lbs. broccoli

6 c. chicken stock
2 c. light cream or evaporated milk
salt and pepper to taste
parsley, minced
croutons

In a large saucepan sauté onion, celery, leek or onion tops, and garlic in butter until vegetables are tender. Rinse and trim broccoli. Cut heads from stalks. Cut stalks into 1-inch slices and separate heads into florets.

Add to the pan the stalks and chicken stock. Bring liquid to a boil over moderate heat. Simmer mixture for 15 minutes. Add florets and simmer mixture for 15 minutes more. Purée broccoli in blender and combine with broth, stir in light cream, and bring soup just to simmer. Add salt and pepper. Ladle soup into heated bowls, garnish with minced parsley, and serve with croutons. Serves 6.

Broccoli Salad

1½ to 2 lbs. broccoli
6 hard-cooked eggs, coarsely chopped
¼ c. chopped onions
½ c. mayonnaise

Steam, cool, and chop broccoli. Mix all ingredients and chill for 12 hours before serving. If served for a buffet supper, place serving dish in crushed ice. Serves 8–12.

Broccoli with Butter-Mustard Sauce and Cheese

½ c. crushed seasoned croutons (or dried bread crumbs with herbs added)
½ c. shredded Cheddar cheese
¼ c. (½ stick) butter
¼ c. flour
½ t. salt
2 c. milk
2 T. prepared mustard
1½ to 2 lbs. broccoli, steamed

Combine crushed croutons or crumbs with cheese for topper. Set aside. Melt butter in small saucepan. Blend in flour and salt until smooth. Remove from heat. Stir in milk. Heat to boiling, stirring constantly. Boil and stir 1 minute. Stir in mustard. Spoon over hot, cooked broccoli and sprinkle with cheese topper. Serves 6.

Broccoli with Ginger and Garlic

1½ lbs. fresh broccoli
2 T. oil
2 T. thin slivers of peeled fresh ginger root
1 clove garlic, sliced thin
2 T. water
1½ T. soy sauce

Trim broccoli, cutting into florets and ¼-inch slices of peeled stems. In heavy skillet heat oil and cook ginger root and garlic until golden. Transfer cooked ginger root and garlic to paper towel to drain.

Add broccoli to skillet and cook, stirring often, until browned, about 5 minutes. In small bowl combine water and soy sauce. Add to skillet and cook until liquid is evaporated, about 1 minute. Serve broccoli sprinkled with ginger root and garlic, if desired. Serves 4.

Chinese Broccoli

1¹/₂ lbs. fresh broccoli
2 T. oil
1 c. chicken stock
salt, pepper, nutmeg
1 T. cornstarch mixed with small amount of water

Trim tough stalk from broccoli. Cut into small stalks. Slice crosswise about ¹/₄-inch thick to tops. Heat oil in large frying pan or wok. Add broccoli and stir-fry over high heat about 1 minute. Add chicken stock and season with salt, pepper, and nutmeg. Cover and allow to steam for 3 to 4 minutes. When just crisply tender, thicken sauce with cornstarch-water mixture. Serve at once over rice. Serves 4 to 6.

Broccoli-Tuna Luncheon Casserole

1¹/₂ lbs. broccoli
2 cans (7-oz.) water-packed tuna, drained
1 can (10 ¹/₂ oz.) condensed cream of mushroom soup
¹/₄ soup can of milk
¹/₂ c. sour cream
1 t. instant minced onion
generous pinch marjoram
2 T. butter, melted, mixed with ¹/₂ c. bread crumbs

Trim tough stalks from broccoli. Cut into small stalks and cook uncovered in boiling water 10 to 12 minutes. Drain. Place tuna in bottom of 2-qt. casserole. Combine mushroom soup, milk, sour cream, onion, and marjoram for sauce. Spoon half of sauce over tuna. Top with broccoli and add remaining sauce. Sprinkle buttered crumbs over top. Bake uncovered in 350° oven until hot and bubbly—about 20 minutes. Serves 6.

Broccoli and Rice Puff

¹/₂ c. chopped onions
2 T. butter
1 can (10 ¹/₂ oz.) cream of mushroom soup
2 c. cooked rice

1 lb. broccoli, steamed
1 t. Worcestershire sauce
¹/₄ t. thyme
2 c. grated Cheddar cheese
4 eggs, separated

Sauté onions in butter until tender. Stir in canned soup, cooked rice, broccoli, Worcestershire sauce, and thyme. Put in shallow 2-qt. baking dish. Bake in 400° oven for 20 minutes.

Meanwhile, beat egg whites until soft peaks form. Beat egg yolks until thick and lemon colored. Stir in cheese. Fold whites into egg yolk mixture.

Take casserole from oven and stir. Spread egg-cheese mixture over top. Return to oven and bake 15 minutes longer or until golden brown. Serves 4.

Broccoli and Ham Casserole

1 lb. cooked ham, finely chopped (about 3 c.)
1¹/₂ lbs. broccoli, chopped (about 4 c.)
¹/₂ c. chopped onion
3 c. shredded Cheddar cheese, divided
6 slices bread, crusts removed
6 eggs
¹/₂ t. dry mustard
1 t. Worcestershire sauce
3 c. milk

Mix together ham, broccoli, onion, and 2 c. cheese. Place trimmed bread on the bottom of a buttered 3-qt. baking dish. Spoon broccoli-ham mixture over bread. Beat eggs with dry mustard, Worcestershire, and milk. Pour over broccoli mixture. Sprinkle top with remaining cheese. Let stand 10 minutes.

Place baking dish in a larger pan of hot water. Bake in a 375° oven 50 minutes or until a knife inserted in the center comes out clean. Let stand 5 minutes before serving. Serves 6 to 8.

Refrigerator-Pickled Broccoli

²/₃ c. cider vinegar
¹/₃ c. olive oil
¹/₄ c. Dijon mustard
2 T. honey
¹/₂ t. curry powder
salt to taste
4 c. broccoli florets
¹/₂ green pepper, cut into ¹/₄-inch wide strips 1 inch long

Whisk together vinegar, oil, mustard, honey, and curry. Add salt and set aside.

Blanch broccoli in boiling water for 2 to 3 minutes. Drain and transfer to a glass container. Pour in marinade and place green pepper strips on top. Cover container and allow to marinate for at least 12 hours. Serves 6.

Broccoli Rabe

This variety of broccoli (also known as Italian turnip, broccoli de rape, rapa, rapini, and broccoletti) is grown for the green tops and tender flower shoots. It is excellent for salads and rich in vitamins. Seeds are available from Page Seed Co., New York (see Resources for address).

Steamed Broccoli Rabe

1 bunch broccoli rabe
$^1/_2$ c. water
1 T. soy sauce
1 large clove garlic, minced
salt, if desired

Wash broccoli rabe, discarding any hollow or coarse stems. Bring water, soy sauce, and garlic to a boil in a large skillet. Add broccoli rabe and steam, covered, over medium high heat for approximately 2 minutes. Uncover and cook until water has evaporated and broccoli rabe is tender. Season with salt if needed. Serves 4.

Spaghetti with Broccoli Rabe
Wear gloves while chopping the peppers!

$1^1/_2$ lbs. broccoli rabe
4 or 5 cloves garlic, minced
4 green onions with tops, chopped
2 small hot red or green peppers, seeded
   and minced

$^1/_3$ c. olive oil
$^3/_4$ lb. spaghettini or linguine
2 t. salt or to taste
$^1/_2$ t. black pepper
$^3/_4$ c. grated Parmesan cheese

Wash broccoli rabe, discarding stem bottoms and yellowed leaves. Cut florets from stems and cut stems into 2-inch lengths. Set aside. Chop any large leaves.

In an extra-large skillet or pan heat oil and gently sauté garlic, onions, and peppers 3 to 4 minutes. Add 4 c. hot water and bring to boil. Break pasta in 2-inch lengths and add to water with seasonings. Boil pasta about 5 minutes, stirring frequently. Add broccoli rabe and 1 more cup hot water or as needed. Boil over high heat, stirring frequently as pasta absorbs water. Add more water as needed to keep pasta from sticking. Boil until pasta is tender but firm (al dente) and broccoli rabe is tender but crisp, 8 to 10 minutes. Serve in large bowl accompanied by grated cheese. Serves 4.

Variation: Slender stalks of broccoli may be substituted.

Broccoli Rabe with Pork Chops

1 lb. broccoli rabe

2 T. olive oil

2 large center-cut pork chops

2 cloves garlic

2 sprigs rosemary

$^{1}/_{2}$ c. dry white wine

1 c. tomato juice

salt and pepper to taste

pork chops

Pull the broccoli rabe while the roots ("turnips") are slightly larger than marbles and the green tops are young and tender. Cut broccoli rabe tops from the turnips, wash, and cut up. Wash the turnips and cut up without peeling. Layer in a kettle some broccoli rabe, salt, another layer of greens, etc., until all greens are salted and in. (Turnips themselves should be mixed in with the greens.) Cover and cook slowly for 20 minutes or until greens are wilted. Drain. Should equal a pint of cooked greens.

Heat oil in large cast-iron skillet and lay chops in it. On each chop place 1 clove of garlic halved lengthwise and run through with toothpick, and the sprig of rosemary. Brown on one side. Remove rosemary and garlic, turn chops, and return herb and garlic. Brown chops on second side. Add wine, cook 10 minutes, then add tomato juice, salt, and pepper.

Cover and cook 45 minutes or until chops are tender. Put drained broccoli rabe in sauce around the chops, spoon more sauce over them, and cook covered for 10 minutes more. Serve at once, after discarding the garlic cloves. Serves 2.

Brussels Sprouts

They look like little cabbages, and that should help us harvest them or buy them from an organic grower when they are still small. Sprouts should have small, tight leaves with a good green color. Also, they should have no strong odor, which is a definite warning of old age.

The name dates back to the 12th century when they were sold in markets on Belgian streets. From there the name spread to northern Europe and in the 19th century it came to the U.S.

Sprouts ripen on the stalk from the bottom up, and when they are harvested by hand they are picked that way. When they are picked by machine, the harvester cuts the entire plant at ground level and feeds it into a machine which strips them from the stalk.

If you find the odor of cooking sprouts objectionable, you may minimize it by dropping a whole walnut into the boiling water.

To prepare sprouts, wash them thoroughly. Slice off the end and cut an X into the stem so it will cook more quickly. Be careful not to cut off too much of the stem because it is the stem which holds the leaves together while cooking.

The simplest way to cook sprouts is to boil them for 10 minutes in an uncovered pan or to microwave them for a few minutes in a covered casserole or steamer with water covering the bottom of the pan. Then drain and add salt, pepper, and butter.

Special Brussels Sprouts

¹/₂ c. real mayonnaise
2 T. grated Parmesan cheese
1 T. prepared mustard
¹/₄ t. salt
dash pepper
1 lb. Brussels sprouts

In a small bowl stir together first five ingredients. Set aside. Cook sprouts for 10 minutes and drain well. Pour sauce over hot sprouts. Serve immediately. Serves 6.

Peppery Sprouts

12 oz. small sprouts, trimmed
¹/₂ c. chopped onion
2 T. olive oil
¹/₄ t. salt
coarsely cracked peppercorns to taste
pinch of cayenne
1 c. sliced mushrooms

Boil sprouts for 10 minutes in lightly salted water until almost tender. Drain and allow to cool. In a skillet cook onion in olive oil for 3 minutes and stir in seasonings. Add mushrooms and cook mixture until mushrooms and onions are lightly browned. Add sprouts and cook, covered, over low heat, for a few minutes more until sprouts are tender. Serves 4.

Brussels Sprouts with Caraway Seeds

1 qt. sprouts
chicken stock
3 T. butter
³/₄ t. salt
¹/₈ t. ground black pepper
2 t. caraway seeds

Wash sprouts, trim off tough outer leaves, and cut small cross in bottom (stem) end. Pour stock to one-inch depth in saucepan. Bring to boil and add sprouts. Return to boil and simmer for 3 minutes, uncovered. Cover and cook for 7 to 10 minutes longer, or until tender, depending on size. Drain. Add remaining ingredients, toss, and serve. Serves 6.

Freezing Brussels Sprouts

Soak sprouts for 30 minutes in salted water (4 t. salt to 1 gallon water) to draw out insects. Rinse and blanch in boiling water for 3 to 5 minutes, depending upon size. Cool, drain thoroughly and pack in plastic containers.

Other Flavorings for Brussels Sprouts

1. Top with tomato sauce and grated American cheese. Bake for 15 minutes at 350°.
2. Combine sprouts with onions, peas, beans, and celery. Add white sauce flavored with nutmeg.
3. Add crisp, crumbled bacon bits or chopped toasted almonds.
4. Pour raspberry sauce over sprouts sautéd in olive oil.

Cabbage, Green

All members of the cabbage family (broccoli, Brussels sprouts, green head cabbage, cauliflower, kale, and kohlrabi) thrive when planted next to bush beans, beets, chard, cucumbers, lettuce, onions, potatoes or spinach. Herbs such as rosemary and sage deter cabbage moths, and dill improves its vigor and growth. Mint and nasturtiums deter moths, ants, beetles and aphids in cabbage. Do not plant cabbage next to pole beans or strawberries if you want any of them to thrive.

Cabbage family members are all cruciferous, and crucifers have been found to be active anti-cancer agents, so they should be included in the diet on a regular basis. The American Institute for Cancer reports that enzymes produced by crucifers are responsible for breaking down cancer-producing chemicals. In addition, members of the cabbage family are good sources of dietary fiber and vitamins A and C.

There are many kinds of cabbage itself, such as Napa cabbage, an elongated, pale green head resembling cabbage and popularized by Chinese workers and restaurateurs in northern California. Bok choy, also called Chinese white cabbage, had a similar introduction to traditional U.S. menus. However, its ribs are wider and whiter than Napa, and it has loose, dark green leaves. All of these cabbages are interchangeable in most recipes calling for green cabbage.

However, in this section we shall be focusing on what is usually thought of when cabbage is mentioned—the round, light green head. Green cabbage should be harvested as needed, once heads have formed. If left too long in the garden, the heads may burst, especially if you have a heavy rain. (Water content in cabbage is very high.) If a head splits, harvest it immediately and use, or refrigerate it in a perforated plastic bag. Left in the garden, it will attract pests. Cut away any damaged or dirty spots and use the remainder.

As mentioned earlier, cabbage is an excellent source of vitamin C. But it is also an inexpensive source, when compared to citrus fruits. However, in order to preserve the vitamins, it is important to keep the cabbage wrapped in plastic before cooking. Cabbage should be stored at the same temperature and humidity as apples and potatoes (32–40° and 80–90% humidity).

There are many excellent recipes for cabbage slaw, one of which, Cabbage Salad with Raw Apples, we have already discussed. Slaw dressings are of two basic varieties: the boiled (mayonnaise) type and the sweet-sour oil and vinegar type. Slaw may be prepared in large amounts, since refrigerating and marinating it improve its flavor. For good sources of slaw cutters, see Resources section.

Processor Slaw

1 small head cabbage, quartered and cored
$^1/_2$ green pepper, seeds and membrane removed
$^1/_2$ medium sweet onion
1 carrot, sliced on bias in chunks

Chop coarsely in processor. Toss with mayonnaise-type salad dressing to which celery seed has been added, if desired.

Old-Time Favorite Slaw

4 c. finely shredded cabbage
$^1/_4$ c. chopped sweet onion
$^1/_4$ c. chopped green or red pepper
1 t. salt
$^1/_4$ t. pepper
$^1/_2$ t. dry mustard
$^1/_2$ t. celery seed
2 T. sugar
3 T. oil
$^1/_3$ c. cider vinegar

Mix vegetables together in a large bowl. Blend remaining ingredients in a blender and pour over vegetables. Toss, cover, and refrigerate overnight, if possible.

Many of us grew up with stuffed cabbage rolls or Pigs in Blankets because the dish was so tasty and so inexpensive. However, the modern cook has less time and consequently searches for substitutes which taste as good but take less time. A good example is the following:

Stuffed Cabbage Casserole

1 medium cabbage, cut up
1 lb. ground lean beef
1 onion, chopped
¹/₂ c. uncooked rice
salt and pepper to taste
1 can (10 ¹/₂ oz.) cream of tomato soup
1 soup can water

Place cabbage in greased baking dish. Brown beef and onion. Stir in rice and place mixture on the cabbage. Season with salt and pepper. Combine soup and water and pour over all. Cover with foil and bake at 350° for 1 hour.

Fried Cabbage

The following recipe is from my husband's experience as Director of the Mountaineer Mining Mission, Fairmont, West Virginia, a cooperative Presbyterian Church (USA) ministry with coal miners and their families. Every fall at the annual Men's Retreat, this fried cabbage was one of the dishes prepared and served at the outdoor dinner.

6 c. finely shredded cabbage
5 T. lard or bacon drippings
¹/₂ t. salt
1¹/₂ T. sugar

¹/₄ t. dry mustard
¹/₂ t. paprika
¹/₂ c. cream
2 to 3 T. vinegar

Melt fat and add cabbage. Fry slowly for 15 minutes, stirring every few minutes. Mix other ingredients and add to cabbage. Heat to boiling point and serve.

Cabbage Pie

7 c. medium-shredded cabbage
16 saltine crackers
2 c. milk
¹/₄ c. (half stick) butter

¹/₄ t. ground black pepper
¹/₄ t. celery seed
1 t. salt

Fill a 1¹/₂-qt. casserole with alternating layers of cabbage and coarsely crushed crackers, having 3 layers of each with cabbage as bottom layer and crackers on top. Heat milk with remaining ingredients and pour over cabbage-cracker layers. Bake in 350° oven for 40 minutes or until lightly browned on top. Serves 6–8.

The best way to preserve cabbage for winter use is to make sauerkraut. As a child growing up in a Mennonite community I helped to make sauerkraut by stamping the kraut with my bare feet (after they had been well scrubbed!) in what appeared to be at the time a "humongous" crock, just as Italian vintners used to crush grapes in a vat. Modern cooks usually preserve sauerkraut in jars or transfer kraut from crocks into jars after it has "worked" sufficiently.

Sauerkraut

Daune Miller Palmer, Dunkirk, New York, in writing her family's memoirs, shared with me her father's recipe for sauerkraut:

> Needed: A clean and scoured crock. For every 5 lbs. cabbage, use 3½ T. salt.
>
> Shred cabbage, pack firmly in crock and mix salt well with cabbage. Repeat, layer by layer, until within 5 inches of top. Press firmly but do not pound.
>
> Keep cabbage covered with juice and cover with 2 or 3 layers of clean cloth, then a plate on top of the cloth, and a rock on top of the plate to keep the pressure steady. Fermentation starts right away.
>
> Give kraut daily care by removing film as it forms. When bubbling stops in about 3 weeks, pack into clean quart jars and process in boiling water for 30 minutes. Add 1½ T. brine to kraut and add water to cover before processing.
>
> Note: If you eat kraut regularly, your supply will hold in the stone jar in a cold room 55 degrees or lower. We packed the sauerkraut and stored it in the cellar refrigerator without processing. There was always enough to distribute to friends and fellow sauerkraut-lovers.
>
> One small warning if you're planning to make sauerkraut: Aromas waft from the cellar to announce that the cabbage is fermenting. The "announcement" lasts 3 weeks. IT'S WORTH IT!

Robert Woodbury, Dunkirk, New York, utilized his knowledge of winemaking (acquired from Woodbury Vineyards) when he preserved a huge crock of sauerkraut for the winter of 1987–88. Page Woodbury, his wife, served it to us in many forms when we were their house guests following the death of Grandpa (Arthur) Towne. The most memorable was Sauerkraut and Kielbasa, a dish which includes potatoes.

Sauerkraut and Kielbasa

1 lb. kielbasa (Polish pork sausage) cut in chunks

1 chopped medium onion

1 qt. sauerkraut, drained and rinsed

3 diced potatoes (peel if you wish)

2 c. water

1 bay leaf

½ t. paprika

Fry kielbasa chunks in large pot. Add onion and sauté until translucent. Add sauerkraut, potatoes, water, bay leaf, and paprika. Simmer, covered, for 30 minutes or until potatoes are tender. Add more water if needed or desired.

Hutterite Mennonite weddings during the thirties and forties invariably included Sauerkraut and Dampfleisch (stewed beef). Both were cooked in large outdoor kettles. Below is a more modest-size recipe from my cousin, Annie Hofer Brockmueller. My father records in his diary that his niece was a fine cook, an extraordinary compliment coming from my father. (She shared her board with our family on a regular basis, especially for Sunday dinners after church services.)

Hutterische Sauerkraut
This is a good accompaniment to roast beef, roast pork,
or any type of meat sausage.

1 qt. canned sauerkraut
1 c. water
¼ c. sugar
2 T. lard
2 T. flour

If the kraut is very sour, pour boiling water over it and drain well. In an enameled or stainless steel saucepan place kraut, water, and sugar. Boil until soft. Make sauce by heating shortening until very hot, adding flour, and browning it in a small cast-iron skillet. Add browned mixture to kraut, mix well and serve.

When cabbage is in season and in great supply it is important to have a way to preserve it fresh for winter use. Freezing coleslaw is a good solution.

Frozen Coleslaw

1 medium head cabbage
1 t. salt
1 grated carrot
1 green pepper
Dressing (recipe follows)

Shred cabbage into a crockery or stainless steel bowl. Sprinkle with salt. Let stand for 1 hour. Drain water, return cabbage to bowl, and add carrot and pepper.

Dressing for Frozen Coleslaw

1 c. vinegar
¼ c. water
1 c. sugar

1 t. mustard seed
1 t. celery seed

Combine and boil for 1 minute. Cool to lukewarm. Slowly pour over cabbage mixture. Put in containers and freeze.

Cabbage, Red

Because red cabbage has a coarser texture than green cabbage, it requires a longer cooking time. Be careful to use a stainless steel knife in cutting red cabbage; otherwise the cut part will turn blue due to a chemical change.

Red cabbage is a very welcome addition to the autumn table because of its festive color and the wonderful way it enhances traditional fall dishes such as roast pork and duck. Fortunately, it teams nicely with a fruit also plentiful in fall—the apple, whose acidic quality helps to maintain the red color. (For that reason, other acidic foods like lemon juice, vinegar, and wine are often teamed with red cabbage.)

The microwave oven makes red cabbage, with its greater "structural integrity," quick and easy to prepare, enabling it to be cooked at a high temperature without any loss of color and flavor.

Hot Cabbage Slaw

4 c. sliced red cabbage	3 T. water
1 large red apple, sliced thin	2 T. cider vinegar
1 T. oil	1 t. caraway seeds
2 T. chopped onion	1 t. salt
2 T. raisins	

Place cabbage and apple in microwave casserole or steamer and set aside. Microwave oil, onion, and raisins in microwave-safe measuring cup for 1 minute on high. Add water, vinegar, salt, and caraway seeds and microwave for 1 minute more. Pour dressing over cabbage-apple mixture and toss to coat. Cover and microwave on high 2–4 minutes, stirring after 1 minute. (Slaw will be limp but still crisp-tender.) Serve in bowls. Serves 4.

Hot Sweet and Sour Red Cabbage

2 T. oil	2/3 c. red wine vinegar
1 medium onion, chopped	2 T. brown sugar, packed
1 large (2 lbs.) red cabbage, shredded	1 t. caraway seeds
2 medium tart red apples, unpeeled and sliced thin	1 t. salt
	1/4 t. pepper

Combine oil and onions in large microwave-safe casserole or steamer. Microwave on high 2 to 3 minutes or until onions are tender. Stir in cabbage, apples, wine vinegar, sugar, caraway seeds, salt, and pepper. Cover lightly and microwave on high 10 minutes. Stir.

Cover again and microwave on medium 3 to 4 minutes more or until cabbage is tender and flavors are mixed. Let stand for 5 minutes before serving. Serves 8–10.

Red Cabbage Slaw

2 c. canned beets, cut into thin strips (julienne-style)
6 c. coarsely shredded red cabbage
1 medium onion, thinly sliced
$^1/_2$ c. vinegar
$^1/_3$ c. sugar

Drain beets, reserving $^1/_2$ c. liquid. In large bowl combine beets, cabbage, and onion. In saucepan combine vinegar, sugar, and reserved beet juice. Bring to boil and pour over vegetables. Toss lightly. Cover and refrigerate overnight, if possible, tossing occasionally. Serves 8.

Calico Coleslaw

3 c. shredded green cabbage
3 c. shredded red cabbage
1 red apple, unpeeled
1 yellow apple, unpeeled
$^1/_2$ c. raisins
$^1/_2$ c. peanuts
$^1/_3$ c. mayonnaise-type salad dressing

Combine all ingredients and add just enough dressing to moisten. Toss lightly. Serves 8 to 10.

Spiced Red Cabbage

4 c. coarsely shredded red cabbage
$^2/_3$ c. water
$^1/_3$ c. red wine vinegar
3 T. apple jelly
$^1/_4$ t. ground cinnamon
dash of ground allspice
dash of ground cloves

Place all ingredients in a large stainless steel saucepan, bring to a boil, cover, and reduce heat. Cook slowly for 30 minutes or until cabbage is crisply tender. Serves 4. Good served with roast pork.

Carrots

Strangely, the carrot is a vegetable hated by children when it is cooked but loved when it is served raw, especially when it is pulled right out of the garden and rubbed clean on shorts or jeans just before being eaten.

Carrots flourish when they are grown with beans, lettuce, onions, peas, peppers, radishes, and tomatoes. Do not plant dill near carrots as it retards their growth. Carrots usually need to be thinned, so enjoy carrots throughout the summer and pull small ones for small visitors. The rest will mature in autumn, but allowing them to mature to more than 1½ inches in diameter may result in woody carrots. Store carrots at the same temperature and humidity as beets, parsnips, and turnips: at 32–40° and 90–95% humidity.

My father's diary records that our family harvested carrots by the bushels in South Dakota in the thirties and forties. I can remember storing them in sand in the house cellar and preserving some large ones whole in paraffin wax. The latter was probably an experiment of my elder sister Pearl, who was very active in 4-H club work at the time. Now, living in the milder climate of Indiana, I allow carrots to remain in the ground as long as possible and then store them in plastic bags in the refrigerator (with green tops removed). On December 31, 1994, shortly before a hard freeze, I harvested two gallons of wonderfully sweet carrots from our backyard garden. During a really mild winter they will not freeze if kept in the ground and pulled as necessary. I have even discovered a perfect carrot from the previous season while planting the spring garden.

One fall I had so many short, stubby carrots that I used them in place of sweet potatoes for the Thanksgiving dinner, a time when my family expects the traditional caramelized dish. No one at the table suspected it was made with carrots instead of yams or sweet potatoes.

Candied Carrots

2 lbs. carrots cut in 2-inch chunks
³/₄ c. firmly packed brown sugar
½ c. orange juice
3 T. butter
³/₄ t. salt
¼ t. ginger

Cook carrots until tender but not mushy. Mix sugar, juice, butter, salt, and ginger in a deep 12-inch skillet. Heat slowly, stirring constantly until mixture comes to a boil. Add carrots and stir well to coat all of them. Simmer, covered, for 5 minutes.

Remove cover and simmer, stirring frequently, until liquid in pan has been absorbed by the carrots. Serves 10–12 at Thanksgiving, when there is an abundance of other food.

Carrots should be scrubbed with a vegetable brush instead of peeled, especially when they are used in pot roast, soups, or casseroles. Too many vitamins are lost if carrots are peeled.

I grew up with ground Carrots and Raisin Salad, the dressing for which was sometimes fresh cream straight from the cream separator spout. (And carrots were scrubbed but not peeled.) A good variation of that combination is to substitute for the raisins some Italian prune plums, pitted and cut in fourths, enhanced with chopped salted peanuts. Cultured sour cream and/or yogurt or mayonnaise may be used as a dressing.

Another good variation of carrot and raisin salad is to add bits of chopped, peeled apple and sweet pickle relish.

Carrot Salad with Apple and Pickle

1 small peeled apple, chopped
2 c. grated carrots
$^1/_2$ c. raisins
3 T. sweet pickle relish
$^1/_3$ c. mayonnaise

Mix chopped apple, carrots, and raisins. Blend pickle relish and mayonnaise and lightly dress carrot mixture. Serve atop crisp salad greens. Serves 6.

Carrot Slaw

3 T. oil
1 T. white wine vinegar
$1^1/_2$ t. caraway seeds
pinch of salt
generous grinding of black pepper
2 c. shredded or ground carrots

Mix oil and vinegar until well combined. Add caraway seeds, salt, and pepper, and shake. Pour over shredded carrots. Chill before serving. Serves 4.

Carrot Crunch Salad

4 medium carrots (2 c. grated)
1/3 c. chopped walnuts
1/4 c. chopped pimiento-stuffed olives
1/2 c. chopped green pepper

1 T. finely chopped onion
1/2 t. salt
2 T. mayonnaise (optional)
crisp lettuce leaves

In a bowl combine grated carrots with chopped walnuts, olives, green pepper, onion, and salt. If desired, blend in mayonnaise. Mix well, cover, and chill thoroughly. Spoon onto lettuce leaves. Serves 4.

Carrot and Cottage Cheese Salad

4 medium carrots (2 c. grated)
1 c. cottage cheese
1 T. finely chopped onion
1/2 t. salt

1/8 t. pepper
1 T. lemon juice
crisp lettuce leaves

In a bowl combine grated carrots with cottage cheese, chopped onion, salt, pepper, and lemon juice, mixing well. Cover and chill thoroughly. Spoon onto lettuce leaves to serve. Serves 4.

Copper Pennies

2 lbs. carrots
1 medium green pepper
1 medium onion
1 can (10 1/2 oz.) condensed tomato
    soup
1/2 c. vegetable oil

2/3 c. sugar
3/4 c. cider vinegar
1 t. dry mustard
1 t. Worcestershire sauce
1 t. salt
1/2 t. pepper

Slice carrots into circle slices. Cook carrots in boiling water or in microwave casserole or steamer until tender but not mushy. Drain. Cut onion into rings. Cut pepper into rings, discarding seeds and membrane. Combine onion and peppers with cooked carrots in heatproof bowl.

Combine tomato soup, oil, sugar, vinegar, mustard, Worcestershire sauce, salt, and pepper in saucepan. Slowly bring to simmer over medium heat. Remove from heat and pour over carrots, onions, and peppers.

Cover and refrigerate overnight before serving cold. This will keep in the refrigerator for 2 to 3 weeks. Serves 8.

Dill Carrots

8 large carrots
boiling water
1 medium onion, thinly sliced
2 T. dillweed
$^2/_3$ c. vinaigrette dressing
1 clove garlic, crushed
1 t. celery seed

Cut carrots into $^1/_4$-inch slices. Place in steamer basket over boiling water and steam until just tender (about 7 minutes) or in a microwave steamer with a small amount of water in bottom for 4 minutes on high. Drain well and turn into serving bowl.

Separate onion into rings and add to carrots. Sprinkle with dill. Pour dressing over vegetables. Add crushed garlic clove and celery seed. Cover salad and chill. Serves 6.

Easy Carrot Casserole I
This is a good dish to bake while ham or meat loaf is baking in the oven.

1 lb. carrots cut in chunks on bias (diagonally)
1 can (10 $^1/_2$ oz.) condensed cream of mushroom soup
$^1/_8$ t. rosemary leaves, crushed
$^1/_8$ t. pepper

Place cut carrots in small glass casserole. Add can of soup, undiluted, to top of carrots. Sprinkle with rosemary and pepper. Cover and bake at 325° for 45 minutes or until tender. Serves 4.

Easy Carrot Casserole II

1 lb. carrots, cut in chunks on bias
$^1/_4$ c. brown sugar, packed
$^1/_2$ t. salt
$^1/_2$ c. water

Place cut carrots in glass baking dish. Spread brown sugar over carrots. Sprinkle with salt and pour water into bottom of dish. Cover and bake at 325° for 45 minutes or until tender. Cover may be removed during the last few minutes to remove moisture and "caramelize" the carrots. Serves 4.

Carrot Potato Burgers

During the early seventies, when our family was living in Chicago, meat prices rose precipitously. I searched for ways to stretch a pound of ground beef with vegetables, grains, and legumes. This recipe was one of my great successes.

1 lb. lean ground beef
1/2 c. finely chopped onion
1 c. shredded raw carrot
1 c. shredded raw potato
1 egg

1 t. salt
1/8 t. pepper
1 t. Worcestershire sauce
2 T. oil

Combine all ingredients but oil and form into 6 or 8 patties. Fry in oil in skillet over moderate heat for about 15 minutes or to the doneness desired, turning burgers once. Serves 6 to 8.

Spicy Carrot Loaves

1 c. vegetable oil
1 3/4 c. firmly packed brown sugar
3 eggs
2 c. shredded carrots
1 can (8 oz.) crushed pineapple, drained
1 t. vanilla
3 c. flour

1 c. uncooked quick or old-fashioned
　ground oats
1/2 c. chopped walnuts
1 T. baking powder
1 t. baking soda
1 t. ground allspice
1 t. ground cinnamon
1/2 t. salt

Grease bottom of 2 loaf pans. Combine oil and sugar, mixing until well blended. Add eggs and vanilla. Mix well. Stir in carrots and pineapple. Add combined remaining ingredients, mixing just until dry ingredients are moistened. Pour into 2 prepared pans.

Bake in preheated 350° oven for 45 to 50 minutes or until wooden pick inserted in center comes out clean. Cool 10 minutes on rack before removing from pans. Cool completely on wire racks. Loaves will keep in freezer for 2 to 3 months if wrapped securely. If frozen, thaw, wrapped, at room temperature, for 2 to 3 hours before serving.

Carrot Cookies

1 1/2 sticks butter (3/4 c.)
3/4 c. sugar
1 c. grated carrots
1 egg

1 t. grated orange rind
2 1/4 c. sifted flour
1/2 t. salt
2 t. baking powder

Cream butter and sugar together. Beat in carrot and egg, blending well. Mix in the rind and dry ingredients, sifted together. Dip out dough by teaspoons onto greased cookie sheet. Bake in 375° oven for 10 to 12 minutes or until cookies are a delicate brown around edges. Loosen from pan while still warm. Cool on a wire rack and store in air-tight container. Yields 5 dozen.

Carrot-Nut Cake

The heavy cream cheese frosting usually found on carrot cake detracts from its wholesome character. This cake has the desired moistness and nutty texture without requiring the frosting.

1 ³/₄ c. flour
¹/₂ t. baking powder
¹/₂ t. salt
1 t. cinnamon
³/₄ c. sugar

¹/₂ c. corn oil
2 eggs
1 c. grated carrot (about 2 medium
    carrots)
¹/₂ c. finely chopped nuts

Grease an 8-inch square baking pan and line bottom with waxed paper. Stir together flour, baking powder, salt, and cinnamon. In a medium bowl beat together sugar and corn oil. Thoroughly beat in the eggs, one at a time. Stir in the dry ingredients in 4 additions, alternately with the carrots, blending just until the batter is smooth after each addition. Begin and end with dry ingredients. Stir in nuts.

Turn into prepared pan. Bake in preheated 350° oven until cake springs back when touched lightly with finger, about 40 minutes. Cool on wire rack for about 10 minutes.

With spatula, loosen sides. Turn out on wire rack. Turn right side up and cool. Store in tightly covered tin box or wrapped in aluminum foil in refrigerator.

Date-Carrot Tea Bread

1 c. chopped dates
2 c. grated carrots
³/₄ c. flaked coconut
¹/₂ c. chopped nuts
2 c. sifted flour
¹/₂ t. salt

1 t. baking powder
³/₄ t. soda
1 t. cinnamon
¹/₂ c. shortening
³/₄ c. brown sugar
2 eggs

Mix together dates, carrots, coconut, and nuts. Sift together dry ingredients. Cream shortening and sugar. Beat in eggs. Stir in dry ingredients. Add date mixture. Mix until well blended. Turn into greased loaf pan and bake at 350° for 1 hour. (From Barbara Krell, Hyde Park, Chicago, who writes, "Reminiscent of our many committee meetings and tea parties on our patio, here is one of my favorites used on such occasions.")

Carrot Marmalade

4 c. cooked, sliced carrots
2 lemons
2 oranges
6 ½ c. sugar

Put carrots and seeded lemons and oranges (including rind) through food grinder (coarse). Save all juices. Add sugar. Cook slowly until thick. Pour hot into hot sterilized pint jars, adjust lids, and process in hot water bath canner for 20 minutes, after water comes to rolling boil, or for 10 minutes at 10 pounds pressure in pressure cooker. Makes 3 pints.

Carrot Pickles

This is a good use for end-of-the-season carrots which, because of a cold climate, will not have a chance to mature.

2 dozen small carrots
1 c. granulated sugar
2 c. vinegar
1 t. salt
1 stick cinnamon
1 T. mixed pickling spices
1½ c. water

Cook carrots until just tender. Drain and remove skins by plunging hot carrots immediately into cold water and rubbing skins off. (Leave small carrots whole but cut larger ones into strips about the length of the small carrots.)

Combine sugar, vinegar, water, and salt. Bring mixture to a boil. Tie spices in a cheesecloth bag and add to sugar-vinegar mixture. Boil for 8 minutes. Pack carrots into hot canning jars, leaving ¼-inch head space. Remove spice bag from syrup and discard. Pour hot syrup over carrots, leaving ¼-inch head space. Adjust lids and bands. Process in hot water bath for 20 minutes after water has come to a rolling boil, or at 10 pounds pressure for 10 minutes in a pressure cooker (for pints).

Cauliflower

Being a member of the cabbage family, cauliflower should be planted near beans, beets, cucumbers, and potatoes. Dill, mint, and nasturtiums deter pests on cauliflower.

Do not expect to grow in the home garden the huge snow-white heads of cauliflower that you can find in the supermarket. Pick when heads are firm, smooth, and about 6 inches around. Once they have gotten yellow or developed loose, mealy curds, they have stayed in the garden too long.

Cauliflower can be stored for a short time in cold and moist conditions, at 32–40° and 80–90% humidity. Keep covered in plastic bags to retain vitamin C.

Florets of cauliflower may be used raw on vegetable trays or in salads. Slice from bottom to top so that they resemble tiny trees in full leaf. Use in tossed green salads, especially with dark spinach leaves and cherry tomatoes, for a pleasing aesthetic as well as gastronomic experience.

Cauliflower is most beautifully served as a vegetable when it is steamed or microwaved whole, placed in a few inches of water stem down. Serve in a bowl of contrasting color. I enjoy serving whole cauliflower in a dark green Fiestaware bowl which I found at a church rummage sale. Cover with lemon butter, sprinkle with Parmesan cheese, or pour on cheese sauce spiced with bits of hot green pepper or pimiento.

Reserve any water that cauliflower has been cooked in for making Cream of Cauliflower Soup. Place any leftover cooked cauliflower in a jar with Italian dressing poured over it; refrigerate and use in a salad the next day.

Cream of Cauliflower Soup

2 small heads cooked cauliflower or equivalent leftover cauliflower
1/4 c. butter
1 small cooking onion
3 ribs celery, diced
1/4 c. flour
4 c. stock (chicken broth and/or vegetable broth)
2 c. scalded hot whole milk
salt and paprika
Parmesan cheese, grated

Sauté onion and celery in butter. Stir in flour. Add stock slowly and bring to boil. Add cooked cauliflower which has been puréed in blender. Add scalded milk. Salt to taste. Serve with sprinkling of paprika and a dash of Parmesan cheese. Garnish with sprig of fresh parsley, if desired.

Low-Cal Mock Cauliflower Lasagne

1 c. fresh cauliflower florets
$^1/_2$ c. cottage or ricotta cheese
$^1/_2$ c. tomato juice
minced parsley
Parmesan cheese

Steam cauliflower until crisply tender. Drain thoroughly. Add cheese and mash together. Place in casserole and top with tomato juice and minced parsley. Sprinkle with Parmesan cheese. Bake in 350° oven for approximately 45 minutes or until cheese bubbles. Serves 1 or 2.

Cauliflower Salad Bowl

1 small head cauliflower
1 small head romaine lettuce
$^1/_2$ large Bermuda or red onion
$^1/_2$ c. sliced stuffed olives
$2^1/_2$ oz. Roquefort or blue cheese, crumbled
bottled French dressing

Break cauliflower into florets and wash thoroughly. If desired, slice florets vertically so pieces resemble miniature trees. Wash, drain, and chill romaine. When romaine is chilled, tear it into bite-size pieces. Slice onion thin and separate into rings. Toss ingredients together, using just enough dressing to moisten. Serve immediately. Serves 4 to 6.

Pickled Cauliflower

1 large head cauliflower
1 c. boiling water
$1^1/_2$ t. salt
1 c. each sugar and vinegar
1 bay leaf
12 cloves and 12 whole allspice

Separate cauliflower into florets and wash in cold water. Use any small green leaves. In a 10-inch covered skillet in boiling water with $^1/_2$ t. salt, boil cauliflower until tender. (Or steam in microwave for 4 minutes.) Drain, reserving water for soup. Turn into a shallow container. In a clean skillet over low heat stir together remaining 1 t. salt, sugar, and vinegar until sugar dissolves. Tie spices in a double thickness of cheesecloth and add. Bring to a boil and simmer 5 minutes. Pour over cooked cauliflower. Add spice bag. Cool. Cover and chill. Remove from marinade before serving.

Pickle-Cauliflower Medley

1 medium head cauliflower
1 c. dill pickle liquid
1 small clove garlic, crushed
1/4 c. chopped onion
4 medium dill pickles, quartered
1/4 c. sliced radishes (if in season)*

Separate cauliflower into florets. Cook cauliflower in boiling salted water until crisply tender, 6 to 7 minutes. Drain. In a shallow dish blend pickle liquid, garlic, and onion. Add cauliflower, pickles, and radishes. Toss lightly until vegetables are coated. Cover and chill at least 12 hours, turning occasionally. To serve, remove from brine.

---

*I often plant radishes in late summer for a fall crop, when they would be "in season."

Canned Cauliflower Pickle

2 medium heads cauliflower
2 c. small white onions
3/4 c. salt
ice cubes
2 qts. white vinegar
1 1/4 c. sugar
2 t. turmeric
2 T. yellow mustard seed
1 T. celery seed
1 hot red pepper pod

Separate cauliflower into florets. Scald and peel onions. Add salt to vegetables. Mix with ice cubes. Cover with more cubes. Let stand 3 hours. Drain. Mix remaining ingredients in large kettle. Bring to boil, stirring to dissolve sugar. Add cauliflower and onions. Cook 10 minutes or until crisply tender. Pack in 5 hot sterilized pint jars. Reheat liquid to boiling. Pour over vegetables in jars, allowing 1/4 inch head space. Adjust lids and bands. Process in hot water bath for 20 minutes after water has come to rolling boil or in pressure canner for 10 minutes at 10 pounds pressure. Remove from canner and cool on wooden rack.

Celery

While celery is not an essential crop for the home gardener to plant because commercially grown supplies are easily accessible and inexpensive year-round, there are now self-blanching varieties of celery plants on the market if the home gardener wishes to approximate the commercial product. (In horticulture, blanching means to bleach by earthing up or covering so as to keep away light and improve appearance, flavor, or tenderness.) However, I have planted the green type and not worried about blanching it since blanching causes loss of vitamins. Because celery consists primarily of water and fiber, it is a heavy feeder and drinker. It grows best in "muck." I have had the best results planting it in low-lying, heavily composted spots. I have also recently grown celery in an outdoor planter and cut stalks as needed. (It even thrives when the planter is moved indoors.)

Raw celery on the relish tray hardly needs mentioning. The ribs stuffed with Cheddar, cream, or Roquefort cheese provide a delicious appetizer, even for children who may shy away from cooked celery. (I have recently discovered that grade school age children will gobble up celery if it is stuffed with peanut butter, and it will be absolutely irresistible if studded with raisins, in which case it is called Ants on a Log.)

Every bit of the celery head should be used. I use fresh leaves and thin stalks for sauces for pasta and in chili; for soups such as borscht and vegetable; and for dressings or stuffings for fowl and pork. Just remember not to use too much celery, usually not more than a cup of diced celery, or the recipe may be diminished in flavor.

Celery leaves are easily dried on a cookie sheet in the gas oven with a pilot light. When dried, they may be stored in small glass jars on your spice rack and used with parsley or other herbs to flavor soups made with chicken stock.

Celery and Cheese Salad

1 c. chopped celery	1/2 c. mayonnaise
1 c. frozen peas, thawed	1 c. shredded Cheddar cheese
1 carrot, grated	salt and pepper
1 t. grated onion	lettuce leaves

Toss together celery, peas, carrot, and onion. Add mayonnaise. Fold in shredded cheese, and season to taste. Serve on crisp lettuce.

Celery, Apple, and Coconut Salad

2 apples, unpeeled and diced	1/4 c. orange juice
1 c. diced celery	salt to taste
1/2 c. flaked coconut	paprika
1 T. lemon juice	lettuce leaves
1/4 c. oil	

Combine apples, celery, and coconut. Sprinkle lemon juice over fruit. Combine oil, orange juice, salt, and paprika. Add to fruit. Chill. Line a salad bowl with lettuce leaves and pile chilled salad in center.

Braised Celery

2 hearts of celery
1 c. chicken stock
3 T. soft butter
1/2 t. salt
1/8 t. pepper

Remove thick outer leaves from celery hearts. Cut hearts lengthwise into 4 sections each. Arrange celery in steel skillet and add chicken stock and butter. Sprinkle with salt and pepper. Bring liquid to a boil, cover, and braise over low heat for 30 minutes, or until tender.

Celery Soup

2 c. chopped celery   *2 T. butter*
1 medium onion, sliced   *2 T. flour*
4 or 5 celery leaves   *3 c. milk*
4 c. leftover vegetable cooking water   *1/2 t. salt*

Cook celery, onion, and celery leaves in 4 c. leftover vegetable cooking water. Season if necessary.

To make the sauce, melt butter. Blend in flour. Add milk and salt. Cook until slightly thick, stirring constantly. Mix in the cooked celery, onion, and celery leaves. (Adapted from a recipe prepared by Marilyn Wollman and Pauline Hofer in a 1950 Freeman Academy cooking class.)

Celery-Potato Soup

1 c. potatoes
1 c. celery
1 qt. milk
2 T. butter
salt and pepper to taste

Dice celery and potatoes. Cook together until soft. Add milk, butter, and seasoning. Bring just to boiling point. Serves 6.

Curried Celery

2 c. sliced celery

1/2 t. salt

1/4 c. water

1 medium baking apple, cored and
    sliced

1/3 c. sliced onion

1 1/2 T. butter

2 t. flour

1 t. curry powder

1/2 t. salt

1/8 t. pepper

Place first 3 ingredients in saucepan. Cover, bring to boiling point, and cook 5 minutes or until celery is crisply tender. Sauté onions in butter until translucent. Push onions to one side of skillet and stir in flour and curry powder. Cook 1 minute. Drain celery and add with apples to onion mixture. Blend. Cover and cook slowly 2 minutes. Add salt and pepper. Serve hot as vegetable with poultry, pork, or lamb.

Garlic

1994 was the year of garlic! Garlic worshippers bought miniature earthenware garlic roasters as well as slicers, and stopped apologizing for garlic breath. In addition, all sorts of claims were made for the health benefits of garlic. It is said to lower blood pressure and cholesterol, reduce the chances of cancer, and provide traces of vitamins B_6 and C.

Garlic *aficionados* may want to subscribe to a quarterly newsletter that provides recipes, tips, and health information published by the Fresh Garlic Association (see Resources section for address). Better yet, visit the annual Gilroy [California] Garlic Festival, which attracts upwards of 90,000 visitors who tour the Christopher Ranch and sample all kinds of garlic products. Among the items for sale is the bumper sticker, "Garlic Lovers Love Garlic Lovers—No One Else Will."

Garlic may be grown in your garden by planting the cloves, root side down. Each will grow into one bulb. You will be able to distinguish it from the growing green onion plant because its leaves or stems are thinner and wavier. My son Karl as a teenager tried to grow garlic as a cash crop. As I recall, he did not make a lot of money that year.

Our family is fond of garlic, but in modest amounts. If a recipe calls for 3 or 4 cloves, I will probably use only one. However, I will vouch for the fact that a head of garlic provides more flavor than a clove does. When my husband and I were dating he learned how to make spaghetti sauce. It was particularly tasty until he learned that when a recipe called for a "clove" of garlic, it did not mean using the entire head or bulb.

Trendy cooks are now using a whole head of roasted garlic to flavor mashed potatoes, pizza topping, pasta sauce, or cream sauce. But if you want to roast a head of garlic you might see if your microwave does the job before going out to buy a new kitchen gadget.

Microwave Roasted Garlic

Place a whole unpeeled bulb on a paper towel. Microwave on High for 1 minute, turn the bulb upside down, and then microwave it for a minute more. Squeeze the cloves to pop the softened garlic out. Use as needed in recipe of choice.

Garlic-Flavored Salad Dressing

1 t. (heaping) celery seed   3 cloves garlic, crushed
2 T. brown sugar   3 green onion tops, minced
1 t. dry mustard   1 t. marjoram
3/4 c. red wine vinegar   1 t. thyme
1 c. olive oil   salt and freshly ground pepper to taste

In a mortar crush the celery seed well. If dried herbs are used, also pulverize them in the mortar. (Green fresh herbs should be minced along with the onions.) Mix sugar and mustard with vinegar; add oil, garlic, onions, and herbs. Add salt and pepper. Keep in a covered jar at least 24 hours before using, but *do not refrigerate,* since the oil congeals. Shake or beat well before tossing on green salad.

Garlic Bread Superb
Use your mortar and pestle for this, if you have one.
If not, a food processor will do.

2 small cloves garlic, minced
1 T. fresh marjoram or oregano, minced (or half a teaspoon of dried, crushed)
2 T. olive oil
1/8 t. salt
1/8 t. black pepper
6 thin slices Italian or sourdough French bread

Place garlic and minced or crushed herbs in mortar. With pestle, grind together, adding oil a little at a time. Add salt and pepper and mix well. Apply with pastry brush to bread slices. Place slices under broiler and brown lightly. Do not allow slices to get hard and dry. Serve hot.

Grapes

Grapes are ripe in early fall and make excellent juice or jelly. My husband is a native of Chautauqua County, New York, which lies south of Lake Erie, so I have benefited from numerous visits to the vineyards which produce Welch's (now a growers' cooperative) grape juice and fine varietal wines. (Local history avers that Mr. Welch, a pious Methodist, was responsible for the widespread use of unfermented grape juice now being used in most Protestant communion services.)

From the Chautauqua County village of Fredonia and the Women's Association of the First Presbyterian Church's recipe collection, *To the Town's Taste* (no date but probably post–World War II) comes Eila Bowen's recipe for:

Grape Juice

Wash and stem Concord grapes. Cover with water. Cook slowly until thoroughly cooked. Strain through a muslin jelly bag. To 1 gallon grape juice add 3 c. sugar (or less if grapes are sweet). Return to fire and, when boiling, seal in fruit jars.

Spiced Grape Jelly

$3^1/_2$ c. sugar
2 c. grape juice
$^1/_2$ t. crushed rosemary leaves
$^1/_4$ t. whole cloves
1 box ($2^1/_2$ oz.) powdered pectin

Measure sugar into bowl and set aside for later use. Pour juices and 1 c. water into 6 to 8 quart kettle. Tie rosemary and cloves in cheesecloth bag and add. Stir in powdered pectin. Place over high heat and stir until mixture comes to a full rolling boil which cannot be stirred down. Add sugar all at once. Mix well. Bring to full rolling boil again. Boil 1 minute, stirring constantly. Remove jelly from heat. Skim off foam with metal spoon. Remove spice bag. Pour at once into half-pint jars, leaving $^1/_2$-inch head space. Seal with lids and bands. Yields 3 half-pint jars.

Grape Pie

Prepare pastry for 2-crust, 9-inch pie. Line pie pan. For the filling: Slip off skins of $5^1/_3$ c. ripe Concord grapes by holding the stemmed grapes between your fingers. Save skins in a bowl. Place grape pulp (with seeds) in a saucepan without water and bring to rolling boil. While hot, rub pulp through strainer to remove seeds. Mix strained pulp with the skins. Mix lightly through the grapes 1 c. sugar and ¼ c. flour. Sprinkle with 1½ t. lemon juice and ¼ t. salt. Pour grape mixture into pastry-lined pan. Dot with 1½ T. butter. Cover with top crust. Carve a design into top crust with sharp paring knife in order for steam to escape. Bake at 425° for 35 to 45 minutes or until crust is nicely browned and juice begins to bubble through design. Serve cool or slightly warm but not hot or you may be burned. (From my mother-in-law, Margaret Shug Towne, who suggested protecting the bottom of your oven with aluminum foil or cookie tin, in case your pie runs over.)

My son Karl in 1994 had a bumper crop of grapes on his vines in Ferndale, Michigan, and called me in panic for all the recipes I had on my hard drive for using Concord grapes. At Christmas time he reported success with the pie recipe and the juice recipe. Patrice, his wife, couldn't understand this burst of enthusiasm for baking and juicing when he could have been making overtime pay for nursing on Saturday. I tried to explain that some tendencies in behavior are transmitted genetically.

Freezing Concord Grape Pie Filling

Follow directions for Grape Pie filling above, except omit salt and butter. Mix all together well and freeze in plastic containers, allowing space at the top for expansion while freezing.

"Vyne" Sauce (Grape Sauce for Fowl)

When I taught Chaucer at Findlay College in the 1960s, the class celebrated the end of the course with a Medieval dinner. This recipe would have been a welcome accompaniment to the baked chicken we ate from wooden trenchers.

1 lb. Concord grapes, pits removed
2 c. red wine
1 c. beef broth
7 T. honey
dash pepper
¼ t. salt
4 egg yolks

Separate grape skins from pulp and the seeds from the pulp as directed above under Grape Pie. Reunite the skins and pulp and soak in red wine for several hours or overnight. In enameled or stainless steel pot gently simmer the marinated grapes and wine with beef broth for 15 minutes. Combine honey, pepper, and salt with egg yolks. Stir in ½ c. hot broth. Then add this mixture to the simmering broth. Remove from heat. Serve with chicken or duck. (From daughter-in-law Carol ("Cricket") Courtney, a devotée of the Society for Creative Anachronism.)

Of course, there is no better use for surplus grapes in season than to make wine, whether you tramp the grapes with your bare feet or not. However, the Townes suggest leaving winemaking to the professionals like the Woodburys, makers of prizewinning Woodbury Wines. For a catalogue write them at Route 1, Dunkirk, NY 14048. (It's all in the family!)

Horseradish

If you like a garnish with zip to it, horseradish is a perennial to consider. It can be grown in almost any leftover corner of your back yard. Five or six roots should be enough for most families, and you probably will have no difficulty finding a gardener who would like to share starter roots with you.

The horseradish root makes its prime growth in the fall when weather turns cool. Roots may be dug from unfrozen ground any time after September.

Horseradish is favored for its medicinal effects. It acts as a decongestant, a stimulant, a laxative, and a diuretic. Its high vitamin C content will persist as long as it is kept in cold storage. It even serves as an analgesic if applied externally as a compress.

Creamed Horseradish
I remember the sweet cream coming directly from the cream separator.
Remove your glasses and prepare to cry while grating or
grinding the horseradish roots!

¹/₂ c. grated horseradish
1 c. sweet cream
¹/₂ t. vinegar (optional)
pinch of salt
pinch of sugar

Grate horseradish and mix with cold, slightly beaten, sweet cream, vinegar, salt, and sugar. Serve with fish, roast beef, or ham.

Variation: Crumbs of homemade white bread may be added to cut the "bite." This will make it more palatable to children.

Horseradish Applesauce

Combine ¹/₄ c. grated horseradish with ¹/₂ c. unsweetened applesauce. Excellent with baked ham.

Variation: Grated beets may be substituted for the applesauce.

Horseradish Dressing

¹/₂ c. mayonnaise
¹/₄ c. sour cream
3 T. grated horseradish
1 c. vinaigrette dressing

Blend mayonnaise, sour cream, and horseradish. Add vinaigrette dressing, stirring until smooth. Makes 1 ³/₄ cups. Serve over cooked potatoes or a combination of potatoes, beets, and green beans or as an accompaniment to roast beef.

Tangy Topping for Baked Potatoes

8 oz. yogurt
2 T. grated horseradish
1 t. Worcestershire sauce
¹/₂ t. salt
¹/₄ t. paprika

Combine yogurt with remaining ingredients and chill. Serve with additional sprinkle of paprika. Makes 1 cup.

Seafood Cocktail Sauce

¹/₂ c. ketchup
¹/₂ to 1 t. grated horseradish, depending upon taste
¹/₂ t. sugar (optional)

Mix all ingredients and serve as a dipping sauce for shrimp or other seafood.

Horseradish Butter

¹/₂ stick (¹/₄ c.) butter
1¹/₂ T. drained prepared horseradish

Cream together the butter and horseradish. Let stand, covered, for at least an hour. Serve with broiled meats.

Kiwi Fruit

Television's Galloping Gourmet first popularized the kiwi fruit, originally called the Chinese gooseberry, a soft, emerald green berry with tiny, edible black seeds. High in vitamin C, kiwis have a unique flavor "like a combination of strawberry and banana with a hint of fig and a dash of lemon," according to a Gurney Nursery ad.

Beautiful when sliced crosswise and added to fruit salads or fresh greens, the supermarket kiwi is large and covered with a fuzzy coat. It is best peeled before being eaten, although I have seen it served at elegant receptions with its coat still on. It is good eaten as if it were a soft boiled egg, with its top cut off and standing in an egg cup.

The hardy kiwi, however, is a hairless berry slightly bigger than a large grape. It need not be peeled. It has been available to home gardeners in the Midwest since the early 1980s. Just be sure to plant at least 1 male plant for every 5–8 female plants! Plants are available from Gurney's Nursery in Yankton, South Dakota (see Resources section. Gurney's also have liberal replacement policies, as I learned in 1993 after a particularly hard spring freeze).

Kiwi plants are climbers and will need a strong trellis. I have planted mine along a fence in a protected area south of the garage. The fruit is harvested in late September or early October. Fruit will keep in the refrigerator for up to 4 months.

Kiwi Fruit Purée

Place fruit in blender and purée until smooth. Store in tightly sealed container up to 1 week in refrigerator or 4 months in freezer. Use purée in the following ways:
1. Make a salad dressing with 1 c. purée and 1 T. sweet mustard.
2. Make a dessert topping with 1 c. purée, 1 c. yogurt, and 1½ T. honey.
3. Make a chocolate sauce with 1 c. melted chocolate chips and ½ c. purée.

Kiwi-Melon Fruit Basket

1 large cantaloupe
1 pint raspberries
1 cup hardy kiwi fruit

Cut cantaloupe into basket with or without handle. Remove melon from shell and dice. Combine melon, raspberries, and kiwis which have been halved. Let stand, covered, in the refrigerator for an hour to meld flavors. Sprinkle with fruit syrup or cranberry juice cocktail, or serve with plain yogurt. Serves 4.

Variation: Before serving, sliced banana may be added.

Kiwi Gazpacho

1 c. water
¹/₄ c. sugar
2 c. strawberries (fresh or frozen)
1 c. raspberries (fresh or frozen)
1 c. hardy kiwis, halved
1 T. lemon juice
4 sprigs fresh mint

Combine water and sugar in small saucepan. Stir to dissolve while heating. Remove from heat and allow to cool.

Purée the berries, kiwis, and lemon juice in blender. Add chilled sugar syrup and blend. Chill in refrigerator until serving time. Serve in chilled glass bowls, decorated with mint sprigs. Serves 4.

Lima Beans

Lima beans are popular in our family picked green from the garden when the bean bulges the pod or dried and shelled when the pods have thoroughly dried.

Microwaved Fresh Lima Beans with Ham Bits

2 c. freshly shelled green lima beans
¹/₄ c. water
¹/₂ to ³/₄ c. leftover bits of ham cut from bone
freshly ground black pepper

Combine shelled lima beans and water in microwave-safe casserole and cook on high for 5 minutes. Add ham bits and cook on high 1 minute more. Grind black pepper over all to taste. (It should not be necessary to add salt or butter.) Serves 2 to 4, depending on whether it is used as main dish or side dish.

Creole Lima Beans

4 T. (¹/₂ stick) butter

4 slices white bread, cut in small cubes
  (2 c.)

1 medium onion, peeled and sliced

¹/₂ small green pepper, seeded and diced
  (¹/₂ c.)

1 T. flour

¹/₂ t. salt

¹/₄ t. pepper

1¹/₂ t. leaf basil, crumbled

2 c. tomatoes, peeled and quartered

2 c. small green lima beans or cooked
  dried lima beans

Melt 2 T. butter in medium skillet. Stir in bread cubes until evenly coated. Place in small bowl.

Sauté onion and green pepper in remaining butter until soft in same skillet. Stir in flour, salt, pepper, and basil. Cook, stirring constantly, until bubbly. Stir in tomatoes. Continue cooking and stirring until mixture thickens slightly and boils 1 minute. Stir in lima beans. Spoon into a lightly greased 6-cup baking dish and sprinkle bread cubes over top.

Bake in 375° oven for 20 minutes or until bubbly and topping is toasted.

Paprika Beans for a Crowd

1 lb. (2¹/₂ c.) large dry lima beans

2 t. salt

2 c. chopped onions

¹/₄ c. soft butter

¹/₂ c. sliced mushrooms

2 T. paprika

2 c. light sour cream or yogurt (or a
  combination of both)

1 t. salt

fresh parsley for garnish

Rinse lima beans, cover with 6 c. cold water, and bring to boil. Simmer 2 minutes and remove from heat. Do not drain, but cover and let stand 1 hour. Add 2 t. salt to beans and water. Bring to boil, reduce heat, cover, and simmer 45 to 60 minutes or until tender. Drain.

Cook onions in butter until translucent. Add mushrooms and paprika. Cook 5 minutes longer. Stir in beans, sour cream or yogurt, and 1 t. salt. Heat through, stirring occasionally. Garnish with fresh parsley. Serves 12.

Southern Succotash

2 c. lima beans

1 lb. green beans

3 large ripe tomatoes, peeled

1 c. corn kernels

2 T. flour

2 T. butter

¹/₂ c. sour cream (at room temperature)

2 t. sugar

1 t. salt

¹/₂ t. pepper

Cook limas and green beans with tomatoes in $^1/_4$ c. boiling water until beans are tender, about 15 minutes. Add corn and cook until done, about 5 minutes. In a separate saucepan prepare a thickened sauce with flour, butter, and sour cream. Add to vegetables. When mixture comes to a boil, add sugar, salt, and pepper. Serves 8.

Luscious Lima Bake

4 slices bacon
1 large onion, chopped
1 can (10 $^1/_2$ oz.) condensed cream of tomato soup
4 c. drained cooked lima beans (12 oz. dried)
buttered bread crumbs

Cook bacon until crisp. Remove from pan, drain, and crumble into bits. Brown onion in bacon drippings. Mix with soup, lima beans, and bacon. Spoon into a casserole dish and sprinkle top with bread crumbs. Bake in 375° oven for 30 minutes or until crumbs are browned. Serves 6 to 8.

Onions

A city in southeastern France, Lyon, has given us the style of cookery known as *lyonnaise,* meaning "prepared with finely sliced onions, particularly designating potatoes prepared with fried onions." *Vive la France!* How boring it would be to cook without onions!

Growing up on a South Dakota farm during the Great Depression, I had plenty of potatoes, eggs, and onions. I can still smell the potatoes and onions frying in a large black cast-iron skillet atop a wood or corncob-burning kitchen range.

I truly pity anyone who does not like onions or with whom onions do not agree. More to be pitied is the cook, usually the woman, who must cook for someone who does not like the flavor of onions. For those of us who love onions, can you imagine a pot roast without onions? Chili con carne without onions? Spaghetti sauce without onions?

We have already discussed the pleasure of pulling those first green onions in the spring garden and adding them to green salads or cottage cheese. Now we focus on the winter onions harvested in autumn, if you haven't already eaten your supply during the summer.

If you planted your winter onions, yellow, red or white, with onion sets readily available in the produce section of most supermarkets, you did not have to wait long before they matured and the stems bent over and dried. If you planted onion seeds and transplanted the seedlings, you waited longer for the harvest!

It is important not to pull onions, unless you plan to use them immediately, before the outer skin has dried, since immature onions bruise easily and do not keep well. Break or crush the stems if there are signs of flower heads. When the stems are dry, dig the bulbs, which can be left on top of the ground until thoroughly cured. This may take 3 to 10 days, depending upon the weather.

Onions may be stored in a well-ventilated attic, in a loft in the garage or barn, or braided and hung from hooks in a warm, sunny porch.

The producers of sweet Georgia Vidalia onions suggest storing them in old panty hose. "Drop one onion in the panty hose, tie a knot, add another, tie a knot, until the panty hose leg is filled. Hang the hose in a basement or cool place, and the onions should last up to 3 months."

Overnight Onion Relish

1 large sweet Bermuda onion
1½ c. finely chopped cabbage
½ c. grated carrot
½ c. chopped green pepper
1 medium tomato, chopped

3 T. sugar
2 t. salt
6 T. vinegar
¼ t. chili powder
¼ t. oregano

Peel and finely chop onion. There should be about 2 cups. Combine onions with remaining ingredients. Cover and refrigerate overnight. Serve with hot dogs, ham, or sausages.

Onion Casserole

2 slices bacon
3 c. quartered and sliced onions
1 c. water
2 eggs
1 can (13 oz.) evaporated milk

⅓ c. water
1 t. salt
⅛ t. pepper
1 t. crushed dillweed or dill seeds

Fry bacon, remove from skillet, drain on paper, and crumble when cool. Pour excess bacon fat from skillet. Add onions and 1 c. water to skillet. Cook 10 minutes. Drain. In mixing bowl, combine remaining ingredients. Stir in bacon and onions. Pour into greased 1½-qt. casserole. Set in pan of water. Bake in 375° oven for 35 to 40 minutes, or until knife inserted halfway between edges and center comes out clean.

Onion Soup

2 T. butter
1 T. oil
3 large (2 lbs.) onions, thinly sliced
6 beef bouillon cubes

6 c. boiling water
2 t. Worcestershire sauce
½ t. salt

In a large, heavy saucepan heat butter and oil. Add sliced onions and sauté over medium heat, stirring constantly, until tender and translucent. Dissolve bouillon cubes in boiling water and gradually add to onions. Stir in Worcestershire sauce and salt. Bring mixture to a full boil and simmer for 5 minutes.

Serve over toasted French bread slices and sprinkle with Parmesan cheese. Or top the bread with shredded mozzarella or Swiss cheese and bake in a 400° oven until cheese melts, about 5 to 8 minutes. Serve hot.

Creamed Onions

This is a traditional Thanksgiving dish.

Find the smallest onions of your harvest. Cut off the root ends, then the stems. Peel outer layers and reserve for other cooking needs, such as diced in the Thanksgiving turkey dressing. Steam the peeled onions over boiling water, covered, for 20 minutes, or until barely tender. (Or microwave in small amount of water in covered casserole or steamer for 5 minutes.) Cover with a standard white sauce and flavor with dash of nutmeg. (From Nancy Dickinson, who served them to us at Thanksgiving, 1975.)

Onion Pie
This is a traditional Amish-Mennonite dish.

pastry for 1-crust, 9-inch pie
2 c. sliced onions
6 strips lean bacon
salt and pepper

Line pie plate with pastry. Fill with thinly sliced onions. Season with salt and pepper. Add 2 T. water. Lay strips of bacon on top. Bake at 350° for 30 to 35 minutes.

Onions and Apples
A fine accompaniment to roast pork.

2 T. soft butter
4 medium onions, sliced
3 large tart apples, sliced
1/2 c. water
1 t. salt

Heat butter in frying pan and add sliced onions. Cook slowly until almost tender. Pare and slice apples. Add apples, water, and salt. Cover and cook until apples are soft. Remove cover and fry until water is absorbed and apples and onions are light brown.

Onioned Rice

1 c. chopped onion
1 c. uncooked white rice
3 T. soft butter
¹/₂ t. marjoram
¹/₂ t. summer savory

1 t. rosemary
3 chicken-flavored bouillon cubes
¹/₂ t. salt
2 c. water

Cook onion and rice in butter until both turn yellow. Add herbs, bouillon cubes, salt, and water. Bring to vigorous boil. Stir to dissolve the bouillon cubes thoroughly. Turn the heat low, cover the pan and simmer 14 minutes. Remove from heat, but leave cover on for 10 minutes or until you are ready to serve. Rice will stay hot for 20–30 minutes. (From Florence Mayfield, Hyde Park Union Church, Chicago)

Onion Cure for Warts

Daune Miller Palmer, Dunkirk, New York, writes in her family memoirs about her baby sitter, Mrs. Stitzinger, who lived on Dove Street and made Daune's wart disappear: "After supper one night we went into the garden. She dug up an onion, cut it and rubbed it against my little wart. Then by the light of the moon (very important part of magic) we buried the onion. Soon the wart disappeared."

Pawpaws

Pawpaw trees, also known as Northern or Indiana Banana trees, grow in an area stretching from Canada to Nebraska to Georgia, and produce our largest native fruit. The pawpaws are 5 to 6 inches long, shaped like short, fat bananas. They appear alone or in clusters on branches, starting out dull green and turning brown when they are ripe, beginning in late August. When ripe, the fruit usually falls to the ground. The bright yellow flesh tastes like a mixture of bananas, papaya, and pineapple. It contains many flat, nickel-sized, shiny brown seeds. The fruit may be eaten fresh or cooked.

Because the fruit is creamy and strong-flavored, many people prefer to use it in fruit bread, cupcakes, or muffins. Simply substitute mashed pawpaw for mashed banana in baking your favorite recipe of banana nut bread or banana cake, for example. I suspect babies and children would enjoy pawpaw pulp (absent the seeds, of course) mixed with their cereal and yogurt. Because of the large seeds it might be more usable as juice.

According to Dr. Jerry McLaughlin of Purdue University, the pawpaw bark is a natural insecticide against squash bugs, cabbage worms, bean leaf beetles, and striped cucumber beetles.

Purdue has planted 600 pawpaw trees in a project with 13 other universities to determine the best growing conditions and the best varieties to encourage for commercial production. If you have a good pawpaw tree growing in your woods or back yard you should contact the New Crops Center at Purdue or Dr. Brett Callaway at Kentucky State University. We are looking forward to the growth of a seedling planted by our son Jon from Michigan stock.

Pawpaw Bread

1 c. white sugar (or substitute brown sugar)
$1/2$ c. shortening
2 eggs
1 c. pawpaw pulp
$1/2$ c. sour milk (or $1/2$ c. sweet milk plus 1 t. vinegar)
1 t. baking soda
2 c. all-purpose flour
$1/2$ c. chopped walnut meats

Cream sugar and shortening together. Beat in eggs. Add pawpaw pulp. Add sour milk and soda alternately with flour, beating in by hand. Add nuts. Bake at 350° for 1 hour in greased loaf pan. Cool upright on wire rack for 10 minutes before turning out of pan on wired rack to cool. Allow to "ripen" for 1 day before slicing and eating. Keeps well in refrigerator or freezer if well wrapped. (Adapted from a recipe for banana bread from my niece, June Hofer Libby, who baked it as a 4-H club member.)

Fiesta Pawpaw Cake

$1/2$ c. vegetable shortening
2 c. cake flour
1 t. baking powder
1 t. soda
$3/4$ t. salt
$1^1/3$ c. sugar
$1/2$ c. sour milk minus 2 T. (or sweet with 1 t. vinegar added)
1 c. pawpaw pulp
2 eggs, unbeaten
$1/2$ c. chopped nut meats (optional)

Cream shortening in a large mixing bowl and sift in the dry ingredients (cake flour, baking powder, soda, salt, and sugar). Add $1/4$ c. of the milk and the pawpaw pulp, and mix until dampened. Add eggs, nut meats, and rest of milk. Beat at low speed until all ingredients are well mixed. Bake in 2 well-greased cake layer pans at 375° for 25 minutes. Remove from oven and cool for 10 minutes on wire racks before turning upside down on wire racks to finish cooling. Frost when thoroughly cooled with boiled frosting of choice. (Adapted from my old favorite recipe [origin unknown] for banana cake, usually used when necessary to use up overripe bananas.)

Pears

The pear is one of the tastiest fruits to grow at home. Whether of the Bartlett, Kieffer, Douglas, or Seckel variety, the pear will find its way into many menus. Owens Nursery in Bloomington, Illinois (for address see Resources section), has even developed a dwarf 5-varieties-in-one tree that will provide pears from August to November.

The pear can be eaten out of hand. It also provides a number of other snacks, the first being a beverage.

Pear Refresher

1 fresh pear
1 chilled liter bottle mineral water, club soda, or ginger ale

Core and slice 1 fresh pear into 8 wedges (or into as many wedges as there are persons present). Place 1 wedge in each stemmed goblet. Pour sparkling mineral water, club soda, or ginger ale over each pear slice. Serve immediately.

Pears lend themselves to a wide variety of salads. Below are some suggestions:

Fresh Pear and Cheese Salad

$^1/_4$ c. Cheddar cheese, grated
$^1/_4$ c. celery, finely diced
1 T. onion, minced
$^1/_4$ t. chili powder
1 T. mayonnaise
2 fresh pears, halved lengthwise, cored and sprinkled with lemon juice to prevent browning
4 lettuce leaves

Combine cheese, celery, onion, chili powder, and mayonnaise and spoon into halved and cored pear halves laid on lettuce leaves. Serves 4.

Green and White Salad

1 package (3 oz.) lime-flavored gelatin
1 c. boiling water
1 c. cold water
1 pear, halved lengthwise and cored

4–6 lettuce leaves
1 T. plain yogurt
1 T. mayonnaise
$^1/_2$ lime, sliced

Pour boiling water over gelatin and stir until dissolved. Add cold water and stir. Cool until gelatin begins to set. Slice or dice pear and fold into gelatin. Pour into molds or shallow square glass dish. Refrigerate until firmly set. Just before serving time, unmold individual salads onto crisp lettuce leaves or cut gelatin into serving sizes and serve on lettuce. Top with mixture of yogurt and mayonnaise. Garnish with twist of lime. Serves 4–6.

Savory Pear Sauté
Serve this with roast fowl, such as duck or turkey.

2 T. soft butter
2 T. minced onions
4 firm but ripe pears

4 T. lemon juice
1/4 t. marjoram

Melt butter in skillet, add onions, and sauté until golden. Cut pears in half lengthwise. Core and cut pear halves into fourths. Coat with lemon juice in a small bowl. Add to skillet. Sprinkle with marjoram and cook over medium heat until pears are heated through, about 5 minutes.

Pear Marmalade
Very good on dark wheat or rye bread, toasted.

2 large pears, peeled, cored and cut into eighths
2 T. water
3/4 c. sugar
2 T. lemon juice

In heavy stainless steel or enameled skillet combine pears and water. Cook, covered, over low heat for 5 minutes or until pears are very soft. Purée in blender and transfer purée to pan. Add sugar and lemon juice. Bring mixture to boil over high heat, stirring. Boil while stirring for 10 minutes or until it is reduced by half and a teaspoon of the purée dropped from a spoon onto a plate holds its shape. Transfer to a heatproof serving bowl and allow to cool. Makes 1 cup.

Pears for After-School Snacks

Wedge and core firm pears. Spread with peanut butter. Sprinkle with sunflower seeds and/or raisins. (Better yet, simply wedge and core the pears. Put out the peanut butter, sunflower seeds, and raisins for the children to spread on the pear wedges.)

Pear in a Bottle

The winemaking Woodburys have perfected a method of getting a full-grown pear inside a wine bottle to make pear brandy. Any guesses how they do it?

Pear Crisp Dessert

3 c. sliced, unpeeled pears

2 T. honey

2 T. water

2 T. brown sugar, packed

$^1/_3$ c. quick-cooking oats

$^1/_2$ t. cinnamon

1 T. soft butter

Arrange pear slices in an even layer in a microwave-safe 9-inch pie plate. Combine honey and water and pour over fruit. Cover with wax paper and zap on high for 5 to 7 minutes or until fruit is soft. Stir together brown sugar, oats, and cinnamon. Cut in softened butter until mixture resembles coarse crumbs. Sprinkle topping over fruit before serving warm. (May be served with vanilla ice cream or whipped topping.)

Poached Pears in Microwave

Pears may be poached in port wine, cranberry juice, or creme de menthe–flavored sugar water for colorful treats for the holidays. Here's the basic recipe for poaching pears in the microwave:

6 fresh pears, peeled

$^1/_2$ c. water

1 c. sugar

1 lemon, sliced

Peel pears, core, but leave stems attached, if possible. Combine water, sugar, and lemon slices in 2-quart microwave-safe casserole. Cover and microwave on high for 3 minutes. Make sure sugar is dissolved. Arrange pears in casserole. Spoon sauce over pears. Cover. Microwave on high for 7 minutes more or until pears are barely tender. Serve warm or chilled. (Sugar water may be flavored as suggested above or with a sprinkling of cinnamon at serving time.)

Pear-Coconut Bread

2 c. flour

1 c. flaked coconut, toasted

1 c. coarsely chopped nuts

$1^1/_2$ t. baking powder

$^1/_4$ t. salt

1 c. chopped peeled pears

2 t. grated lemon rind

1 T. lemon juice

$^1/_3$ c. soft butter

$^2/_3$ c. light corn syrup

2 eggs

2 T. milk

$^1/_2$ t. vanilla

Preheat oven to 350°. Grease 9x5x3-inch loaf pan. In medium bowl stir together flour, coconut, nuts, baking powder, and salt. In small bowl stir together pears, lemon rind, and juice. In large bowl with mixer at medium speed, beat together butter and syrup until smooth. Beat in eggs until well mixed. Beat in milk and vanilla. Stir in flour mixture just until moistened. Stir in pear mixture. Turn into prepared pan. Bake 55 minutes or until toothpick inserted in center comes out clean. Remove from oven and let rest in upright position for 10 minutes before turning out on wire rack. Cool completely. (This bread slices best on second day.) Makes 1 loaf.

Asian Pears

Perhaps you have enjoyed the crunch of an Asian pear, which reminds you more of an apple than a pear. Most are imported from Asia. However, U.S. nurseries have developed Asian pear trees which compete favorably with the Oriental varieties.

Miller Nurseries of New York (see Resources section for address) have developed the Chojuro and Shinseiki varieties of Asian pear. These trees are ornamental and yield pears of the fancy "salad" quality. Claims Miller: "Left to ripen on the tree, they're so rich, juicy, and flavorful they put market Asian pears to shame." (That's because Asian pears for American tables must be picked green, shipped, and held in markets before being sold.) Because they are hybridized for the crowded Oriental landscape, they grow only head high and can produce fruit the first year.

Asian pears, I feel, are so special that cooking them would be a waste.

Peppers

Peppers come mild and   hot; green, red, yellow, and even chocolate colored. Mild green bell peppers may become mild red bell peppers if left on the plant long enough, but early picking of mature green peppers encourages further production. In some areas of the Midwest green bell peppers are called mangos, but they are not to be confused with the tropical fruit.

Peppers are an excellent source of vitamin C and should find their way to every relish tray when they are in season. Even finicky children will enjoy eating fresh green pepper slices if placed within their reach while they are playing or reading. Simply remove stem, membrane, and seeds and cut into strips or rings.

Peppers are one of the few vegetables that require no blanching before freezing. Simply dice surplus green peppers as they are produced, freeze on a cookie sheet, and store, frozen, tied in a double plastic bag. Then, when they are needed, remove the desired amount for cooking or flavoring.

Peppers combine well with other vegetables such as onions, celery, tomatoes, and corn, not to mention dried beans. Cooked with beans and cheese, peppers provide a complete protein dish.

In California many cooks roast red peppers. To roast peppers, wash and dry them thoroughly. To char them over an open flame, spear them on a long fork, preferably with a wooden handle, and turn them close to the flame until they char

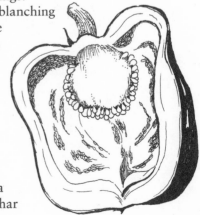

and blister all over. Or place them on a broiler rack 2 or 3 inches from the source of heat. As each pepper is ready, place it in a plastic bag and seal. This makes removal of the skin easier with your fingers.

If the only reason for roasting peppers is to remove their skins for general cooking, it is easier to drop them into boiling water and peel, just as for tomatoes. However, more nutrients will be retained if skins are left on. (More fiber and time will also be saved.)

Recipes for stuffed green bell peppers are legion, all of them good. Early recipes, i.e., recipes published forty years ago, called for blanching peppers in hot water for about 5 minutes, but modern recipes do not. However, if you wish to reduce the crunch, microwaving is useful.

Tuna Salad in Microwaved Boats

2 large green bell peppers, halved
    lengthwise
2 cans (6 ¹/₂ oz. each) water-packed
    tuna, drained and flaked
¹/₂ c. mayonnaise

1 carrot, chopped
1 celery stalk, chopped
¹/₂ medium onion (red preferred),
    chopped

Place pepper halves on plate. Microwave on high for 1 minute. Chill. Combine remaining ingredients and chill. Spoon tuna mixture into pepper halves to serve on lettuce leaf. Serves 4.

Stuffed Peppers with Beef and Rice

6 to 8 green peppers
1 c. rice, parboiled
1 lb. lean ground beef
1 medium onion, chopped

1 T. chopped parsley
¹/₂ t. salt
¹/₄ t. black pepper
2 c. fresh tomato pulp

Cut off tops of green peppers, remove stem, seeds, and membranes but save the tops. Precook rice and drain. Brown ground beef, add chopped onion, and cook until tender. Mix beef, rice, onions, parsley, salt, and pepper together.

Stuff peppers, put on tops, and stand upright in flameproof casserole or Dutch oven. Pour tomato pulp over peppers and cook slowly for 30 to 40 minutes. Serves 6 to 8.

Variation: 1 t. chili powder may be added to stuffing mix.

Microwaved Stuffed Green Peppers

Reduce recipe above by half to serve 4. Cut ¹/₂ inch from stem end of peppers and set aside for later use. Remove seeds and membrane. Place 2 T. water in microwave-safe casserole or steamer. Arrange peppers, cut side down, in the water. Cover and microwave on high for 2 to 4 minutes or until crisply tender.

Remove peppers from dish and cool and drain. Remove stems from pepper tops. Chop tops and add to rice and meat mixture. Spoon evenly into pepper cups and place back in microwave casserole. Spoon tomato pulp over stuffed peppers. Cover and microwave on medium 10 to 15 minutes or until peppers are tender. Let stand, covered, for 3 minutes. Serves 4 when served with crusty French bread.

Autumn Mélange

$^{1}/_{2}$ lb. smoked turkey sausage

$^{1}/_{2}$ onion, sliced

1 large green bell pepper, cut in chunks (or $^{1}/_{2}$ red pepper and $^{1}/_{2}$ green pepper)

1 small clove garlic, minced

3 large mushrooms, sliced

$^{1}/_{2}$ lb. Swiss chard (stalks and leaves chopped separately)

2 potatoes, peeled and diced

1 bay leaf

1 c. water

salt and pepper to taste

Slice sausage diagonally into chunks and brown in cast-iron skillet. Add onion, green pepper, and garlic. Sauté until browned. Add mushrooms, chopped chard stalks, and diced potatoes. Add bay leaf and water. Bring to boil. Add chopped chard leaves after chard stalks and potatoes have become tender. Simmer with skillet covered for 15–20 minutes. Season to taste. If excess moisture remains, remove cover until most moisture has evaporated. Serves 2–4, depending upon appetites.

Now come the recipes for using hot peppers. *Beware—always use rubber gloves when preparing jalapeño peppers so as to avoid burning your hands. Also, be careful not to get pepper juice in your eyes!*

Uncooked Caribbean Spaghetti Sauce

2 medium tomatoes, peeled and chopped

1 clove garlic, minced

1 medium onion, chopped

1 jalapeño pepper, seeded and finely chopped

1 T. cilantro or parsley, chopped

salt and freshly ground pepper to taste

$^{3}/_{4}$ c. olive oil

$^{1}/_{4}$ c. wine vinegar

Mix tomatoes, garlic, onion, pepper, cilantro, salt, pepper, oil, and vinegar together and let stand for at least half an hour before using in order for flavors to meld.

Serve the sauce over 1 lb. spaghetti, cooked *al dente*. Leftover sauce should be refrigerated and used within a few days over grilled hamburgers or steaks.

Jalapeño Corn Bread

1¼ c. yellow cornmeal

½ c. white flour

2 t. baking powder

1 t. baking soda

1½ t. salt

2 eggs

1 c. buttermilk or sour milk (made by adding ½ t. lemon juice or vinegar to sweet milk)

½ c. sour cream or plain yogurt

1 can (6 oz.) cream-style corn

4 T. melted butter or bacon drippings

1 jalapeño pepper, minced

½ c. grated sharp Cheddar cheese

Preheat oven to 350°. Generously grease a 10-inch baking dish or cast-iron skillet, using bacon grease, if available. Combine cornmeal, flour, baking powder, baking soda, and salt. Combine eggs, buttermilk, sour cream, and creamed corn. Stir in melted fat and minced jalapeño. Combine cornmeal mixture and buttermilk mixture, being careful not to overbeat—just make sure dry ingredients are all moistened. Pour into prepared baking dish. Top with grated cheese. Bake 1 hour or until top is dark golden brown. (From Sheila Gwynn, Fairmont, West Virginia.)

Southwestern Cheese Wafers
These are good served as a before-dinner nibble or as a light snack with fruit.

½ c. butter, softened

½ c. grated sharp Cheddar cheese

6 T. yellow cornmeal

1 t. Worcestershire sauce

½ c. plus 2 T. flour

1 T. minced jalapeño pepper

In a large bowl, cream butter and cheese well. Add cornmeal, Worcestershire sauce, flour, and pepper. Mix thoroughly. Lightly flour a large board and turn dough onto board and shape into a cylinder about 2 inches in diameter. Wrap in plastic wrap or wax paper and chill 1 hour. (Dough may be frozen.)

Slice roll into ¼-inch slices and bake on ungreased baking sheet for 10 minutes in preheated 375° oven. Serve warm or at room temperature.

Jalapeño Dip

1 jalapeño pepper, minced

1 lb. small curd cottage cheese

¼ t. salt

1 t. seasoned salt (optional)

2 t. lemon juice

Blend all ingredients together. Serve with taco chips.

Fresh Pepper and Tomato Salsa

3 jalapeño peppers, seeded and membraned
2 large tomatoes
2 green onions or small yellow onion
1 clove garlic
1 t. red wine vinegar
1 T. chopped fresh cilantro or parsley

Combine all ingredients in blender container and process to desired consistency. Serve with tortilla chips. Refrigerate any remaining salsa and use within a few days on scrambled eggs. (From Jonathan Towne.)

Canned Hot Pepper Mix

2 lbs. small pickling cucumbers, with skins left on
3 carrots, scrubbed, and cut on the bias into $^1/_4$ inch slices
1 medium red or green bell pepper, seeded and membraned, cut into 4-inch strips
1 small cauliflower, separated into florets
4 "banana" peppers
$1^1/_2$ c. canning (kosher) salt
4 quarts water
10 c. white vinegar
2 c. water
$^1/_4$ c. sugar
2 T. prepared horseradish
2 cloves garlic
3 or 4 jalapeño peppers, cut in half

Wash cucumbers, trim ends, and cut into half-inch slices. Combine $1^1/_2$ quarts sliced cucumber with carrots, bell peppers, cauliflower, and onion. Dissolve salt in 4 quarts water and pour over vegetables. Let stand 1 hour.

Meanwhile, remove seeds from banana peppers and cut into $1^1/_2$-inch slices. Measure $1^1/_2$ quarts and set aside. Prepare 8 pint home canning jars and lids according to manufacturer's instructions.

Combine vinegar, 2 c. water, sugar, horseradish, and garlic. Simmer 15 minutes. Remove garlic. Drain vegetables. Pack peppers and other vegetables in hot jars, leaving $^1/_4$-inch head space. *With rubber gloves* add a piece of jalapeño pepper to each jar. (Jalapeño peppers will have seeds and membranes intact.) Carefully pour hot liquid over vegetables, leaving $^1/_4$-inch head space. Remove air bubbles with wooden spoon. Adjust caps. Process pints 10 minutes in boiling water bath canner. Makes 8 pints.

Green Pepper Jelly

6 large green bell peppers
1¹/₂ c. cider vinegar
1 t. crushed, dried red pepper
6 c. sugar
¹/₂ t. salt
1 bottle pectin
green food coloring (optional)

Put half the green peppers and half the vinegar in a blender container. Cover and purée. Pour puréed green peppers into a large enameled or steel saucepan. Repeat the process with remaining green peppers and vinegar. Add crushed dried red pepper, sugar, and salt to the puréed green peppers. Bring pepper mixture to boil and add bottled pectin. Boil until it thickens when dropped from a spoon, about 20 minutes. Add a few drops green food coloring, if desired.

Pour into hot sterilized half-pint jars, leaving ¹/₄-inch head space. Cover with lids and bands. Invert jars for a few seconds and stand jars upright to cool. Yields 4 half pints. (From Emily Chenette, who serves it over a block of cream cheese in a beautiful crystal dish to spread on tiny wheat crackers.)

West African Groundnut Stew

This is a nourishing one-dish meal, great for low-cholesterol diets.

1 c. uncooked rice
1 medium onion, thinly sliced
2 T. vegetable oil
2 or 3 T. barbecue sauce
1 c. peanut butter, chunky style
³/₄ c. to 1 c. cold water

4 small hot banana peppers, chopped
Accompaniments:
¹/₂ c. each chopped apples, tomatoes, pineapple tidbits, bananas, orange slices, etc.

Prepare the rice according to package directions or use 2 c. cold water, bring to boil, and simmer for 12–14 minutes, or until all water is absorbed.

While rice is cooking, sauté onion in oil. Add barbecue sauce. Over low heat, add peanut butter. Slowly add water, mixing continuously until peanut butter is of desired consistency (like sour cream). Add hot peppers. Cook, stirring continuously, until hot.

Serve over rice and pass the accompaniments listed above. Serves 4. (From Natalie Ashanin, who learned it in Ghana, West Africa.)

Persimmons

If one lives in Indiana for any length of time, one will eat wild persimmons in some form, probably in pudding. The persimmon is 1 to 1½ inches in diameter, the largest berry produced by any American forest tree, a member of the ebony family. They contain several large, flat seeds which must be removed by rubbing the pulp through a colander. However, the effort is worth it because persimmons are rich in iron, potassium, and vitamin C.

Persimmons ripen around the time of the first frost and fall to the ground when ripe. They may be harvested by shaking the branches gently so that the plump, soft fruit will fall onto an old bed sheet or piece of plastic. If you harvest them too early, you will know it, for your mouth will pucker from the high tannic acid content of the unripe fruit.

Each year the town of Mitchell in southwestern Indiana holds a Persimmon Festival which highlights the many ways in which persimmons may be used. Canned persimmon pulp may be ordered from Dymple's Delight in Mitchell (see Resources for address).

Persimmon Pudding

A traditional Thanksgiving or Christmas dish. The pudding will "fall" as it cools. It can be reheated, covered, in a low-temperature oven for 15 to 20 minutes. It is best when cut into squares and served warm with whipped cream or ice cream. Or spoon it into ice cream cones and top with a dollop of whipped cream.

1 c. sugar	1 t. baking soda
1 pint persimmon pulp	dash salt
1 c. flour	2 c. milk
1 t. baking powder	2 T. butter

Mix sugar and pulp. Add flour, baking powder, baking soda, and salt, which have been sifted together, alternately with the milk. Pour into 9 x 13-inch greased ovenproof glass pan. Add butter. Bake 1½ hours at 325°. (From Jeanne Hammond, who got it from her mother, Susan Weldon. Jeanne and her husband, Evan, lived for many years just over the line from Indiana in Martinsville, Illinois, where they gleaned persimmons from an old tree on Evan's family's farm.)

Refrigerator Persimmon Cookies

1 c. persimmon pulp	³/₄ c. chopped nuts
1 c. sugar	1 lb. graham crackers, crushed
1 c. small marshmallows	

Mix together all ingredients. Shape mixture into a roll and refrigerate to chill until firm. Slice into rounds to serve. Keep leftovers refrigerated. (One of the recipes on a can of Dymple's Delight persimmon pulp.)

Persimmon-Nut Bread

1 c. persimmon pulp
1 c. sugar (half white, half brown, packed)
2 eggs, lightly beaten
2$^1\!/_2$ c. flour
1 T. baking powder
$^1\!/_2$ t. salt
$^1\!/_2$ c. butter, melted
1 c. chopped walnuts

Combine pulp, sugar, and eggs in a bowl. Into another bowl sift together flour, baking powder, and salt. Add flour mixture alternately to pulp mixture with butter and combine well. Fold in walnuts and pour into buttered glass loaf pan. Bake at 325° for 1 hour or until cake tester comes out clean.

Canning Persimmon Pulp

Remove flower caps from wild persimmons and run through colander to remove pits. Pour pulp into hot, sterilized pint jars. Adjust lids and bands. Process for 30 minutes in hot water bath canner. Cool on wooden rack. Use in any recipe calling for persimmon pulp.

Freezing Persimmon Pulp

Follow directions for canning pulp (above). After pulp has been put through the colander to remove pits, package it in pint or half-pint plastic containers. Cover, allowing air space for expansion. When needed, thaw in container and follow recipe for using fresh pulp. (From Jeanne Hammond, Columbus, Ohio.)

Note: Jeanne emphasizes clear labeling. Once in her family a container of chicken livers was mistaken for persimmon pulp!

Plums

Plums come in all sizes and colors, ranging from the golden plums originating in Japan to the purple prune plums of European origin, most of which now come from California. However, we emphasize here the native plum, which is found all over the U.S. along streams and lakes, wherever soil is moist. I remember a thicket of plum trees in the northwest quarter of my family's farm in South Dakota adjacent to a section line, making it easy to watch the ripening process and to pick at the opportune time. My father often returned from his evening walks around the farm with ripe plums bulging his bib overall pockets.

Wild plums are tangy and tough-skinned but excellent for jams and baking.

Fresh Plum Sauce

1 c. fresh plum quarters, with pits removed
¹/₄ c. white corn syrup
1 T. lemon juice
sugar to taste

Purée plum quarters in blender. Add corn syrup and lemon juice. Sweeten to taste with sugar. Serve on sliced peaches, ice cream, pancakes, or waffles.

Wild Plum Jam

1 lb. wild plums
1 c. water
1 c. granulated sugar

Clean plums, removing stems and damaged areas. Cook in water until skins pop and pulp is tender, 10 to 15 minutes. Cool. Run through colander to remove seeds. Add sugar and heat slowly until sugar is dissolved. Then cook rapidly until thick. Cool slightly, stirring occasionally. Pour into hot, sterilized jars and seal. Or pour into jam dishes and store in refrigerator. Yields 1 to 2 cups jam.

Chinese Plum Sauce
This makes a great dipping sauce for shrimp, beef, and vegetables.

1 c. Wild Plum Jam (recipe precedes)
¹/₂ c. dry sherry
¹/₂ t. ground cloves
¹/₂ t. ground anise seed
¹/₂ t. ground fennel
up to ¹/₂ c. dry mustard, depending upon tang desired

Combine all ingredients except mustard in blender. Add mustard a little at a time to get desired tanginess. Yields 2 cups. (From Solomon Grundy's Restaurant, Berkeley by the Bay.)

Plum Pudding

1 c. sugar

1/2 c. butter

1 egg

5 T. buttermilk, low-fat yogurt, or sour
milk (made by adding 1/2 t. lemon
juice to sweet milk)

1 c. wild plum pulp with seeds removed
according to instructions above

1/2 c. walnuts, chopped

1 1/8 c. flour

1 t. cinnamon

1/2 t. (scant) ground allspice

1 t. baking soda

Cream sugar and butter together. Mix together egg and buttermilk and add to creamed mixture alternately with other ingredients. Mix all together well and bake in greased and floured glass loaf pan at 325° 35 minutes or until toothpick comes out clean. (From Adeline Kaufman, Marion, South Dakota.)

Plum Bread

1 c. mashed overripe plums

1 1/2 c. all-purpose flour

1 t. baking powder

1 t. baking soda

dash salt

1/2 c. soft butter

1 c. sugar

2 eggs

1 t. vanilla

1/2 c. sour cream or yogurt

1/2 c. chopped pecans

Preheat oven to 350°. Grease loaf pan. Mash plums with fork or blend in electric blender until mashed but not puréed.

Sift together dry ingredients. Beat together butter and sugar until light and fluffy. Add eggs and vanilla. Beat again. Stir in mashed plums and sour cream.

Gently stir in flour mixture and pecans. Spoon batter into greased pan and bake for 45–50 minutes until toothpick inserted in center comes out clean. Let stand upright 5 to 10 minutes before turning upside down on wire rack to cool completely. Do not slice until cool.

Plum Kuchen
This is an old, traditional German recipe.

2 c. flour

1 T. baking powder

1/2 t. salt

2 T. sugar

6 T. butter

1 egg

2/3 c. milk

4 c. sweet, juicy plums (about 1 1/2 lbs.),
cut into eighths

2 T. butter, melted

3/4 c. sugar

1 t. cinnamon

Blend together flour, baking powder, salt, and sugar. Cut in the butter until mixture resembles coarse crumbs. Beat together the egg and milk; stir into flour mixture until well blended. Spread dough in greased baking pan (about 8 x 12 inches). Arrange plums in rows, overlapping slightly, and press into dough. Pour melted butter evenly over plums. Mix sugar with cinnamon and sprinkle over top. Bake in 400° oven for 30 minutes. Serve warm. Serves 8 to 9.

Freezing Plums

To freeze individually, wash, halve, and pit plums and spread on cookie sheet. Freeze until firm. Pack into plastic containers or freezer bags. Seal tightly and return to freezer.

To freeze plums in syrup pack, boil 1 c. sugar with 2 c. water until sugar dissolves. Refrigerate syrup to chill. Wash, halve, and pit plums. Pack in plastic containers and cover with chilled syrup, leaving 1/2 inch air space for pints. Cover tightly and freeze.

Popcorn

Popcorn, the food that made Hoosier Orville Redenbacher famous, is easy to grow, fun to pick and shell, and not fattening! One of my favorite Midwestern female farmers, Carol Gail Eigsti of Morton, Illinois, shared a box of popcorn on the cob with us a few years ago and we enjoyed it for several years, shelling it as we needed it and storing it in a covered glass jar in the refrigerator. My granddaughters, Ariana and Bernadine Kaufman, enjoyed shelling it by rubbing one cob against another while we sat on our low brick wall in the back yard. (You might shell it over prepared soil and watch the kernels germinate and sprout within a few days.)

It is foolish to pay good money for packages of popcorn to microwave when it is so easily and inexpensively grown in your garden.

Popcorn (without butter) makes a filling low-calorie snack. Try it at your next cocktail party!

Popping Corn

To pop corn over direct heat, use a skillet with tightly fitting cover. Cover bottom of pan with cooking oil to depth of approximately 1/8 inch. Place over high heat. Pour in 1/2 c. white or yellow kernel popcorn. Cover and shake until popping ceases. Pour into large bowl and season with salt if desired.

Popping Corn on Cob in Microwave

When popcorn is ready to harvest, allow corn to dry completely. Strip off the husk. Place corn, still on the cob, in a brown paper bag. Fold bag closed. Place in microwave and microwave on high for 3 minutes or until popping slows down.

Cheesy Corn

Add $1/3$ c. dry grated sharp Cheddar cheese to $1/4$ c. melted butter. Pour over freshly popped, salted corn. Toss lightly and serve at once.

Parmesan Currycorn

Sprinkle 1 t. Parmesan cheese and $1/4$ t. curry powder over 1 c. popped corn.

Baked Caramel Corn

2 c. light brown sugar	pinch of cream of tartar
2 sticks (1 cup) butter	dash of salt
$1/2$ c. light corn syrup	8 qts. popped corn
$1/2$ t. baking soda	

Preheat oven to 200°. Mix brown sugar, butter, and corn syrup in heavy saucepan. Bring to boil. Cook to soft ball stage (234 to 238° on candy thermometer). Remove from heat.

Add baking soda, cream of tartar, and salt. Mix with wooden spoon.

Drizzle caramel sauce over popped corn which has been placed in two large pans. Stir popcorn in order to coat each kernel with caramel sauce.

Bake for 1 hour, stirring occasionally. Pour out on waxed paper. When cool, store in tightly covered containers. Makes 8 qts.

Popcorn Ball Uglies

$2/3$ c. light or dark corn syrup	$1/2$ t. salt
$2/3$ c. sugar	2 qts. popped corn

Boil syrup, sugar, and salt together for 2 minutes, stirring constantly. Gradually pour over popped corn and toss until coated. Grease hands with butter and shape corn into balls. Insert wooden sticks. (If the popcorn mixture cools during shaping, place it over low heat.) Makes 6 popcorn balls.

To decorate for Halloween, dip candy corn, chocolate chips and licorice laces in syrup and apply immediately. Or, thinly spread syrup over popcorn ball and sprinkle with colored sugar or coconut. (Children will enjoy participating in this activity.)

Potatoes

Until recently God's gift to poor people, the potato has come into disfavor with dieters. However, its caloric value is equal to that of a same-size apple. Rich in vitamins B and C, plus minerals and protein, the potato with milk is a complete food source, supplying all needed nutrients. That explains why early rural Midwest pioneers who subsisted on potatoes and milk did not get scurvy or suffer from malnutrition. As a matter of fact, potatoes and milk may be considered "soul food" for their comforting quality in younger and older stomachs. A recently widowed older gentleman told me that he eats a microwave-baked Idaho potato and milk every day to ensure sufficient nutrients.

Although I ate pieces of raw potato as I watched my elders peel potatoes, I would not recommend that today. Nor do I recommend canning or freezing potatoes. Potatoes keep so well in their natural state in a cold, moist basement (32 to 40°, 80–90% humidity) that all you need do to keep a good supply through the winter is remove and use first any that are cut or bruised. As with apples, one rotten potato can spoil the whole barrel!

Canning potatoes is a total waste of time and nutrients. And why would anyone buy a can of potatoes when they are so easily cooked for 20 minutes in boiling water? Home freezing of potatoes is not recommended because home freezing equipment does not lend itself to the quick-vacuum partial dehydration and instant freezing that commercial freezing equipment is capable of.

If you as a gardener cannot wait until the potato plants have dried to harvest the tubers below them, you may want to steal some tiny new potatoes by digging carefully around the perimeter of the potato plant, being careful not to disturb the roots too much. If you are lucky enough to find some tiny new potatoes, wash them gently and boil them in their skins until tender, approximately 20 minutes. Drain and serve with butter and chives or parsley. Or shake them gently in a skillet of melted butter or olive oil to which fresh dill has been added.

Potatoes Rosemary

3 T. butter
2 T. olive oil
10 small new potatoes
1 t. dried rosemary, crushed
1 t. salt
$^1/_8$ t. black pepper

Melt butter and combine with olive oil. Put potatoes in casserole. Pour butter and oil over them. Sprinkle with salt, rosemary, and pepper. Bake uncovered at 400° for 45 minutes, until crisp and brown. Unbelievably good! Serves 4. (From Helen Smith, Business and Professional Women's Club, Hyde Park Union Church, Chicago.)

Unless there are loud protests from members of your family, it is best to serve potatoes in their jackets rather than peeled. Because many vitamins and minerals are lodged just below the skins, peeling removes many nutrients. Cooking potatoes with their jackets on also helps to retain the shape of the potato, even if halved or quartered, in pot roasts, stews, chowders, soups, etc.

More times than not I now make potato salad with skins intact, but if you wish to remove the skins, always do so after cooking the potatoes. Then pour the dressing over the potatoes as soon as possible because flavor deteriorates somewhat after potatoes get cold. It is also best to use leftover boiled potatoes cold rather than to reheat them. Reheating results in lowering the nutritive value of any vegetable. But good exceptions to this rule are the following two recipes: Potato Dosas from South India and Potato Griddle Scones.

Potato Dosas

1 c. cold mashed potatoes
1 c. whole wheat flour
2 T. oil
salt, pepper, herbs

Mix potatoes into flour with hands. Add seasonings. Press dough as flat as possible on board and then roll out as thin as possible. Cut out with round biscuit cutter and cook in oil in skillet. Press down and flip over at intervals until both sides are crisped and speckled dark brown. Serve hot.

Potato Griddle Scones

2 c. flour
1 t. salt
1 T. baking powder
3 T. fat (preferably bacon drippings)
1 c. cold mashed potatoes
1 egg, beaten
¹/₃ c. milk

Sift together dry ingredients. Cut in fat with pastry blender. Blend in the potatoes. Mix egg and milk and add to first mixture. Mix slightly. Form mixture into a ball, roll out ³/₈ inch thick, and cut into squares. Place scones on a hot, greased griddle or frying pan. Bake slowly, turning several times to cook through. For a main dish, pour creamed meat, fish, or vegetables over the scones. Serves 4 to 6. (From "Potatoes in Popular Ways," U.S. Dept. of Agriculture.)

Potato, Yogurt, and Cucumber Salad
This is a Greek favorite.

1 lb. boiling potatoes
1/4 c. plain yogurt
1 small clove garlic, minced and mashed with 1/4 t. salt
1 T. fresh chopped mint or 1 t. dried mint, crumbled
1 unpeeled small cucumber, seeded and cut into thin slices

Cook diced and peeled potatoes in salted water about 10 minutes. Drain in colander held beneath cold water. In a bowl combine yogurt, garlic, mint, and cucumber. Add potatoes, stir, and chill. Serve on lettuce leaf.

Niçoise-Style Potato Salad

Begin by marinating leftover boiled potatoes in French or vinaigrette dressing at close of meal. Complete salad at future time by adding cooked chilled green beans, cherry tomatoes, onions, celery, etc. Use black olives or anchovies as a garnish.

Potato, Beet, and Herring Salad
This salad was served on stage during a performance of Henrik Ibsen's
The Wild Duck, *produced in 1978 by the Repertory Theatre at Christian Theological Seminary, Indianapolis. Realism of stage properties as well as costumes and design is essential to Ibsen's drama. When the pickled herring could be smelled from the audience during dress rehearsal, we knew the play would be successful.*

1 c. diced boiled potatoes
1 c. diced cooked beets
1/2 c. diced celery
1 T. minced onion
1 T. minced parsley
1 c. diced pickled herring marinated in sour cream

Mix all ingredients together in a bowl and serve, chilled, over lettuce.

Pennsylvania Dutch–Style Hot Potato Salad

2 lbs. potatoes (6 medium)
$^1/_4$ lb. bacon, diced
1 medium onion, chopped
$^1/_2$ c. cider vinegar

$^1/_2$ c. beef broth or bouillon
$^1/_2$ t. salt
$^1/_4$ t. pepper
$^1/_4$ c. chopped fresh parsley

Cook unpared potatoes in boiling water for 20 minutes. Drain, peel while hot, and slice $^1/_4$-inch thick.

Fry bacon and onion in large skillet until light brown. Remove from heat and drain off excess bacon drippings. Add vinegar, broth, salt, pepper, and parsley to bacon mixture. Stir in sliced potatoes and heat through. Serves 4 to 6. A good accompaniment to baked ham.

Quick Vichyssoise

Vichyssoise is as American as apple pie. The cold potato and leek soup was created by Louis Diat, the French chef of the Ritz-Carlton Hotel in New York City. Its inspiration was a hot peasant soup that Diat remembered from his childhood. To "ritzy" it up, Diat puréed the soup, added heavy cream and chives, and served it chilled. This is a lower-caloried version.

4 medium potatoes, diced, or part cauliflower, if fewer calories are desired
3 medium onions, sliced
$3^1/_2$ c. milk or part evaporated milk, if richer soup is desired
salt and pepper
yogurt or Cottage Cheese Sour Cream (recipe follows)
chopped chives

Cook potatoes and onions in small amount of boiling water until soft. Purée in blender. Add milk and seasonings. Heat slowly, stirring constantly. Serve hot or cold. If served cold, beat until smooth before serving. Garnish with yogurt or cottage cheese, sour cream, and chopped chives and/or parsley.

Cottage Cheese "Sour Cream"

1 c. cottage cheese
1 t. lemon juice

Purée in blender. Serve. Refrigerate any remaining in closed container.

Baked Potato with Low-Cal Topping

4 baking potatoes

$1^{1}/_{2}$ t. chopped parsley

$^{1}/_{2}$ c. creamed cottage cheese

$1^{1}/_{2}$ t. chopped chives

$^{1}/_{4}$ c. plain yogurt

$^{1}/_{4}$ t. salt

$1^{1}/_{2}$ t. blue cheese

$^{1}/_{8}$ t. pepper

Scrub potatoes. Prick with fork. Bake in 425° oven for about 1 hour or until soft. (To reduce cooking time, microwave in microwave-safe steamer with small amount of water in bottom on high for 10 minutes. Then, to crispen the skins, bake in conventional oven for 5–10 minutes.)

Meanwhile, place remaining ingredients in blender container. Blend until smooth. Spoon 2 T. topping over each potato. Serves 4.

Low-Cal Potato-Tomato Scallop

4 c. sliced pared potatoes

1 t. salt

2 tomatoes, sliced

$^{1}/_{4}$ t. pepper

$^{1}/_{4}$ c. sliced green onions with tops

2 beef-flavored bouillon cubes

2 T. grated Parmesan cheese

$^{1}/_{2}$ c. boiling water

Place layer of potatoes in a $1^{1}/_{2}$-quart casserole. Cover with tomato slices. Sprinkle with sliced green onions, Parmesan cheese, salt, and pepper. Repeat until all ingredients are used. Dissolve bouillon cubes in boiling water. Pour over potatoes. Cover and bake in 325° oven for 1 hour. Remove cover and bake 15 minutes longer. Serves 6.

Potato Kugel

6 potatoes, peeled and cubed

dash of pepper

1 onion, coarsely cut

$^{3}/_{4}$ c. flour

3 eggs

4 T. melted butter

$^{1}/_{2}$ t. salt

Blend potatoes in electric blender, $^{1}/_{2}$ c. at a time, adding a small amount of water to facilitate blending. Drain in a sieve. Rinse with cold water. Repeat until all potatoes are grated. Work quickly to minimize discoloration of potatoes.

Blend onion until grated. Combine with potato in bowl. Beat in eggs, salt, pepper, and enough flour to make a batter that will drop from spoon. Melt butter in 9 x 9-inch baking pan in microwave. Stir into the batter. Pour batter back into the pan in which the butter was melted. Bake at 375° about 40 minutes or until brown and crisp at edges. (From Ardinelle Duncan, President, Findlay College Faculty Spouses, early 1960s.)

Potato Latkes or Pancakes

4 large potatoes, grated in electric blender as for Potato Kugel, above
3 T. matzo meal, cracker meal, or flour
3 eggs, beaten
1 t. salt
$^{1}/_{4}$ t. pepper
1 large onion, grated
oil for frying

Peel potatoes and keep covered with cold water until ready to grate. Grate potatoes in blender until only coarsely grated. (Do not purée.) Do only a small batch at a time, putting the grated potatoes in colander to drain.

Squeeze out excess moisture. Mix with matzo meal, beaten eggs, salt, pepper, and onions. Heat oil in large skillet to about $^{1}/_{2}$-inch depth. Drop mixture by tablespoonsful into hot oil. Flatten slightly with spoon. Cook until golden brown and crisp on one side. Turn and cook the other side. Serves 6.

Microwaving Potatoes

The microwave oven is a great boon to potato lovers. I remember the mid-fifties, when microwave ovens were introduced into the Moundridge, Kansas, community by the local furniture dealer and mortician. Amish women, watching the demonstration, said, "But how would you make gravy?"

Later I saw the delight of my cousin, Harry Tiahrt, then one of South Dakota's German bachelor farmers, who could come in from a hard day's work in the fields and fix himself a wonderful baked potato "in no time"!

I resisted the attempts of my husband to buy a microwave oven until the early nineties, and now cannot imagine life without it! Many office workers and teachers have discovered the joys of a baked potato luncheon. Before leaving home in the morning they combine yogurt, herbs, and seasonings in a container to be stored in an insulated bag or office refrigerator. At the office they pierce a cleaned potato once with a fork on top and bottom, place it on a 9-inch paper plate, and microwave it on high for 3–5 minutes, depending upon size.

Microwave Fries

$^{1}/_{2}$ t. garlic salt
$^{1}/_{4}$ t. paprika
$^{1}/_{8}$ t. pepper
1 t. oil
1 large potato, quartered
2 T. grated Parmesan cheese

Combine seasonings and oil in medium bowl. Cut each potato quarter into 4 or 5 thin wedges. Toss potato wedges in seasoning mixture in closed paper bag until evenly coated. Arrange potato wedges, cut sides down, on microwave-safe plate. Sprinkle potato wedges evenly with Parmesan cheese. Microwave at high for 5–7 minutes, or until potatoes are tender. Rotate dish once if your oven does not have a rotating tray. Let stand 1 minute before serving. Serves 1 or 2.

Pumpkins

Unfortunately, too many Americans think of pumpkin only at Halloween and Thanksgiving time, first as jack-o-lanterns and then as pumpkin pie. However, its uses are many, particularly when you consider its long-lasting properties when fresh—if it is treated with respect—and when you consider it as a substitute for winter squash and sweet potatoes. Furthermore, it can easily be canned and/or frozen for use year-round.

Other nationalities use pumpkin curried, stuffed with meat, fried in oil, or puréed in soup. But first it should be considered simply as a vegetable.

Baked Pumpkin
A traditional Native American dish.

1 medium pumpkin, peeled and cubed
$1/2$ c. brown sugar
1 T. melted butter
cinnamon or nutmeg, as desired

Place pumpkin in baking pan. Sprinkle with sugar and butter. Cover pan with foil and bake in preheated 350° oven for 30 minutes or until tender. Serve topped with cinnamon or nutmeg.

Pumpkin Purée

When preparing whole pumpkins for pies and other uses it is much more time and energy efficient to use the oven than to cut and dice large amounts of pumpkin.

Preheat oven to 325°. Cut pumpkin in half crosswise, trying to make an even cut so that the cut ends will rest evenly on a flat surface. Remove seeds and stringy membranes. Place pumpkin, shiny skin side up, on a greased cookie sheet and bake until pumpkin feels soft to the touch from the outside, approximately 75 minutes. Remove from oven.

When pumpkin has cooled, remove pulp with a large metal spoon. The pulp may be used at once in a recipe, canned, or frozen in plastic containers. Be sure to allow half an inch for expansion when freezing. A 6-lb. pumpkin yields about $4^{1}/2$ c. purée, which can be used for bars and bread in addition to pie.

Pumpkin Soup

2 T. butter
1 c. chopped onion
1 clove garlic, minced
2 stalks celery, chopped
1 T. ginger root, minced

4 c. pumpkin purée
2 t. curry powder
$1/4$ t. ground cinnamon
$1/8$ t. ground nutmeg
3 c. apple juice

Melt butter in large saucepan over medium heat. Sauté onion, garlic, celery, and ginger root. Add pumpkin purée and spices. Stir to blend well. Add apple juice. Heat to boiling, cover, and reduce heat. Simmer for 15 minutes. Serve hot or cold with dollop of plain yogurt. For thinner soup, add water. For smooth consistency, purée vegetables in blender before adding pumpkin purée.

Spicy Pumpkin Bread

$1^{1}/_{2}$ c. sugar
$1^{2}/_{3}$ c. flour
1 t. soda
1 t. salt
$1/4$ t. baking powder

$1/2$ t. each cinnamon, nutmeg, ginger,
   and cloves
1 c. canned pumpkin
$1/2$ c. cooking oil
$1/2$ c. water
$1/2$ c. chopped nuts

Combine all above ingredients and mix well. Bake in greased loaf pan at 350° for 1 hour. (From Sharon Creighton, Findlay College Faculty Spouses.)

Pumpkin Pie

Make pastry for a 9-inch, 1-crust pie (or buy pie shell for deep-dish pie). Line pie pan, building up a high, fluted edge. For the pie filling, combine the following:

1 $3/4$ c. mashed cooked pumpkin
$1/2$ t. salt
1 $3/4$ c. evaporated milk
2 eggs
$2/3$ c. brown sugar (packed)

2 T. granulated sugar
$1^{1}/_{4}$ t. cinnamon
$1/2$ t. ginger
$1/2$ t. nutmeg
$1/2$ t. cloves

Beat all above ingredients together with an electric mixer. Pour filling into pastry-lined pie pan. Bake at 425° until a table knife inserted in center comes out clean, 45 to 55 minutes. Serve slightly warm or cold with whipped topping.

Pumpkin Cake

1/2 c. butter
1 c. sugar (half white, half brown, packed)
1 c. baked pumpkin purée
1 c. flour
1/2 t. baking soda

1 t. cinnamon
1/2 t. nutmeg
1/8 t. cloves
dash salt
1/2 c. seedless raisins, chopped
1/2 c. walnuts or pecans, chopped

Beat together butter and sugars until creamy. Blend in pumpkin. Stir together flour, baking soda, cinnamon, nutmeg, cloves, and salt. Add raisins and nuts. Stir flour mixture into pumpkin mixture and mix well. Spoon into greased 9 x 9-inch glass baking dish. Bake at 350° for about 50 minutes, testing for doneness with toothpick.

Pumpkin Drop Cookies
Recipe makes enough for Halloween Trick or Treaters.

4 1/2 c. sugar
3 c. pumpkin purée
1 1/2 c. shortening
3 eggs
7 1/2 c. flour (sifted)
1 1/2 t. salt
4 1/2 t. cinnamon

1 1/2 t. ginger
1 1/2 t. cloves
3 T. baking powder
2 1/4 t. soda
2 1/4 c. raisins and/or nuts
1 T. vanilla

Cream together sugar, pumpkin, shortening, and eggs, and add remaining ingredients. Mix all together thoroughly. Drop by teaspoons or tablespoons on greased cookie sheets and bake at 375° for 12 to 15 minutes, depending upon size. May be frosted with confectioners' sugar frosting. (From Betty Wheeler, Findlay College Faculty Spouses.)

Toasted Pumpkin Seeds

Children of all ages love these, but encourage them to hold the spitting contest outdoors, not in the house!

Remove seeds from 1 pumpkin, spread them on a cookie sheet, and let stand in a dry place overnight or until they are dry. Rub off any stringy membranes clinging to seeds. (Drying the seeds before removing the membrane saves time and energy.)

Dot each cup of seeds with 3 T. butter and toast the seeds in preheated 375° oven, shaking pan frequently, for 7 to 12 minutes or until golden brown. Transfer seeds to a brown paper bag to absorb any residue of butter, and sprinkle with salt or seasoned salt. Store in airtight container.

Tomatoes, Green

After a light frost and as soon as a killing frost has been forecast, pick all the green tomatoes in your garden. Believe it or not, there are ways in which you will be able to use all of them, even several bushel baskets full. Large tomatoes that have started to ripen will ripen indoors. (Remember that tomatoes purchased in supermarkets have been picked green.) Wrap the tomatoes in newspapers and place them in a single layer in shallow boxes in a dark and cool place in your basement. But be sure to check them frequently and use them as they ripen.

Fried green tomato slices are a delicacy all too little known and appreciated. The popular 1992 movie *Fried Green Tomatoes* lent credence to their use. Below is a country recipe sure to please those with a hankering for "down home cookin'."

Fried Green Tomatoes

4 medium, firm green tomatoes
1/4 c. flour
2 T. oil or bacon drippings
1/4 c. brown sugar
salt and pepper to taste

Cut thin slices from both ends of tomatoes, then slice each tomato crosswise into 3 uniform slices. Dredge in flour. Heat fat in frying pan.

Fry tomato slices on one side. Sprinkle with brown sugar. Turn and fry the other side until lightly browned. Season with salt and pepper. Good served with ham.

Variation: Dip tomato slices in beaten egg, then dredge in flour, coating completely, then in egg mixture, then in seasoned crumbs, so that each slice is completely coated. Fry in 1/3 c. oil in large skillet. Sauté about 3 minutes on each side, until they are nicely browned. Keep hot. Add more oil if needed. Serve with hot tomato sauce, if desired.

Seasoned Bread Crumbs: These may be made by whirling dry or stale bread in the food processor and adding seasonings such as basil, oregano, thyme, parsley, sage, and rosemary.

French Fried Half-Ripe Tomatoes

4 medium tomatoes, half ripe
1/2 c. all-purpose flour
2 1/2 t. salt
2 1/2 t. sugar
1/4 t. pepper
3/4 c. evaporated milk
oil for frying

Wash tomatoes, but do not peel them. Cut into ³/₄-inch slices. Place on paper towels to drain. Combine flour, salt, sugar, and pepper. Dust tomatoes in flour mixture on both sides. Add evaporated milk to remaining flour mixture to make a thick batter. Dip floured tomatoes in batter. Fry in hot oil ¹/₂-inch deep until golden brown on both sides.

Baked Green Tomatoes

6 medium green tomatoes
2 T. melted shortening
¹/₂ t. salt
¹/₄ t. pepper
¹/₂ c. seasoned bread crumbs

Wash and remove stem ends of 6 tomatoes. Place in greased baking dish. Brush with melted shortening, salt, and pepper. Add just enough hot water to cover bottom of dish. Sprinkle with seasoned bread crumbs. (See above under Fried Green Tomatoes). Bake in preheated 375° oven for 45 minutes.

Marinated Vegetable Salad

1¹/₂ lbs. potatoes
¹/₂ lb. zucchini (about 3 small)
1¹/₂ c. sliced celery
2 red, ripe tomatoes (quartered)
2 green tomatoes (quartered)
7 T. olive oil

4 T. white wine vinegar
3 T. minced fresh parsley
¹/₂ t. salt
¹/₂ t. basil, crushed
¹/₂ t. oregano, crushed
freshly ground black pepper to taste

Boil potatoes in jackets until just tender. Cool before peeling. Trim and slice zucchini ¹/₈ inch thick. Place potatoes, zucchini, celery, and tomatoes in a large bowl. Combine dressing ingredients and pour over vegetables. Toss gently and chill for at least 2 hours. Serves 6 to 8.

Green Fresh Salsa

This recipe was inspired by a green tomato and a cucumber
partially eaten by squirrels. I simply cut away the damaged area,
washed the vegetables carefully, and proceeded.

juice of 1 lime
1 small green tomato
8 sprigs mint
1 small cucumber, peels included
1 small jalapeño pepper

1 small clove garlic
1 small onion
1 small yellow squash
¹/₄ c. diced cantaloupe

Blend all in electric blender. Yields 1 c. salsa.

Green Tomato Chutney

3 lbs. green tomatoes

2 c. chopped onions

2 c. raisins

1 pint cider vinegar

1½ c. firmly packed brown sugar

2 T. Worcestershire sauce

1 T. salt

1 t. dry mustard

Dip tomatoes in boiling water for a few seconds, then peel. Chop to make about 2½ quarts. Place in large heavy saucepan. Add remaining ingredients. Mix well. Bring to the boiling point. Reduce heat. Simmer, uncovered, until thickened, about 45 minutes. Pack, hot, into hot sterilized canning jars, leaving ¼ inch head space. Seal with caps and screw lids. Immerse in hot water bath canner, cover, and process for 15 minutes after water comes to a hard rolling boil. Remove jars from water and cool on wooden rack. Makes 3 pints. Good served with curries and other Indian dishes.

Chow Chow
Good served with roast beef, lamb, or ham.

10 green tomatoes

5 medium onions

1 c. chopped red bell peppers

¼ c. salt

1½ c. white vinegar

2¼ c. white sugar

1½ t. whole black pepper

1 T. whole allspice

Dice tomatoes and slice onions. Add chopped peppers. Mix all in a crockery bowl. Sprinkle with salt and let stand for at least 2 hours. Drain and discard liquid. Add vinegar and sugar to vegetables. Tie whole black pepper and whole allspice in a small muslin bag. Place everything in a large stainless-steel saucepan, bring to a boil, and cook until soft, about 10 minutes. Remove spice bag. Pour chow chow into hot sterilized pint or half-pint jars and adjust lids. Process in hot water bath for 10 minutes, counting from time water returns to a rolling boil. If any jars do not seal, store them in refrigerator and use them first.

Green Tomato Mincemeat

4 qts. small green tomatoes, quartered

3 lbs. apples

2 lbs. raisins

1½ c. white sugar

⅔ c. brown sugar

1 T. cinnamon

1 T. salt

1 t. allspice

1 t. cloves

1 t. nutmeg

⅓ c. vinegar

Grind green tomatoes, unpeeled apples, and raisins in grinder or food mill. Place all ingredients in a large kettle, mix together, bring to boil, and simmer for 1 hour. Stir often, as mixture will scorch easily. Put in hot sterilized jars and seal. Process in hot water bath canner for 15 minutes after water has come to a rolling boil. Makes 6 pints.

Variation: Bake in large covered enamel roaster at 325° for 3 hours or until all elements are tender and the color is brown. Cool and freeze in plastic containers— quart-size or whatever size is appropriate for the size of pies you normally bake.

Green Tomato Mincemeat with Apple Pie

Prepare pastry for 2-crust 8-inch pie. Pour into lined pastry shell 1 pint of green tomato mincemeat. Slice peeled apple over the mincemeat to fill out the pie, if desired. Sprinkle with cinnamon sugar and dot with butter, if you like. Cover with top pastry and cut slits in top with sharp paring knife so steam can escape. Bake at 425° for 30 minutes or until top crust is nicely browned.

Green Tomato Mincemeat Rice Stuffing for Poultry

1/2 c. chopped onion
2 T. butter
3 c. cooked rice
2/3 c. green tomato mincemeat
ground cooked giblets (heart, liver, gizzard) from bird to be roasted
1 t. blend of parsley, sage, rosemary, and thyme

Sauté onions in butter until tender but not brown. Add rice, ground cooked giblets, herbs, and mincemeat. Blend and heat thoroughly. Serve as side dish, or stuff duck or turkey before roasting. (Bake in a covered casserole alongside the roaster any amount of stuffing that does not fit into cavity or cavities of fowl roasted. Stuffing baked in a casserole will need additional moisture from water or broth.)

Note: Green tomato mincemeat may be substituted for commercial mincemeat in any recipe. If the mincemeat is too "runny," add more dry ingredients such as flour or crumbs. Also, more apple and raisins may be added to "stretch" the mincemeat.

Turnips

The turnip as a vegetable is considered a "poor relation," yet it is quite versatile, easy to grow, and can be eaten both for its greens and its root, like the beet. It is also high in vitamin C and, because it is 90% water, low in calories.

Grits and Turnip Greens

1 lb. ham hock
4 c. water
1 t. salt
3 lbs. turnip greens,* washed and drained

Simmer meat in water about 45 minutes. Add salt and turnip greens. Cook until tender. Drain and serve hot with hominy grits, prepared according to package directions. Vary the menu by serving yellow corn bread with the meat and turnips when the leftovers, if any, are served.

———

*Small, immature turnips may be included with and cooked with the greens.

Cream of Turnip Soup

1 lb. white turnips, peeled and thinly sliced
3 T. plus 2¹/₂ T. butter
2 leeks or 4 scallions (white part only), thinly sliced
2¹/₂ T. flour
4 c. hot milk
salt, pepper, and nutmeg
¹/₂ c. heavy cream or evaporated milk

Place sliced turnips in boiling water in a large, heavy saucepan or enameled cast-iron pot and boil 3 minutes, then simmer gently until soft. Drain well. Place in a large mixing bowl and stir in 3 T. butter and the leeks or scallions. Set aside.

In the same pot, over low heat, melt remaining 2¹/₂ T. butter and blend in flour. Gradually add milk. Season with salt, pepper, and nutmeg. Simmer gently 5 to 6 minutes, stirring constantly with wire whisk, until slightly thickened.

Add vegetable mixture and simmer 15 minutes, then pour soup back into mixing bowl. Purée 1 c. at a time in blender. Return puréed soup to pot. Reheat, taste for seasoning, and, just before serving, add ¹/₂ c. heavy cream or evaporated milk.

Turnip Pudding

1¹/₂ lbs. turnips, peeled
1 t. salt
3 eggs, separated
3 T. butter, melted
1 t. salt
1 c. fine dry bread crumbs
1 c. milk
¹/₂ c. grated Cheddar cheese

In a saucepan, cover the peeled, sliced turnips with boiling water. Add salt, cover, and cook until tender, about 20 minutes. Drain and mash turnips. Set aside.

In a small bowl, beat egg whites until stiff. In a larger bowl, beat egg yolks. To yolk mixture add melted butter, salt, bread crumbs, milk, and cheese. Blend in turnips. Mix well. Fold in beaten egg whites. Transfer to a 2-qt. casserole. Place casserole in a large pan containing hot water and bake in a preheated 350° oven for 1 hour, or until set in center.

Braised Turnips

1^1/$_2$ lbs. turnips
^{2}/$_3$ c. chicken stock or beef stock
^{1}/$_4$ c. butter
salt and pepper

Trim, peel, and quarter turnips, cutting quarters to form uniform shapes. In large saucepan boil turnips in salted water for 5 minutes. Drain into colander.

In a skillet large enough to hold turnips in one layer, heat the stock with butter over moderate heat until butter is melted. Add turnips and salt and pepper to taste. If necessary, add enough stock to reach halfway up the sides of the turnips. Bring liquid to a boil and simmer turnips, covered, for 15 to 20 minutes or until tender. Transfer turnips with slotted spoon to heated serving dish. Reduce liquid over high heat, stirring, until it is thickened, and pour it over the turnips.

Turnip Salad with Caraway-Mustard Dressing

2 lbs. turnips, peeled
3 T. white wine vinegar
3 T. lemon juice
2 t. crushed caraway seed
2 t. Dijon-style mustard
1^1/$_2$ t. sugar
^{3}/$_4$ t. pepper
^{1}/$_2$ t. salt
^{1}/$_2$ c. plus 2 T. olive oil

Cut turnips into 1^1/$_2$ inch strips a quarter inch wide. Drop strips into kettle of boiling salted water. Return water to a boil and cook turnips for 2 minutes. Drain in colander and refresh them under running cold water. Drain, pat them dry with paper towels, and transfer them to a salad bowl.

In a small bowl beat together vinegar, lemon juice, caraway seed, mustard, sugar, pepper, and salt. Add olive oil in a stream, beating. Toss turnips with the dressing and chill salad for at least 6 hours.

Other uses for turnips: Turnips may be served raw, peeled and sliced onto a vegetable tray or in strips on a relish tray. They may also be grated and added to a pasta salad as you would celery or green onion.

Turnips are an integral part of the meat and vegetable pastries eaten as finger food by the Cornish people in mining communities of Wisconsin. When Dr. Alfred R. Edyvean retired as Executive Director of the Repertory Theatre at Christian Theological Seminary, Indianapolis, pasties (pronounced with a short *a*) were served for the dinner entrée, celebrating Edyvean's roots in Cornwall, England, and his pioneering accomplishments in religious drama.

Cornish Pasties

pastry for 2 9-inch crusts
½ lb. uncooked lean ground beef
½ c. diced raw potatoes
½ c. diced raw turnips
½ c. diced raw carrots
¼ c. chopped onion
1 t. salt
⅛ t. pepper

Divide pastry dough into 4 parts and roll each part into an 8-inch circle. Mix beef, raw vegetables, salt, and pepper. Place ¼ of the mixture on half of each circle.

Brush edges with water. Fold pastry over filling and turn lower edges up over top edges. Seal well. Prick top with fork to allow steam to escape. (To glaze top, brush with cream, if desired.) Place on baking sheet. Bake at 350° for 1 hour. Serve hot or cold. Makes 4 servings.

Notes on Turnips: Turnips keep well, like potatoes, if stored in a cool place. Also like potatoes, they may be boiled and served with butter, salt, and pepper. Or they may be mixed with potatoes, carrots, celery, and onion for a vegetable medley. Because turnips are less caloric than potatoes, they will add flavor and bulk without adding calories.

Turnips may be planted as late as Labor Day in moderate climates such as Indiana's for a good crop, especially turnip greens. They may be left in the ground until a heavy freeze is imminent. Then lop off the tops and treat like carrots, storing them in damp sawdust, sand, or moss.

Turnips are good roasted with other root vegetables, such as carrots, parsnips, onions, and potatoes. Also, when caramelized at high temperatures (500° oven in a roasting pan with olive oil for 35 minutes), they add a lot of flavor to winter soups.

Winter Squash

Winter squash consists of those varieties with a hard skin, such as acorn, Hubbard, butternut, and turban—all those which are ready in autumn before a heavy freeze and will keep in a cool place for several months for use in winter. Unlike the yellow summer squash and zucchini, they will be a dependable source of squash pulp for use in many recipes year-round—from soup to desserts.

Blossoms of squash can be stuffed, used to fill an omelet, made into fritters, or sliced and added to a light soup just before serving.

Spaghetti Squash

A relative newcomer in the squash family, spaghetti squash is so named because when it is baked, its interior comes out looking like strands of spaghetti. And it is appropriately thought of as an autumn vegetable because its bland flavor calls for the addition of sauces made from tomatoes, peppers, and onions—all of which will likely still be in large supply during the autumn months. Unlike pasta, however, it is low in calories compared to the traditional bases for spaghetti sauce.

Spaghetti squash lends itself to preparation in the microwave oven, making it a splendid family supper that can be prepared without "slaving over the hot stove all day."

Baked Spaghetti Squash Combo

1 medium spaghetti squash (about 3 lbs.)
1/4 c. olive oil
1 cup ham, cut in thin slivers
3/4 c. frozen peas, thawed
1/2 c. sliced mushrooms
2 egg yolks, beaten
3/4 c. half and half
1 c. grated Parmesan cheese

Pierce squash in many places with fork or skewer. Place it on paper towel or in shallow glass baking dish. Microwave, uncovered, on high for 15 minutes, turning over at least twice during that time. Let stand 4 minutes. Press surface to see if it yields. If it does not, microwave another 3 to 4 minutes. Split squash lengthwise, discard seeds, and fork strands free from shells. Reserve shells.

Combine 6 c. squash with remaining ingredients and toss together gently. Pile mixture into reserved shells and place shells in shallow baking dish. Cover with plastic wrap and poke several holes in the wrap. Microwave on high for 8 to 10 minutes or until piping hot.

To bake in conventional oven, pierce the unbaked squash, place on cookie sheet, and bake for 1 hour at 350° or until it yields to the touch. Remove from oven, let rest until cool enough to work with, and then split squash lengthwise, discarding the seeds and fluffing the "spaghetti" strands.

Turn into buttered baking dish with remaining ingredients. Bake for 15–20 minutes or until hot.

Or, if you want to be really efficient, bake the spaghetti squash when you have room in the oven, while preparing something else, and store the "spaghetti" strands in the refrigerator for a future meal, at which time they may be warmed in the microwave.

Almond-Maple Squash

2 medium butternut squash (about 2¹/₂ lbs. total)
salt
5–6 T. butter
³/₄ c. maple syrup
¹/₂ c. toasted slivered almonds

Cut squashes in half, cutting just between the long neck and the "bowl" or "bulb" of the squash in order to remove seeds easily. Remove seeds and place, cut sides down, on greased cookie sheet in preheated 325° oven. When the squash is soft to the touch (about 45 minutes), remove from oven and allow to cool. When cool, remove squash rind or spoon pulp out of shell. Add butter and mash until smooth. Stir in syrup and turn into greased glass baking dish. Sprinkle with almonds. Bake, uncovered, at 350° for 20 minutes or until heated through.

Squash-Turkey Casserole
An excellent do-ahead dish using leftover roast turkey; simply freeze until needed.

2 lbs. squash (may be any variety—Hubbard, turban, acorn, butternut, etc.)
¹/₂ c. chopped onion
2 T. butter
2¹/₂ c. Herb-Seasoned Croutons (recipe follows)
¹/₂ t. salt
¹/₈ t. pepper
1 c. turkey broth (from "boiling down" the Thanksgiving turkey carcass)
2 c. turkey bits picked from turkey carcass before "boiling down"
¹/₂ c. shredded sharp processed American cheese

Halve squash and remove seeds. Place, cut sides down, in greased shallow baking pan. Bake at 325° for 45–60 minutes or until tender. Remove from oven and cool. When cool, remove pulp from squash and mash. Should yield about 3 cups.

In saucepan, cook onion in butter until tender. Stir in croutons, salt, and pepper. Add broth and toss. Stir in squash and turkey. Turn into 1 1/2 quart greased freezer-safe casserole and freeze for future use.

To serve, bake frozen casserole, covered, in 400° oven for 1 1/2 hours. Uncover, top with cheese, and continue baking 15 minutes more.

Herb-Seasoned Croutons

Cut stale bread into cubes. Toast in cast-iron skillet, tossing with herb-flavored butter. Herbs you may choose from include parsley, sage, rosemary, thyme, celery leaves, tarragon, summer savory, marjoram, dill, chives, etc.

Shoestring Supper

2 acorn squash
1 lb. bulk sausage
1/2 medium onion, chopped
2 cans (8 1/4 oz. each) crushed pineapple, well drained
2/3 c. stuffing mix or Herb-Seasoned Croutons (recipe precedes)
2 to 4 T. butter, melted
salt

Halve squash and remove seeds. Bake, cut sides down, on greased cookie sheet, until tender. Meanwhile, brown sausage in skillet. Add onions. Sauté until soft but not brown. Drain all fat. Stir in pineapple and 1/2 c. stuffing mix. Blend well. Brush half of butter over squash. Sprinkle with salt. Spoon sausage mixture into squash boats, packing lightly. Blend remaining stuffing with butter. Sprinkle over filling. Bake on cookie sheet at 350° about 15 minutes.

Variations: After squash has been baked, fill with grated apple, cinnamon, brown sugar, and 2 or 3 Vienna-style canned sausages. Return to oven and continue baking 20 minutes. Or, stuff cavity with sautéd onion and celery and add combination of baked beans and frankfurters. Top with shredded American cheese. Bake 15 minutes more or until cheese melts.

Microwave Spicy Squash Boats

3 acorn squash (about 1 lb. each)
salt
1½ c. natural cereal (such as Muesli, with raisins and dates)
1 c. thin celery slices
¾ c. finely chopped apple
½ c. condensed chicken broth
⅓ c. butter, melted
¼ c. chopped onion
½ t. curry powder
¼ t. salt
⅛ t. ground ginger

Pierce squash with sharp knife. Place whole squash on 12-inch round microwave tray. Cook on high for 4 minutes. Cut squash in half lengthwise. Remove seeds and membrane. Place squash, cut side down, on microwave tray. Pour water into tray about ¼ inch deep. Loosely cover with plastic wrap. Cook on high for 9 to 11 minutes or until squash is tender, rotating tray ½ turn after each 3 minutes of cooking if you do not have rotating tray.

For the stuffing, in medium bowl combine remaining ingredients and mix well. Let stand for 5 minutes and mix again. Turn squash cut side up. Spoon about ½ cup stuffing into center of each half. Loosely cover with plastic wrap. Cook on high for 4 to 5 minutes or until stuffing is heated through, rotating tray ½ turn after each 2 minutes of cooking if you do not have a rotating tray. Let stand covered for 5 minutes before serving. Serves 6.

Winter Squash Cake

¾ c. butter
1½ c. sugar
½ c. molasses
3 eggs
1½ c. baked squash pulp
3 c. flour
4 t. baking powder
½ t. salt
¾ t. baking soda
¾ t. cinnamon
¾ t. ginger
¾ t. nutmeg
¾ c. milk
½ c. chopped walnuts or pecans

Cream together butter and sugar until creamy. Add molasses, eggs, and baked squash pulp. Mix until smooth. Sift together dry ingredients. Set aside ½ c. Add dry ingredients alternately with milk to squash mixture. Beat until smooth. Stir together reserved flour and nuts and blend in.

Pour batter into well-greased and floured bundt pan. Bake at 350° for 45 to 50 minutes or until toothpick inserted in center between tube and outside of pan comes out clean. *Do not underbake!* Let cool upright in pan on wire rack for 20 minutes. Invert cake onto serving plate.

If desired, serve with whipped cream flavored with dash of cinnamon. I like to place a narrow glass filled with whipped cream in the hole in the cake's center.

Variation: Applesauce is a good substitute for whipped cream (and lower in calories!).

New England Squash Pie
This is similar to pumpkin pie but lighter in flavor.

pastry for 1 9-inch crust
1 3/4 c. mashed baked squash pulp
1 t. salt
1 1/2 c. milk
3 eggs
1 c. white sugar
1 t. cinnamon
1/2 t. nutmeg
1/2 t. ginger
1 T. butter, melted

Pour into unbaked pastry shell and bake at 425° for 30 minutes or until knife inserted in center comes out clean. Cool on wire rack and served with whipped topping.

Yams (Sweet Potatoes)

While sweet potatoes are smaller, sweeter, and drier than yams, one can use essentially the same cooking methods for both. In fact, I use yams, sweet potatoes, pumpkin, winter squash, even carrots—whatever I have a surplus of—interchangeably in recipes.

Small sweet potatoes are the perfect size serving for children, and I have fond memories of baking them in the wood or corncob-burning cookstove oven at home or atop the pot-bellied heater in South Dakota's rural Sunshine School, District #26. That was the only way we pupils could get a hot school lunch. We would slit the skin and drop in a pat of butter; then we waited impatiently for the potatoes to cool enough so we could devour them.

Yams combine nicely with fruit such as apples, prunes, raisins, pineapple, peaches, or apricots. They are the perfect accompaniment to pork and ham.

Pork Chops with Yams and Apples
This is a favorite fall dish.

6–8 pork chops, depending on size
1–2 T. bacon drippings, if chops are trimmed too lean to provide grease to sauté
1 large onion, sliced
2 lbs. baked or boiled yams, peeled
3 unpeeled cooking apples, quartered and cored
1 t. salt
2 T. brown sugar
1 c. liquid (apple or pineapple juice, drained water from cooking yams, chicken
   stock, or plain water)

In a large cast-iron skillet brown the pork chops in their own fat, if possible. If not, add bacon drippings. Push chops to one side and sauté onion. When onion is golden brown, place some pieces of onion atop each chop. Peel previously baked or boiled yams, slice in half or quarters, depending upon size, and place around the chops. Between the chops stick quartered apples. Sprinkle salt over dish, followed by sprinkling of brown sugar. Pour liquid over contents and cover. Bake in 350° oven for 30 minutes or until chops are tender. Serves 4.

Bacon-Stuffed Sweet Potatoes

6 medium sweet potatoes
$^1/_8$ t. pepper
6 strips bacon, cooked crisp, drained on paper, and crumbled

Bake sweet potatoes in 400° oven for 35–40 minutes until soft. Slit the top of each potato, squeeze sides to push up pulp, and scoop out inside, being careful not to break shells. Mash pulp until fluffy, folding in pepper. Add crumbled bacon and mix well. Spoon into shells. Bake in 400° oven for 15 minutes more, or until lightly browned on top.

Candied Sweet Potatoes

4 to 6 sweet potatoes, depending upon
   size
$^1/_4$ c. butter
$^1/_2$ c. brown sugar

2 T. water
2 T. dark corn syrup
$^1/_4$ t. nutmeg

Boil whole sweet potatoes (or yams) in water to cover for 15 minutes (or steam in covered microwave-safe casserole or steamer for 7 minutes on high). Drain and peel. Cut into chunks. Melt butter in heavy pan. Stir in sugar, syrup, nutmeg, and water.

Add yams, stirring well. Simmer, covered, for 10 minutes, then uncovered for 5 minutes or until tender.

Variation: Omit syrup, water, and nutmeg. Place chunks of cooked sweet potatoes or yams in buttered casserole. Sprinkle ¼ c. brown sugar over potatoes and dot with butter. Cover and place in hot oven. Oven temperature can be regulated to suit any other dishes that are being baked at the same time. Baking time, of course, depends upon oven temperature and the number of other items in the oven, but will be approximately 30 minutes.

Yam Soufflé

4 large yams	*2 T. brown sugar*
5 T. butter	*2 eggs, beaten*
½ t. salt	*2 T. white wine or orange juice*
¼ t. pepper	*½ t. cinnamon*

Bake yams in foil at 450° for about 1 hour or until soft. (Or steam in microwave-safe covered casserole or steamer until soft.) Remove skins. While still warm, mash with 4 T. butter. Add salt, pepper, sugar, eggs, and wine. Beat until fluffy. Pour into large buttered casserole. Sprinkle with cinnamon and dot with remaining tablespoon butter. Bake in 350° oven for 15–30 minutes until heated through, depending upon whether you started with cold or warm baked yams. Serves 6.

Savory Sweet Potato Puff

4 medium sweet potatoes	*1 t. baking powder*
½ c. milk	*½ t. dried leaf marjoram, crumbled*
½ c. butter, melted	*¼ t. dried leaf thyme, crumbled*
4 large eggs	*¼ t. salt*

Cook sweet potatoes in boiling water to cover for 20 minutes, until soft. (Or microwave for 7–10 minutes in covered steamer on high.) Peel when cooled. In a large bowl, mash sweet potatoes until smooth. Beat in milk, butter, eggs, baking powder, and spices until light and fluffy.

Turn into greased 2-quart casserole. Bake at 350° for 45 to 50 minutes until golden brown and a knife inserted in center comes out clean. Serves 6.

Gran Slam Yam Cookies
These cookies are good Halloween treats.

1½ c. all-purpose flour

½ c. packed brown sugar

½ t. baking soda

½ t. salt

½ c. butter

⅓ c. creamy peanut butter

1 c. cooked and mashed yams

¼ c. light corn syrup

½ t. vanilla

6 oz. chocolate chips, melted

Stir together flour, sugar, soda, and salt. Cut in butter and peanut butter with pastry blender. Stir in yams, syrup, and vanilla. Blend well.

Shape mixture into 48 balls, about 1 inch in diameter. Place half the dough balls on ungreased baking sheets. Flour the bottom of a flat-bottomed drinking glass. Flatten each dough ball to a 2½-inch circle. Spread cookie circles with melted chocolate, using about 1 t. per cookie.

Place remaining dough balls on a lightly floured sheet of waxed paper. Flatten each with glass bottom to a 2½-inch circle. Place circles atop chocolate covered circles. Seal edges with tines of fork. Bake at 350° for 18–20 minutes or until light brown. Cool on wire racks and store in covered container in refrigerator.

Sweet Potato Bundt Cake

4 medium sweet potatoes

3 c. flour

2 t. baking soda

½ t. baking powder

1 t. ground cinnamon

½ t. ground allspice

¾ t. salt

1½ c. sugar

1 c. firmly packed brown sugar

1 c. butter, softened

4 large eggs

2 t. grated orange peel

⅔ c. orange juice

1 c. chopped pecans or walnuts

confectioners' sugar

Cook sweet potatoes in boiling water to cover 20 minutes or until soft. (Or steam in microwave casserole on high for 10 minutes or until soft.) Cool, peel, and mash.

Sift together flour, baking soda, baking powder, cinnamon, allspice, and salt. In a large mixing bowl beat sugars, butter, and eggs until light and fluffy. Beat in sweet potatoes and orange peel. Add dry ingredients alternately with orange juice. Stir in chopped nuts.

Pour batter into buttered and floured 12-cup bundt pan. Bake at 350° for 55 to 60 minutes or until cake tester inserted into center of cake comes out clean. *Do not underbake!* Cool upright for 5 minutes on wire rack. Invert onto rack. Cool thoroughly. Sprinkle with confectioners' sugar. Serves 12–16.

Southern Sweet Potato Pie

Follow recipe for New England Squash Pie (above, under Winter Squash), except use sweet potatoes or yams instead of squash.

PART FOUR

Herbs in Pots

Herbs such as basil, chives, dill, oregano, and thyme are easy to grow in pots indoors so long as they get plenty of sun. They can also be started indoors in cold weather and transplanted outdoors when the weather warms.

Use 4-inch clay pots with good drainage holes and fast-drying potting soil. Line pots with clean pebbles or broken old clay pots and fill with soil to within an inch of the top, allowing room for watering.

Sow 8 to 10 seeds in each pot and sprinkle more soil on top. Water and keep warm and moist, setting pots in a protected place. Cover pots with clear plastic sheeting that has holes punched in it for air to circulate.

As herbs begin to sprout, remove plastic and set pots on sunny windowsill. Water only when soil feels dry, perhaps once in 5 to 7 days, depending on humidity of the room. Water carefully with warm but not hot water. As seeds grow, thin by pulling out smaller and weaker seedlings to make room for 2 or 3 of the healthier young plants in each pot.

After a few weeks you may begin to harvest fresh leaves or replant the herbs outdoors. To develop bushy, sturdy plants, pinch out the top growth between your thumb and forefinger.

Marjoram

Marjoram is a perennial and easy to grow. It thrives in a sunny window in well-drained soil. It may be substituted for basil in many recipes, but is more subtle than basil. It is delicious on brown bread sandwiches when its leaves are spread thickly on cream cheese, making it an ideal winter sandwich. It does become more pungent when it is dried.

Shepherd's Pie with Marjoram

1 lb. lean ground beef
1 large onion, diced
1 clove garlic, minced
1 T. marjoram leaves
1 T. flour

1 c. water
salt and pepper to taste
1 lb. potatoes, peeled and mashed
1 T. sesame seeds (optional)
1 T. butter (optional)

Cook ground beef, onion, and garlic in skillet until nicely browned. Add marjoram leaves and cook thoroughly. Sprinkle flour over meat, cook a little longer while stirring and add liquid. Season with salt and pepper. Turn meat mixture into an ovenproof dish and top with mashed potatoes. Spread sesame seeds and butter over top of mashed potatoes, if desired. Bake in 350° oven for 45 minutes. If the top is not browned, put under the broiler for a few minutes before serving. (This is a variation of the popular favorite of the cook at Fairview Presbyterian Church, Katie Brown, who serves it occasionally to the Ben Ezra senior citizens group.)

Marjoram Vinegar

Fill a glass bottle or cruet with marjoram leaves and pour the best wine vinegar over them. Cover with stopper and leave on a sunny windowsill for 2 weeks. Strain and use in tossed green salads.

Oregano

Oregano is very popular in Italian cookery. It is one of the marjorams, but more pungent, so it should be used more sparingly. Like marjoram, it grows well on a sunny windowsill in well-drained soil.

Tomato Salad with Oregano Dressing

4 large firm tomatoes
1 T. oregano, freshly snipped
4 T. olive oil
salt and pepper to taste

Wash, dry, and slice tomatoes. Arrange on platter. Sprinkle with salt, pepper, and fresh oregano. Pour olive oil over all. Chill in refrigerator. Serves 4.

Pizza
This recipe makes enough dough and topping for two 18" pizzas. If you want to make only one pizza, store the other half of the dough in refrigerator or freezer for later use and reduce topping ingredients by half.

1 package active dry yeast
1³/₄ c. warm water (110–115°)
3¹/₂ to 4 c. sifted all-purpose flour (or half white bread flour and half whole wheat flour)
¹/₂ t. salt
¹/₂ T. olive oil (approximately)
1 c. tomato sauce

salt and pepper to taste
2 T. fresh oregano snips
1 large green pepper, cut in strips
1 lb. lean ground beef or 1 lb. bulk pork sausage or ¹/₄ lb. pepperoni slices
1¹/₂ c. shredded mozzarella cheese

Sprinkle yeast on warm water in large mixing bowl. Stir to dissolve. Add 2 c. of the flour and salt. Beat well with electric mixer or rotary egg beater. Stir in remaining flour. Turn onto floured board and knead until smooth and elastic, about 10 minutes. Place in lightly greased bowl, turn dough over to grease top, and cover with waxed paper and cotton dish towel. Let rise in warm place until doubled, about 30 minutes. (In winter you may want to set bowl in kitchen range oven with door open, if you have a pilot light.)

Turn onto board and knead long enough to force out large bubbles. Divide in half. Roll each half to make an 18-inch circle. Stretch each circle to fit an oiled 18-inch round pizza pan. Using pastry brush, brush ½ T. olive oil over surface of dough circle. Spread tomato sauce over dough and season with salt, pepper, and fresh oregano leaf snips. Lay slices of fresh green pepper over tomato sauce (or use the equivalent of frozen pieces of green pepper). Spread meat (browned and drained ground beef or sausage) or pepperoni slices over the green pepper and top with mozzarella cheese. Bake in 450° oven for 20 to 25 minutes. Serve hot with tossed green salad and a glass of Woodbury cabernet.

Rose Geranium

Eat the geraniums? Yes! Rose geraniums, that is. For a "different" winter flavor, try using rose geranium leaves to bake a cake.

Rose geraniums need full southern sun. Use general purpose potting soil and 5 to 6-inch pots, according to the size of the plant. Keep them quite dry during the fall and winter months. Barely water them enough to keep them alive. As spring approaches, increase the water but do not keep them constantly wet. Permit the soil to become fairly dry between waterings.

Rose geraniums do not bloom as spectacularly as the garden geraniums do, but they make attractive, fragrant potted plants. They may reward you with clusters of lavender flowers in May, but do not be disappointed if they do not. Prune them down once a year, preferably in the fall, as they will grow several feet tall if not pruned.

Rose Geranium Cake

Mix an ordinary "butter" cake batter, or mix up a yellow cake from a boxed cake mix. Take a few rose geranium leaves, wash them, dry them with a dish towel or napkin, and lay them in the bottom of the greased cake pans before pouring the batter into the pans. Bake as usual. When you turn out the cake, lift off the leaves and ice as usual.

Rose Geranium Jelly

Make apple jelly as usual. Before pouring it into jelly glasses, place one washed and dried leaf in each glass. Now pour in the jelly and seal as usual.

Rose Geranium–Flavored Tossed Salad

Add finely minced rose geranium leaf to mixed greens (mesclun) in a tossed salad for unusual flavor. It is particularly good with mild-flavored lettuce varieties.

Rose geranium leaves may also be used in sorbets, butters, and as garnishes.

Rosemary

Rosemary grows nicely in a pot on a sunny windowsill in winter. It will grow from seed, but it is quicker and easier to propagate from cuttings, preferably taken in late August or September. It enjoys well-drained soil, as do most herbs.

Rosemary leaves give off a pungent flavor and complement pork and fowl beautifully, but it can easily be overdone. I never make a turkey dressing or stuffing without rosemary (in addition to parsley, sage, and thyme).

Chicken Rosemary

1 3-lb. chicken fryer, cut in parts
1 can (10½ oz.) cream of chicken soup
1 t. rosemary leaves, crumbled

Cut meaty parts from chicken and lay in glass baking dish. (Cover bony parts with water in a kettle and simmer for later use in soup.) Spread undiluted can of cream of chicken soup over all parts of chicken pieces, making sure to cover all. Sprinkle crumbled rosemary leaves over all. Bake at 350° for 1 hour or until dish is nicely browned on top. Serve with potatoes baked in oven at same time and a tossed green salad. Serves 4.

Rosemary Bread

1 loaf crusty French bread
½ t. salt and pepper (mixed)
3 oz. butter
2 T. fresh rosemary, finely chopped

Mix salt, pepper, and rosemary with the butter until smooth. Make diagonal cuts every inch or so along the loaf, cutting ⅔ of the way through the loaf. Spread rosemary butter on each slice until it is all used up. Wrap well in foil and store in refrigerator until needed. When ready to serve it, preheat oven to 400° and heat loaf (wrapped in foil) for 5 to 10 minutes, opening the foil near the end of time to allow moisture to escape and bread to crispen a bit. Serves 6 to 8.

Sage

Sage does not survive most Midwest winters, so if we want to have it year-round, we must grow it indoors. Fresh sage during the winter is a special treat because the gray-green fresh leaves are far more flavorful than the dried leaves are. If you love the smell of turkey roasting with sage dressing made from the dried herb, you will find fresh sage dressing out of this world!

Sage can be grown from seed or from nursery plants. If buying a nursery-started plant, choose compact plants and test the taste of the leaves. The surface should have a light, overall patterning of very little bumps, not coarse raised ones.

Because sage trails somewhat, it is best to plant it in a hanging pot. Hang near a partially sunny window, keep moist, and fertilize regularly. Or you may cut a sage plant growing indoors back to 10 inches. Because of its woody structure, it may be cut into topiary form or shaped into bonsai.

Sage is good for flavoring cheese, dumplings, biscuits, pastry for pot pies, poultry, or as a "rubbing" for all meats before roasting. In the summer you will enjoy sage on yellow squash and tomatoes. Below are two good recipes for winter use.

Roast Dumplings with Fresh Sage

$1^1/2$ T. finely chopped fresh sage

2 large onions

4 c. fresh white bread crumbs

salt and pepper to taste

1 egg

2 T. melted butter

Wash sage leaves, pick them off the stalks, and chop them fine. Peel and finely chop onions and place in bowl with sage, bread crumbs, salt, and pepper. Add lightly beaten egg and melted butter. Mix all ingredients with a fork. With floured hands make about 14 balls. Add dumplings to hot drippings around a beef or lamb roast about 35 minutes before the end of cooking time. Also delightful served with pork roast and sauerkraut.

Sage Focaccia

4 to $4^1/2$ c. flour

1 t. sugar

$1^1/2$ t. salt

1 package active dry yeast

2 T. olive oil

2 T. fresh chopped sage

1 $^3/4$ c. lukewarm water

1 medium yellow onion

Reserve 1 c. of the flour. Mix together flour, sugar, salt, yeast, and one T. of the olive oil. Make a well in the center and add the water, mixing until well combined, adding enough reserved flour to form a soft and slightly sticky dough.

Transfer dough to lightly oiled bowl, turning to coat with oil. Let rise until double in bulk, about 1 hour.

Slice half the onion into thin slices and set aside. Finely chop the other half and knead it into the dough along with half the sage. Press the dough into a well-oiled jelly roll pan or cookie sheet with rims (about 15 x 10 inches).

Let rise until barely puffy, about half an hour. Meanwhile, sauté the remaining sliced onion and sage in the remaining olive oil. Spread evenly over top of focaccia. Bake in preheated 375° oven for 40–45 minutes or until golden brown.

Transfer to wire rack and let cool for 10 minutes. Serve warm with cheese, olives, and red wine.

Tarragon

Tarragon grows in light, well-drained soil in a pot on a warm and sunny windowsill. It is best to start tarragon from a cutting or root division. It complements poultry nicely and adds a uniquely different flavor to stuffing or dressing.

Chicken Livers with Tarragon

1/2 lb. chicken livers
2 T. butter
1/2 clove garlic, finely minced
1 t. chopped fresh tarragon

1 t. white flour
1/2 c. red or white wine
salt and pepper to taste

Wash chicken livers, cut in half, and simmer gently in butter with garlic until they turn color. Do not overcook! Add tarragon and flour. Season with salt and pepper. Turn livers until flour browns. Gradually add wine, stirring until gravy is smooth and thickened. Serve over boiled rice. Serves 2.

Tarragon Vinegar

Place a few sprigs of tarragon in a glass bottle or cruet. Pour wine vinegar over, cover with stopper and infuse for 2 weeks. Makes a very handsome gift. The tarragon need not be removed from the bottle. Tie with a bow and present!

Thyme

Thyme is easy to grow. It can be propagated by root division or by placing cuttings in sand in late winter. The plants will flourish in light, well-drained soil in a warm and sunny location.

Thyme is often used to flavor meat loaf or meatballs, soups, poultry stuffings or dressings, and some root vegetables such as onions, beets, and parsnips.

Turkey Stuffing

1 stick butter
1 large onion
3 large celery ribs with leaves attached
1 c. parsley sprigs
1 T. fresh thyme

1 t. crumbled sage
1/2 t. crumbled rosemary
8 cups cubed, dried and oven-toasted
*   leftover bread, including corn bread*
salt and pepper to taste

Melt butter in bottom of large saucepan. Add onion and celery, chopped. Sauté until lightly browned. Chop parsley sprigs and add. Mix together remaining herbs, seasonings, and bread. Combine all in large saucepan. With large spoon stuff cavities of turkey that has been thoroughly washed and salted. Secure stuffing with string or skewers. (This amount will stuff a 15-lb. turkey.) Roast at 325° for approximately 3 hours in covered roaster or until pink juices no longer run when bird is pierced. Remove the cover in final minutes of baking to brown the skin.

Beets with Thyme

4 to 6 medium beets
¹/₄ c. water
1 T. butter
¹/₂ t. salt
1 t. fresh thyme leaves

Wash beets thoroughly and retain tap root and 1 inch of tops, if possible, so beets do not bleed while cooking. Place in microwave-safe casserole, add water, and cook on high for 10 minutes or until tender. Plunge into cold water before handling beets. When cooled enough to handle, slip skins from beets and cut off tap root and remainder of top. Slice or dice, add salt and butter. Reheat in microwave briefly, if desired. Sprinkle with fresh thyme leaves. Serves 4.

Herb Butter

¹/₂ c. salted butter
¹/₄ c. unsalted butter
¹/₈ t. cayenne pepper
¹/₂ t. kosher salt

2 T. chopped parsley
1 t. thyme leaves
1 t. chopped chives

In a small saucepan over heat, melt butter. Add cayenne and salt. Just before serving, add parsley, thyme, and chives to butter mixture and stir to mix. Brush on hot ears of corn. This makes enough for 12 ears of corn. (From Ellen Walsh.)

Herb Vinegar

herbs of choice
sterilized jars
2 c. quality red, white, or wine vinegar

Pick herbs in the morning after dew has dried. Wash and gently dry. Strip leaves from stem. Pack herbs into a sterilized jar. Use a spoon to bruise leaves. Pour vinegar over herbs to cover completely. Seal jar. Place jar at room temperature in a dark place to steep for a week or longer. Shake every 2 to 3 days. Leave longer for a more intense flavor. Strain vinegar through a coffee filter. Add more sprigs of herbs to a sterilized decorative bottle. Pour strained vinegar over fresh herbs. Seal tightly. (From Ellen Walsh.)

Indoor Winter Harvests

Although the snow may be falling outdoors, it is still possible for the avid gardener to be planting and harvesting indoors. There are many varieties of vegetables especially suited to growing indoors in containers.

Tomatoes are a case in point. Small Fry, Tiny Tim, Hybrid Patio, and Spartan Red are all varieties of tomatoes suited to window or home greenhouse cultivation. In order to substitute for bees and breeze, just give the plants a gentle shake each day to distribute pollen. And beware of temperature falling below 55 degrees.

When it comes to growing green peppers indoors, the small Italian sweet pepper plants produce an abundance of 5- to 6-inch peppers. Peppers do nicely as houseplants in a sunny window if they are pruned to keep them compact.

Leaf lettuce also makes an attractive potted plant 6 to 10 inches tall, and it needs no transplanting. Lettuce produces almost instant crops. Thinnings may be eaten in 3 weeks. Successive plantings at 10-day intervals will keep you supplied. Remember that Bibb lettuce and romaine are more manageable than Black Seeded Simpson, which grows fast but bolts.

Cucumbers may be sown indoors in peat pots very early in spring or late winter and transplanted to permanent containers outdoors after all danger of frost has passed. Or they may be sown indoors directly into permanent containers, allowing at least a gallon-capacity container for each plant. The Pot Luck variety of cucumbers has been bred especially for container growing. It is extremely compact. Its stems are no longer than 18 inches, yet the plant produces 6- to 7-inch dark green cucumbers for use fresh. The Peppi variety of cucumbers is a good pickler and grows on a slightly larger vine. Patio Pik vines bear cucumbers that may be pickled when small or sliced for use fresh when they are larger.

Kale

When the ground is frozen hard in winter, you can still harvest kale, especially if it is planted along a fence near the house and easily accessible though protected under a blanket or mulch of straw, hay, or leaves. It is important not to smother the crowns of the plant with mulch. Just tuck the mulch closely around the stem and toss it lightly over the crown in severe climates, and brush snow away when you want to snap off a few leaves for dinner. In a mild-winter climate such as Indiana usually has, you can harvest kale most of the winter and almost every winter.

Kale Hodgepodge

This is a hearty peasant dish from Holland. A Prussian version of the dish uses oatmeal and bits of ham or bacon as substitutes for the potatoes and wieners.

3 lbs. kale
2 lbs. potatoes, peeled
1 c. chicken or beef stock
¹/₂ lb. wieners
salt and red pepper flakes to taste

Strip curly kale leaves from stems. Throw stems on the compost pile. Wash leaves thoroughly. Cook in boiling, salted water to cover for 25 minutes or until tender. (Or steam in microwave covered casserole for 10 minutes on high.) Drain and chop coarsely.

Boil potatoes and drain. In saucepan put chicken or beef stock, cooked kale, wieners, and cooked potatoes. Simmer for 15 minutes, uncovered, until stock has almost evaporated. Serve on hot platter. Season with salt and red pepper flakes.

Scalloped Kale

3 c. cooked curly kale leaves (stripped from tough stems)
3 hard-cooked eggs, chopped
1 c. medium white sauce
1 c. grated Cheddar cheese

Combine kale with eggs and white sauce. Arrange in alternate layers with cheese and bake in 400° oven for 15 minutes. Serves 6.

Kale with Ham

2 lbs. kale
1 lb. cooked boneless ham, sliced ¹/₂-inch thick
1 t. yellow mustard seed, cracked in grinder or with mortar and pestle
1 t. dried summer savory
1 qt. water
salt and pepper to taste

Strip curly leaves from kale stems. Throw stems on compost pile. Tear leaves into pieces. Cut ham into ¹/₂-inch cubes, leaving fat on. If there is no fat on the ham, add enough butter or oil to fry the ham cubes. Fry ham until it is golden. Stir in cracked mustard seed and summer savory. Add water and kale. Bring to a boil. Reduce heat and simmer, covered, until tender. Drain. Stir in salt and pepper to taste. Serves 4 if accompanied by mashed potatoes, corn bread, or hominy grits.

Kale is also very useful as a garnish, especially on large trays of food at receptions where the appearance of freshness for long periods of time is important. The leaves seem almost indestructible and will withstand a lot of abuse! If you need a few leaves of kale for garnish after snow has fallen, just brush the snow away and snap off the leaves. They are so hardy they will not show frost damage.

Panned Kale with India Relish

1½ lbs. kale
½ t. salt
¼ t. pepper
1 T. butter
2 T. India relish or chopped sweet cucumber pickle

Wash kale well. Strip leaves from stem. Throw stems on the compost pile. Chop leaves coarsely and cook with small amount of water about 15 minutes or until tender. Drain and season with salt, pepper, and butter. Garnish with India relish or cucumber pickle. Serves 4.

Kale and Black-Eyed Peas

1 c. minced fresh kale
2 c. cooked black-eyed peas (cowpeas)
1 carrot, minced
¼ c. minced leeks
juice and pulp of ½ lemon
1 t. red wine vinegar
½ t. dried basil
½ t. dried sage
2 t. olive oil
pinch dry mustard

Place vegetables in large bowl. In small bowl, whisk other ingredients. Pour over the vegetables and toss. Serves 4.

Kale, Barley, and Mushrooms

1 medium onion, chopped
1 clove garlic, minced
2 T. chives, minced
1 T. olive oil
1 c. shredded cooked kale

2 c. cooked barley (½ c. raw)
½ t. dried thyme
2 T. mild white vinegar
2 large mushrooms, chopped, or 2 T. canned mushrooms

Combine onion, garlic, and chives. Sauté lightly in oil. Add kale, barley, thyme, vinegar, and mushrooms. (If using fresh mushrooms, sauté them with onion and garlic.) Serves 4.

Kale Soup

¹/₂ lb. fresh kale
4 c. chicken broth
pinch salt
¹/₄ t. black pepper
3 medium potatoes, peeled and sliced
1 t. oil
1 clove garlic, minced
4 slices lemon

Wash kale and discard discolored leaves. Remove leaves from tough stems and discard stems on compost pile. Shred leaves as fine as possible. In saucepan, combine chicken broth, salt, pepper, and potatoes and cook until potatoes are tender. Remove and mash potatoes. Return to broth, add oil and garlic, and bring to a rolling boil. Add shredded kale and boil, uncovered, for 5 minutes. Serve with lemon slices. Serves 4.

Leeks

Leeks, related to onions, are considered the "poor man's asparagus" in France. They may be harvested from under a snow cover, making them a richly aromatic winter vegetable. (Since the average leeks mature at 110 to 130 days, you may see snow before they are ready to harvest.)

Although giant leeks are available on the market and are great for soups and stocks, the tender, sweet baby leeks are a luxury usually available only to home gardeners.

If your leeks are growing too slowly, feed them with fish emulsion or liquid kelp. If you have a short growing season, start them indoors 4 to 6 weeks before the frost-free date. Leeks may be mulched with compost when they are the size of pencils.

To clean leeks, remove the roots and most of the green tops; then make a slice vertically from the top almost through the bottom, avoiding a cut through the bottom to prevent the leeks from falling apart. Hold the leek open and swish it up and down in a pan of water to flush out all possible grit.

Microwave Leek Soup

1¹/₂ T. butter

1 clove garlic, minced

1 lb. leeks, cut into ¹/₂-inch pieces

2 c. chicken broth

¹/₄ t. salt

pepper

1 c. plain yogurt

Combine butter and garlic in covered microwave-safe casserole and microwave on high for 2 minutes. Stir leeks into casserole and microwave on high 5–7 minutes. Purée mixture in blender. Return purée to casserole. Stir in broth and seasonings. Cover and microwave on high for 8 minutes. Stir in yogurt. Serve soup hot but not boiling, garnished with crisp seasoned croutons, if desired. Serves 4.

Vichyssoise
A quicker, low-calorie version of this soup
can be found in Part III, Autumn.

3 medium leeks, sliced

1 medium onion, sliced

2 T. butter

4 medium potatoes, peeled and sliced

4 c. chicken broth

2 c. half and half

¹/₂ t. salt

¹/₈ t. white pepper

chopped watercress or chives for
    garnish

Sauté leeks and onion in butter until golden. Add sliced potatoes and chicken broth. Simmer until potatoes are tender. Purée in blender and stir in half and half, salt, and pepper. Serve hot or chilled (over ice cubes) and garnish with cress or chives. Serves 4 to 6.

Leeks and Other Winter Vegetables, Oven Roasted

4 T. olive oil

4 small leeks

6 small red potatoes

4 large carrots, quartered

2 medium onions, peeled and quartered

2 red bell peppers, cored, seeded, and
    cut in 8 pieces

¹/₂ t. thyme

¹/₄ t. salt

¹/₄ t. pepper

Preheat oven to 400°. Coat oblong baking dish with 2 T. olive oil. Cut leeks in half and wash thoroughly to remove grit. Scrub potatoes and carrots to clean.

Arrange all vegetables in baking dish and drizzle with remaining oil. Sprinkle with thyme, salt, and pepper.

Roast 1 hour or until vegetables are tender to fork. Baste with pan juices occasionally. Serve hot. Serves 6.

Maple Syrup

Maple sap on average contains about 2$\frac{1}{2}$% sugar, so it takes about 35 gallons of sap to produce a gallon of syrup. That gives one an idea of how precious a gift a quart of maple syrup is. Our son Jonathan, who lives with his family on a small farm near Bangor, Michigan, and taps his own trees, has blessed us many times with such a gift.

The best time for collecting sap is from January to spring when there is a wide variety of temperatures, from sunny days to frigid nights. This fluctuation is what makes the sap "run." A column in the *Indianapolis Star* by Sally Falk Nancrede on February 17, 1995, indicated that mid-February is the peak season in Indiana, with "maple syrup boils" being held "from Terre Haute to Conner Prairie, Evansville to Merrillville. . . . The weather has to freeze and thaw for sap to flow; nights have to dip down to about 28 degrees and days have to get up to 40 degrees." The column listed nine sites for festivals featuring both old and new techniques for "maple sugarin'."

Because maple syrup is so precious I use it primarily as flavoring. If you have maple trees to tap you may use it more generously.

Mapple Slices

4 *large cooking apples*
2 *T. butter*
3 *T. maple syrup*
1 *T. water*
1 *t. lemon juice*
$\frac{1}{4}$ *t. cinnamon*

Peel and core apples. Cut into $\frac{1}{4}$-inch slices. In a cast-iron skillet heat butter over moderate heat and cook apples, turning them until they are tender and golden. Stir in other ingredients and cook until apples are thoroughly glazed. Serve with ice cream. Serves 6.

Baked Maple Apples in Slow Cooker

Wash cooking apples, core, and remove peeling at top and bottom of apple. Stuff core with raisins. Stand apples upright in one layer in slow cooker (Crock-Pot). Pour maple syrup into cavity over raisins. Plug in and cook until tender, following instructions on your appliance.

Mapled Yams or Sweet Potatoes

This recipe works equally well with carrots, squash, or pumpkin pieces.

1 lb. yams or sweet potatoes
$^1/_4$ c. maple syrup
2 T. butter

Boil in water the yams or sweet potatoes until tender. Drain and cool before peeling. Slice into a casserole. Pour maple syrup over all and dot with butter. Bake uncovered at 350° until heated through and top is nicely glazed. Baste with the syrup occasionally while they are baking. Serves 2–3.

Parsnips

When my elder sister, Pearl, left home in the autumn of 1942 to teach seventh- and eighth-graders in Irene, South Dakota, for the exorbitant salary of $100 a month, she took with her a gunnysack of parsnips from our garden to sell to the town's café. Daddy, Ruth, and I were scandalized! But we shouldn't have been, because those of us who were left behind did not know how to prepare the parsnips anyway. However, the café in Irene where Pearl took her meals had a cook who was well acquainted with parsnips and shared her recipes with Pearl, some of which are included here.

Johnny's Selected Seeds in Albion, Maine (see Resources for address), offers a new variety called Cobham Improved Marrow, from England's leading parsnip breeder. It has the highest sugar content in their tests and is selected for resistance to canker. The firm reports that the sweet flavor of parsnips is brought on by freezing. "A portion of the crop may be dug after heavy frosts in late fall for winter use and the balance left in the garden for use as soon as the roots can be dug in spring. Preserve your spring dug parsnips by freezing."

Another way to store parsnips if you do not have an old-fashioned root cellar is to pack them in sphagnum moss. Layer the damp moss in the bottom of a plastic plant flat left over from spring planting, add the parsnips, and cover them with another layer of damp moss. Enclose the flat in a large plastic bag and store it in a cool location, such as an unheated garage.

When preparing this whitish, carrot-like vegetable, it is important to scrape (but not peel) and cook by boiling or microwaving whole, using just enough water to cover the parsnips. (Use less water if microwaving.) Cover the pot and cook just until they are tender. They may be served with butter or cream sauce, mashed, as patties, sautéed in fat until lightly brown, French fried, or even shredded in salad.

Autumn Vegetable Soup

2 T. butter
$^1/_2$ c. onion, chopped
1 clove garlic, minced
4 stalks celery or chard, including
    leaves, chopped
3 medium parsnips, scraped and finely
    chopped
2 carrots, chopped

$^1/_2$ c. parsley stems and leaves, chopped
2 c. chicken broth, defatted
2 c. milk
salt and pepper to taste
1$^1/_2$ t. dried tarragon, crushed
dash nutmeg
plain yogurt (optional)
fresh tarragon sprigs (optional)

Melt butter in heavy saucepan over low heat. Add vegetables and cook, covered, until soft, stirring occasionally and adding water if necessary. Slowly add broth and milk, stirring frequently until mixture comes to boil. Reduce heat to low and simmer, stirring constantly, until thickened. Add seasonings and mix well. Remove from heat and serve in bowls. Garnish with dollop of plain yogurt and fresh tarragon sprig, if available. Serves 8.

Sautéd Parsnips

6 medium parsnips, scraped
1 t. salt
2 T. butter

Cook scraped parsnips in salted water until tender but not soft. Drain and cool. Slice lengthwise and sauté in butter. Serves 4 to 6.

Baked Parsnips

6 medium parsnips, scraped
$^1/_4$ c. water
1 t. salt
2 T. butter

Parboil the scraped parsnips for 7 minutes in microwave-safe casserole or steamer to which salted water has been added. Drain and allow parsnips to cool before handling. Cut in quarters lengthwise and arrange in greased casserole dish. Dot parsnips with butter. Bake at 375°, uncovered, until parsnips are lightly browned. Serves 4–6.

Fried Parsnips

6 medium parsnips, scraped

1/4 c. water

1 t. salt

2 eggs

2 T. milk

1 c. flour and/or cracker crumbs

4 T. butter

Parboil scraped parsnips in salted water in microwave-safe casserole or steamer for 7 minutes until tender but not soft. Drain and cool. Slice lengthwise and dip in egg and milk mixture, then dredge in flour or cracker crumbs. Fry in hot butter. Serves 4–6.

Puréed Parsnips

*This is a Scandinavian stand-by that is good
with beef or baked ham.*

7 medium parsnips, peeled and trimmed

1 t. salt

1/4 t. mace (or nutmeg, if you can't find mace)

1/2 t. butter

Place parsnips and salt in saucepan, cover with water, and cook until tender, about 20 minutes. Drain water, saving it for later use in soup, and purée parsnips, a few at a time, in electric blender until smooth. If the purée is too thick, add some of the reserved cooking water. Add mace and butter. Serves 4.

Parsnip Fritters

1 lb. parsnips, scraped

1 egg, lightly beaten

2 T. flour

2 T. softened butter

1 t. grated onion

salt and pepper to taste

beaten egg

fresh bread crumbs

Cook parsnips in boiling salted water or microwave until tender. Drain, purée in a blender, and pour into a bowl. Add egg, flour, butter, onion, and seasonings.

Divide mixture into 12 portions, roll them in flour, and form into cylindrical shapes. Dip each cylinder in beaten egg and roll in fresh bread crumbs.

Fry them in deep fat fryer or in skillet containing an inch of hot oil (360°), turning once, until golden in color. Lift from oil with slotted spoon and drain on brown paper bags turned inside out. Serve in heated dish.

Variation: Instead of making fritters, turn the parsnip mixture into parsnip pancakes. (Omit dipping in beaten egg and bread crumbs.) Fry tablespoonsful of the mixture in a small amount of oil on a hot griddle as you would potato pancakes. Serve with meat, as a substitute for potatoes.

Roasted Parsnips

Parsnips, like most large root vegetables, respond nicely to roasting. Added to a pot roast, they pick up some of the meat flavor. Cooking them with the pan covered will ensure they are tender. Then remove the cover, stir them to combine juices, and continue roasting uncovered. They will glaze beautifully.

But meat is not essential to roasting. Parsnips may be roasted with other vegetables such as carrots, potatoes, yams, onions, and turnips. Or they may be roasted alone.

4 medium parsnips, peeled, stem end trimmed, and cut in half lengthwise
1 clove garlic, minced
1 T. olive oil
salt and pepper to taste
herbs such as parsley, thyme, or marjoram, if desired

Heat oven to 400°. Toss parsnips, garlic, and olive oil in bowl. Season with salt, pepper, and herbs. Place in covered baking dish. Bake in oven for about 20 minutes, removing cover and basting parsnips with juices occasionally. Water may be added if necessary. When tender, remove cover and bake until browned, no more than 20 minutes more.

Garlicky Roasted Mixed Winter Root Vegetables
This dish may include parsnips, potatoes, beets, turnips, onions, sweet potatoes, carrots, etc.

1 whole head garlic
2 lbs. mixed vegetables (including parsnips)

2 T. olive oil
salt and pepper to taste

Preheat oven to 400°. Break garlic head or bulb into cloves. Set aside. Peel root vegetables and cut into chunks. Put chunks into low-sided roasting pan large enough to hold them without crowding. Toss with oil. Sprinkle with salt. Roast, uncovered, shaking vegetables every 15 minutes, until tender and evenly browned, about 45 minutes. Add unpeeled garlic cloves during last 20 minutes of baking. Sprinkle with pepper when done. Remove garlic cloves before serving to protect persons who may be interacting with the public within the next few days. Serve hot. Serves 4.

Rutabagas

Rutabagas are sometimes called swedes or Swedish turnips, but they are much larger than turnips and yellow instead of white. Rutabagas have a lot in common with carrots, yams, squash, pumpkins, and sweet potatoes; consequently they will respond to the same treatment as those other yellow vegetables. They may also be combined nicely with potatoes, onions, and leeks. Be sure to remember them when roasting other winter root vegetables.

Microwaved Rutabaga and Carrot Purée

1 large rutabaga
6 medium carrots
¹/₄ c. water
1 T. butter
salt and pepper to taste

Peel rutabaga and scrub carrots clean. Cut into chunks and place in microwave-safe covered casserole. Add water and microwave on high for 7 to 10 minutes, depending on size of vegetables. Purée in blender. Season with salt and pepper, if desired. Serve in warmed bowl with butter swirled into the puréed vegetables. Serves 6.

Variation: Substitute potatoes, onions, and leeks for the carrots.

French-Fried Rutabagas

¹/₂ medium rutabaga
1 t. sugar
¹/₂ c. cornmeal
1 t. salt
1 egg, slightly beaten
vegetable oil for deep frying

Peel rutabaga and slice lengthwise into ¹/₄-inch strips. Parboil 5 minutes in small amount of boiling water with the sugar. Drain well and cool.

Combine cornmeal and salt on waxed paper. Dip strips of rutabaga in egg, then roll in seasoned cornmeal. Fry without crowding in deep fat heated to 370° until lightly browned.

Remove strips from fat with kitchen tongs and place on baking sheet lined with paper towels. Keep warm while frying remaining strips, or warm in 350° oven.

Note: Leftover rutabaga sticks freeze well. To reheat, spread in shallow pan and heat in preheated 350° oven until warmed through.

Piquant Rutabaga

3 c. diced peeled rutabaga (about 1 lb.)
2 T. butter
1 T. brown sugar
2 T. soy sauce
1 T. lemon juice
1 t. Worcestershire sauce

Cook rutabaga in small amount of boiling water for 20 minutes or until tender. Drain. Melt butter, add remaining ingredients, and heat gently. Pour over cooked rutabaga and mix gently. Serves 4.

Soybeans

In February of 1995 the Indiana Farmers Union got a $385,000 loan to support a project involving on-farm processing of soybeans, one of the major farm crops in Indiana, Illinois, and other Lower Midwest states. A soybean press will be set up on the farm of Robert G. Leader near Brookston, which is close to Purdue University. It will produce oil and other soybean products.

This news reminded me of our Chicago days during the mid–1970s when the price of meat skyrocketed and I searched for ways to provide more economical high-protein dishes for our family. The Hyde Park Co-op, where we bought our groceries, helped by printing soybean recipes to try, some of which we found satisfactory if not delicious.

If you do not grow your own, you will find that soybeans are available from many farmers in the Lower Midwest. You may even want to pay a visit to the farm during harvest time in late fall and get some beans directly from the farmer's combine or wagon. Just be careful to sort them carefully to remove foreign matter such as stones or dirt. Rinse in several baths of water.

Basic Preparation of Soybeans

Rinse beans, put in saucepan, and add 3 c. water for each cup of beans. Let stand for 6 to 8 hours or overnight. Add more water, if necessary, to cover beans. For each cup of raw beans (measured before soaking), add 1 T. vegetable oil, 1 small onion, chopped, 1/4 c. diced celery (leaves and all), 1 bay leaf, and 2 whole black pepper-corns. Bring to boil, lower heat, and simmer for 3 hours or until tender. (A slow cooker or Crock-Pot is very useful here, but you must allow extra time for the beans to cook.) Add 1 t. salt after beans are tender. Serve over rice for a delicious high-protein meal.

Variations: Add tomatoes, green peppers, carrots, garlic, etc., and any spices such as cumin or chili which you enjoy in other bean dishes.

To Make Soybean Paste

Soybean paste may be substituted for garbanzos or chickpeas when making hummus. Soak beans and cook as directed above. Drain well. Force through sieve or colander. (1 c. cooked soybeans yields about 2/3 c. paste.)

Soy Burgers

2 c. cooked soybeans
1 chopped onion
1 T. dried parsley
1 egg
2 T. milk
$^1/_4$ t. pepper

salt to taste
flour for dipping
2 T. bacon drippings or vegetable oil for
    frying
barbecue sauce or ketchup

Mash beans. Add onion, parsley, egg, milk, and seasonings. Shape into patties. Dip patties into flour and chill for 1 hour. Brown patties in fat or oil. Serve with barbecue sauce or ketchup. Serves 6.

Soy Snacks

Roast cooked soybeans (drained) in oven for 30 minutes at 350°, or until brown. Sprinkle with desired seasonings (such as Mrs. Dash, lemon butter, etc.) while warm.

Tofu

During our sabbatical in California in the early 1980s we learned to enjoy tofu in a variety of ways. Tofu is soybean curd, just as cheese is milk curd. You may not eat it often enough to justify making it yourself, but you should know that it is possible to do so and to get the health benefits (reputed to be the reduction of menopausal symptoms, lower cancer risk, etc.) by including it in your menus regularly. An Indiana company, Kyoto Food Corp. of Terre Haute, is tapping into the market for this new (or old) health food.

Starting Seedlings for Spring Planting

At least six to eight weeks before the average last frost date (around mid-May for central Indiana), it is high time to plant seeds indoors for plants to be transplanted later in the garden. But my friend Ed Becker gets the itch in early February.

Vegetables to be started indoors are those which require a longer-than-usual growing period in which to bear fruit. Among them are tomatoes, peppers, broccoli, cabbage, eggplant, and parsley.

Of course, a greenhouse is the ideal place for sowing seeds indoors, but if you do not have access to one, you can grow seedlings in front of a few sunny windows, below windows if you have a skylight, or under grow-lights in the basement, which is what Ed Becker does.

Plants may be started in nursery flats, small clay or plastic pots, or old coffee cans with holes punched in the bottom for drainage. But peat pots or Jiffy cubes, which can be planted directly in the garden without disturbing roots, are best.

Covering the newly seeded containers with glass, plastic, or newspaper for a few days will hasten the germination process. When sprouting is noticed, remove the covering and give the seedlings full sunlight. A good temperature range for germination of most seeds is 65 to 75°.

If the growing seedlings become crowded in flats or pots, thin them or transplant some into larger pots so all will have more space for proper root development. Water the seedlings often enough to keep soil moist but not water-saturated. Turn containers every other day or so to allow full light to reach all parts of the plant. Naturally, the plant will grow in the direction of the light source.

Before planting outdoors, seedlings should be hardened off in a protected area of a cool porch for a few days.

Sprouts (Alfalfa, Bean, Wheat)

One type of growing which you can continue to pursue during the winter despite frigid temperatures outside is sprouting, an activity which has grown more popular in recent years as many persons have become more health- and diet-conscious.

Classics for sprouting are mung beans, garbanzo beans, lentils, wheat berries, and alfalfa seeds. But people who are really "into" sprouting also use fenugreek, watercress, sunflower, radish or mustard seeds, and other whole grains and beans.

Be sure that the seeds you sprout are meant for food and have not been treated for planting! A health food store is usually a good source of seeds for sprouting.

Sprouts are most nutritious when eaten within a couple of days, so check them regularly. Depending upon what you sprout, the crop may be ready by the second or third day. Sunflower seeds are sweetest when the sprouts are only $1/3$ of the length of the seed. Sprouts from mung beans, lentils, and most other beans can be eaten the third day. Alfalfa sprouts take about five days.

Follow these general procedures for all sprouts: Sort through seeds to remove any possible stones or other debris. Soak about $1/3$ c. of your selection in a wide-mouth quart or larger jar of cool to tepid water overnight. (If you want to grow mung bean sprouts long or to grow alfalfa sprouts, use a jar larger than quart size.)

The next day, rinse the seeds in cool water and drain them thoroughly. An easy method of rinsing and draining is to fasten a piece of cheesecloth or nylon netting over the mouth of the jar with a thick rubber band. Water will go in and out, but the seeds will stay behind. Alfalfa seeds will require very fine netting, obviously. Keep the jar in a dark place on its side and slightly elevated so excess moisture can drain out. Place a damp towel over the mouth of the jar; seeds want air but they do not want to dry out.

Rinse sprouts 2 times a day, morning and evening, during the winter. (If you are sprouting during the summer, rinse 3 times a day.) Remember that sprout-soaking water is rich in vitamins. Use it to water your houseplants.

Alfalfa Sprouts

Nutritionally, alfalfa sprouts are equivalent to lettuce. They contain large amounts of vitamin C and are easily digested. So, if you grow tired of the limp lettuce offerings during the winter for your sandwiches and salads, try alfalfa sprouts. My husband, during a sabbatical in Berkeley, was forbidden by library rules to bring his lunch into the library, so he ate a sandwich at a local eatery each noon. One of his favorites was avocado and tomato slices topped with alfalfa sprouts on rye bread.

Follow the directions given above for other sprouts during the first 3 days. Then, on the third day, pour the sprouts into a 3-quart (or bigger) bowl and flood with water. If the sprouts have clumped, separate them gently. Pour the sprouts and water into another bowl, leaving the unsprouted seeds behind at the bottom of the first bowl. Strain and drain well, letting them grow as before. Keep the bowl covered with a small towel or with plastic.

Continue to rinse the sprouts a couple of times a day and keep them in a dark, cool place until each has 2 tiny leaves. Now, when you flood them with water, you can swish them gently to wash off the brown seed casings. This last step is not required, but it does produce more elegant sprouts.

Drain the sprouts for the last time and spread them out on a glass or plastic dish (a 9 x 13-inch baking dish is fine). Cover with clear plastic or waxed paper and set them in a cool, lighted place. (Don't let them get too warm, or they will rot.) In a few hours they will be bright green and ready to eat. Store in the refrigerator, closely covered.

Alfalfa sprouts are delicate and pretty, but don't let your enthusiasm for the sprouts overtake you. Alfalfa contains small amounts of natural toxins called saponins. According to the Marion County [Indiana] Cooperative Extension Service, such natural toxins do no harm if the food is not eaten in large quantities.

Alfalfa sprouts may be found on almost every salad bar these days, and for good reason. They also make a fun growing project for children. My granddaughters enjoyed watching the "hair" sprouting from decorated eggshells which they had painted with faces. Simply moisten cotton balls stuffed into eggshell halves propped in an egg carton, sprinkle with alfalfa seeds, and watch them sprout "hair."

Delightful Sprout Salad

1 c. alfalfa sprouts
1 large or 2 small heads Boston lettuce
$^1/_2$ c. raw apple, chopped
$^1/_4$ c. feta cheese, crumbled
8 cherry tomatoes, halved
3 T. chopped parsley
$^1/_2$ c. whole black olives, pitted
4 very thin slices Vidalia onion

Tear lettuce into bite-size pieces. Toss all ingredients together and dress with oil and vinegar. Serve with hot French bread. Makes a good main course for lunch.

Favorite Sprout Sandwich

¹/₂ to 1 c. alfalfa sprouts
2 slices whole-grain bread or pita bread
¹/₂ ripe avocado
2 thick slices tomato
2 T. mayonnaise
2 squeezes lemon juice

Cut avocado in half. Smear one section with lemon juice, leaving pit in. Cover tightly with plastic wrap and store in refrigerator for tomorrow's sandwich. Remove flesh from remaining avocado half. Add mayonnaise and lemon juice and mash. Spread on bread and add tomatoes and sprouts.

Bean Sprouts

No longer do you need to buy your bean sprouts in a can, the contents being half water. Nor do you need to buy brown, wilted or dry sprouts from the Oriental foods section of your supermart. You can now grow your own with dried mung beans or soybeans.

Soybeans require special attention because the sprouts mold easily. Remove the non-sprouting beans as soon as they are obvious. Rinse the sprouting beans at least 3 times daily, and disentangle them when you do. Do not expect a long tail to develop. Sprouted soybeans are ready to eat after 3 days.

Mung beans will produce longer tails, but they need complete darkness while they sprout. Also, they need a larger jar in which to sprout so that they will not crowd one another. Seed casings will float off if you swish sprouts gently in a basin of water during the last rinsings.

Soybean sprouts must be cooked at least 5 minutes to destroy harmful enzymes. Other bean sprouts do not require cooking, but they will be more flavorful if you dip them for 5 seconds or so in very hot water just before adding them to salad or sandwich. Rinse quickly in cold water, pat dry, and serve.

Oriental Bean Sprout Salad

4 c. crisp greens, including spinach
1 c. bean sprouts
¹/₄ c. toasted slivered almonds
¹/₂ c. thinly sliced water chestnuts
Oriental Dressing (recipe follows)

Place first 4 ingredients in salad bowl. Just before serving, toss with Oriental Dressing.

Oriental Dressing

$^1/_2$ c. finely chopped green onions

$^1/_8$ t. dried coriander, ground, or $^1/_2$ t.
  fresh cilantro

$^1/_4$ c. chopped fresh parsley

2 T. minced fresh ginger root

1 T. soy sauce

1 c. sour cream

2 T. mayonnaise

2 T. cream (optional)

Combine all ingredients and mix well. Serves 6.

Chinese Apple Salad

1 large tart apple, cut in chunks

1 c. sliced mushrooms

1 c. bean sprouts

$^1/_2$ c. celery, sliced diagonally

$^1/_4$ c. green pepper, thinly sliced

Chop Suey Dressing (recipe follows)

Combine apples, mushrooms, bean sprouts, celery, and green pepper. Toss with dressing. Diced cooked pork, chicken, or shrimp may be added. Serves 8.

Chop Suey Dressing

3 T. oil

2 T. cider vinegar

1 T. soy sauce

$^1/_4$ t. salt

$^1/_4$ t. pepper

Combine all ingredients and mix well.

Bean Sprouts and Sauerkraut Salad

$1^1/_3$ c. bean sprouts

2 c. sauerkraut, drained

$^2/_3$ c. chopped celery

$^2/_3$ c. diced peppers, red and green
  preferred

$^1/_3$ c. Vidalia onion

$^3/_4$ t. celery seed

$^3/_4$ c. sugar

$^1/_3$ c. salad oil

$^1/_3$ c. cider vinegar

Mix vegetables and seasonings. Blend sugar, oil, and vinegar and heat to blend. Cool before pouring over vegetables. Allow to marinate for several days in the refrigerator before serving.

Vegetarian Fried Rice

2 T. peanut oil
1/2 t. salt
2 eggs, lightly beaten
2/3 c. thinly sliced green onions

1 c. fresh bean sprouts
3 T. soy sauce
3 c. cold cooked rice
freshly ground black pepper to taste

Heat oil in uncovered wok at 350°. Add salt and eggs. Scramble quickly, breaking into small pieces with spatula. Add onions and stir-fry for 2 minutes. Add bean sprouts and stir-fry for 1 minute. Add soy sauce, rice, and pepper. Stir-fry until heated through, about 1 minute. Serve immediately. Serves 4–6.

Quick Chop Suey

1/2 lb. ground beef
1 onion, sliced
3/4 c. celery, sliced diagonally
3 c. fresh bean sprouts
1 c. beef broth or bouillon cubes
    dissolved in hot water

1/2 c. sliced mushrooms
1 T. cornstarch
2 T. soy sauce

Sauté together ground beef, onion, and celery. Add bean sprouts, mushrooms, and broth. Cover skillet and simmer for 5 minutes. Combine cornstarch and soy sauce. Add to beef mixture, stirring constantly. Cook until thickened and smooth. Serve over hot rice. Serves 4–6.

Wheat Sprouts

Sprouting wheat softens the tough outer coating of the kernel, making it more edible. The dry seed is also transformed into a living raw vegetable with multiple nutrients.

1 c. cleaned, untreated, high-quality wheat (directly from farmer is best)
2 c. room-temperature water

Divide wheat into 2 one-quart wide-mouth fruit jars or use 1 one-gallon jar. (A restaurant-size dill pickle jar works fine.) Rinse wheat well in several waters. Cover washed wheat with double its amount of water.

Place one thickness of nylon net, to act as a strainer, over the opening of the jar. Use heavy elastic band or fruit jar ring to hold the net securely in place. (A piece of nylon stocking could be used in place of net.)

After soaking for 12 hours, drain. Save water for cooking, since it contains some nutrients. Shake bottle to remove excess moisture. Place jar upside down and tip against edge of small sauce dish to allow for more drainage and air circulation. Place on countertop and cover with paper sack to keep out light.

Successful sprouting requires warmth, darkness, moisture, and ventilation. Twice each day, morning and night, give the seeds a fresh-water rinse (with room-temperature water) and return, tipped in the saucer.

Wheat should sprout 36 to 48 hours from beginning of soaking time, depending on room temperature. Sprouts are best when they are as long as the grain. Use immediately. Growth can be retarded by storing in the refrigerator. Never keep for more than one week.

Sprouted Wheat Bread

Grind 2 c. sprouted wheat, using fine disc of food grinder, and knead into the bread dough just before shaping into loaves. Add this amount of sprouted wheat to any whole wheat bread recipe calling for 11 to 12 c. of whole wheat flour and yielding 3 or 4 large loaves. Rising action will be somewhat slower, and you will need to bake the loaves about 10 minutes longer.

Ground sprouts may also be added to quick breads such as muffins and waffles, and are good in meat loaf. They impart a nutty and delicious flavor.

Broiled Sprouted Wheat Patties
Nutritional yeast and soy flour are available in health food stores.

2 c. whole wheat berries, sprouted	1 t. salt
1 c. walnuts, chopped	3 T. nutritional yeast
1 onion, chopped	1 sprig parsley
1 c. milk	1 egg
1 T. soy flour	2 c. whole-grain bread crumbs (about)

In food processor whirl all ingredients except bread crumbs until finely ground. Turn into bowl and add enough crumbs to make mixture stiff. Shape into 6 patties. Arrange on oiled cookie sheet and broil on each side until golden brown. Serves 6.

Wheat Grass for Salads

Wheat grass is a good source of nutrition and dietary fiber. If you have indoor cats, give them a pot of their own. They love to nibble fresh grass.

Place rich, black dirt in shallow container. Moisten dirt thoroughly. Allow all water pools to soak in. Sprinkle with a layer of wheat so that no grain of wheat is on top of another. Sprinkle dry black dirt on wheat until wheat is just covered. Cover with burlap or similar loose-weave material. Sprinkle briefly with water several times a day until shoots appear. Remove cloth and sprinkle several times a day until shoots are 6 inches high. Cut shoots off near the ground and wash. Use wheat grass in salads or chopped in meat loaf.

Watercress

Normally watercress grows along streams where its roots are constantly wet—often actually in the water. But it can be grown in winter on the windowsill.

Watercress requires a very "humusy" soil—60% humus, 10% sand, and 30% good soil. You could probably substitute African violet potting soil to grow just a pot or so of watercress.

Put a few small pieces of limestone, if available, in the bottom of the pot. (Or use broken bits of clay pots.) Keep the pot in a deep saucer of water at all times.

Watercress can be started from seeds, but it is easier to root cuttings. Purchase a nice fresh bunch, with no bruised stems. Make the cuttings about 4 or 5 inches long, and put half the length into water. Use well water or rain water; watercress does not like the chemicals in city tap water. Change the water daily and keep the jar in bright light. When the roots are about 2 inches long, pot the cuttings, water well, and set the pot in a saucer of water. Watercress does best in a cool but sunny place. Occasionally feed it a little plant food.

Watercress makes a nice garnish for meats and is a pleasant addition to salads. It also makes delicious sandwiches.

Hot and Sour Chinese Soup

2 T. oil
1 medium onion, slivered
3 carrots, diagonally sliced thin
1 clove garlic, minced
1 T. fresh ginger root, peeled and
    minced
4 c. chicken broth
1 c. water
2 T. soy sauce

2 c. white mushrooms, cleaned and
    sliced thin
1 handful watercress, cleaned, thick
    stems removed
1 c. frozen pea pods
1 c. fresh bean sprouts
1/4 c. rice wine vinegar
2 t. sesame oil
dash red pepper flakes

Heat 2 T. oil in heavy pot over medium heat. Add onion and carrots. Cook, stirring constantly, for 3 minutes. Add garlic and ginger. Cook, stirring, for 1 minute more.

Add chicken broth, water, and soy sauce. Bring to boil and cook, partially covered, for 2 minutes. Add mushrooms and watercress. Boil, partially covered, for 1 minute more. Add frozen pea pods. Boil long enough to thaw pods. Turn off heat and add bean sprouts. Cover and let rest for 2 minutes.

Stir in rice wine vinegar, sesame oil, and red pepper flakes. Heat through, adjust seasonings, and serve immediately. Serves 6 to 8.

Frozen Watercress Salad

1 3-oz. package cream cheese
3/4 oz. (about 1 1/2 T.) Roquefort or blue cheese
1/4 c. mayonnaise
1 1/2 T. lemon juice
1/2 t. salt
2/3 c. heavy cream, whipped
1/3 c. finely cut watercress

Blend cream cheese with Roquefort or blue cheese until mixture is smooth. Add mayonnaise, lemon juice, and salt. Fold in whipped cream and watercress. Place in glass loaf pan and freeze until firm. Slice and serve. Serve surrounded by sliced oranges on a lettuce leaf. Serves 6 to 8.

Watercress Spread

8 oz. cream cheese
2 T. milk
1/4 c. watercress, finely chopped
salt and pepper to taste

Mix together. Bring to room temperature before serving. Spread on dark, whole wheat, or rye bread. Makes 1 1/4 c. spread.

Cream of Watercress Soup

4 thin slices onion, finely chopped
1 qt. milk
2 c. finely chopped leaves and stems of watercress
1 egg, slightly beaten
1/2 c. heavy cream or evaporated milk
1/4 t. nutmeg
salt and pepper

In medium saucepan scald milk with onions. Add watercress and gently simmer 15 minutes. Stir a little of hot milk mixture into beaten egg and return to saucepan, stirring constantly. Add cream and nutmeg. Reheat carefully without letting soup come to boil. Salt and pepper to taste. Purée in blender if desired. Serves 6.

Watercress and Radish Stuffing for Baked Fish
I especially like this stuffing with Icelandic cod filets.

¹/₄ c. chopped onion
¹/₄ c. chopped radish
3¹/₂ T. butter
³/₄ c. watercress leaves and stems, chopped fine
¹/₄ t. salt
¹/₈ t. pepper
2 c. soft bread crumbs
¹/₂ c. clam juice

Cook onion and radish in butter for 5 minutes. Add watercress, salt, and pepper. Mix in bread crumbs, moisten with a little water, and toss well.

Wipe two 1-pound fish filets with damp paper towel. Rub both sides with garlic, salt, and pepper. Place 1 filet in greased baking pan and spread stuffing to cover. Place other filet on top. Hold in place with 2 or 3 skewers. Dot top with butter. Pour in ¹/₂ c. clam juice and place in 375° oven. Baste several times while cooking. Bake 20–30 minutes or until fish flakes easily. Remove to warm platter and garnish with parsley. Serves 4 to 6.

Stir-Fried Watercress and Other Greens

2 T. cooking oil
1-inch piece ginger root, peeled and minced
1 clove garlic, peeled and minced
1 c. watercress leaves and stems, cut in 2-inch lengths
4 c. greens (whatever is available—kale, lettuce, mustard, cabbage, broccoli)
1 T. sesame oil
1 T. soy sauce

Heat oil in wok or skillet over medium heat. Add ginger root and garlic. Stir for a few seconds or until they begin to brown.

Add watercress and other greens. Turn quickly to mix with oil, cooking for 2 minutes or so, depending upon structural integrity of greens.

Add sesame oil and cook for 1 minute. Add soy sauce and serve over rice.

RESOURCES

Books

Bubel, Mike, and Nancy. *Root-Cellaring*. Emmaus, PA: Rodale Press, 1979.

Courter, J. W., C. C. Zych, and M. C. Shurtleff. *Growing Small Fruits in the Home Garden*. Urbana-Champaign, IL: University of Illinois College of Agriculture, Cooperative Extension Service, Circular 935, 1972.

Healthy Harvest: A Directory of Sustainable Agriculture and Horticulture Organizations. Washington, DC: Potomac Valley Press, 1985.

Kluger, Marilyn. *Preserving Summer's Bounty*. New York: M. Evans & Co., 1979.

Lappe, Frances Moore. *Diet for a Small Planet*. New York: Ballantine Books, 1971.

Longacre, Doris Janzen. *More-with-Less Cookbook*. Scottdale, PA: Herald Press, 1976.

Minnich, Jerry, and Marjorie Hunt. *The Rodale Guide to Composting*. Emmaus, PA: Rodale Press, 1987, 1988.

Pioneer Tradition: Modern Nutrition. Freeman, SD: Freeman Junior College Women's Auxiliary, 1961.

Towne, Marian Kleinsasser, *Bread of Life: Diaries and Memories of a Dakota Family, 1936–1945* (Freeman, SD: Pine Hill Press, 1994).

Winn, Grace, ed. *Simply Delicious: Quantity Cooking for Churches*. Ellenwood, GA: Alternatives, 1983.

Women's Association of First Presbyterian Church. *To the Town's Taste*, 2nd ed. Fredonia, NY: *Fredonia Censor*, n.d.

Yepsen, Roger B., Jr., ed. *The Encyclopedia of Natural Insect and Disease Control*. Emmaus, PA: Rodale Press, 1984.

Periodicals

Fanning, Roberta A. "The Organic Home Nursery," *Mother Earth News*, No. 14 (March, 1972), pp. 20–25.

Kozelka, Art. "Grow Your Own Transplants Indoors," *Chicago Tribune*, March 16, 1975, Section 11.

Milne, C. G. "Some Rules for Growing Vegetables," *Indianapolis Star*, Section 6, p. 10, n.d.

Newsletter of the Fresh Garlic Association, Box 2410, Sausalito, CA 94966–2410.

"Organic Producers Computer Commodity Board is Now on Line," *Michigan Organic News*, Vol. 38, #4 (Winter, 1989), pp. 11–12.

"The Urban Gardener," *Chicago Tribune* Magazine, March 23, 1975.

Leaflets

"Apples in Appealing Ways," Leaflet #312, USDA Bureau of Human Nutrition and Home Economics, September 1951.

"Best-Ever Zucchini Recipes," Marion County [IN] Extension Service, Indianapolis, IN.

Carbonneau, M. C. "Gardening in Containers," Circular #997. Urbana-Champaign, IL: University of Illinois Cooperative Extension Service.

Evers, William D., and April C. Mason. "Freezing Vegetables at Home," Leaflet HE–134. West Lafayette, IN: Purdue University Cooperative Extension Service.

Frank, Janet. "Salad Greens." E. Lansing, MI: Michigan State University Cooperative Extension Service.

Hopen, H. J., et al., "Vegetables for Mini Gardens," Circular 1036. Urbana-Champaign, IL: University of Illinois Cooperative Extension Service.

"It's Plum Time!," Leaflet D–29, Consumer Cooperative of Berkeley, Inc. Richmond, CA.

Kerr Home Canning and Freezing Guide. Kerr Research and Education Department, Sand Springs, OK.

Mason, April C., and William D. Evers. "Freezing Fruits at Home," HE–133. W. Lafayette, IN: Purdue University Cooperative Extension Service.

"Nutritional Facts from So Fresh Produce Co.," Franklin Park, IL.
"Potatoes in Popular Ways," Leaflet 295. USDA Bureau of Human Nutrition and Home Economics, February 1944.
"Produce and Pesticides: A Consumer Guide to Food Quality and Safe Handling." FDA Office of Consumer Affairs, 5600 Fishers Lane, Rockville, MD 20857.
"Snap Peas," Leaflet 2894–4. Burpee Seed Co., Clinton, IA 52732.
"Ten Short Lessons in Canning and Freezing." Kerr Research and Education Department. Sand Springs, OK.
Wott, John A. "Small Plot Gardening," HO–124. W. Lafayette, IN: Purdue University Cooperative Extension Service.
Wott, John A. "Tomatoes," HO–26. W. Lafayette, IN: Purdue University Cooperative Extension Service.

Organizations for Information

Capital City Garden Project, Marion County Cooperative Extension Service, 9245 N. Meridian St., #118, Indianapolis, IN 46260. (317) 253-0871 or 848–7351.
Healthy Harvest, 1424 16th St., N.W., Suite 105, Washington, DC 20036.
Indiana Organic Growers Association, 1730 S. 950 E., Zionsville, IN 46077. Attn: Lynn Jenkins.
Indianapolis Clean City Committee, Inc., 445 N. Pennsylvania #330, Indianapolis, IN 46204. (317) 327–7000.
Indianapolis Star Food Section, Donna Segal, ed., P.O. Box 145, Indianapolis, IN 46206.
National Farm Worker Ministry, P.O. Box 302, Delano, CA 93216.
Northwest Cherry Growers, P.O. Box 2696, Yakima, WA 98902 [information on preparing and preserving sweet cherries].
Organic Growers of Michigan, Southwest Chapter, 26041 CR 681, Bangor, MI 49013.
Pacific Kitchen, 217 6th Ave., N. Seattle, WA 98109 [cherry recipes].
State of Indiana Department of Agriculture, Office of Lt. Gov. Frank O'Bannon, State Capitol Building, Indianapolis, IN 46204 [list of certified organic growers].
Toxic Action Project, 3951 N. Meridian St., Indianapolis, IN 46208.
United Farm Workers of America, P.O. Box 62, Keene, CA 93570.

Seed and Nursery Mail Order Catalog Companies

Burpee Seeds, Clinton, IA 52732.
Henry Field's Seed & Nursery Co., 415 N. Burnett, Shenandoah, IA 51602.
Gardens Alive! Natural Gardening Research Center, 5100 Schenley Place, Lawrenceburg, IN 47025.
Gurney's Nursery, 110 Capital St., Yankton, SD 57079 [seeds and plants, including hardy kiwis].
Le Jardin du Gourmet, Box 75, St. Johnsbury Ctr., VT 05863-0075.
Johnny's Selected Seeds, Foss Hill Rd., Albion, ME 04910.
J. W. Jung Seed Co., Randolph, WI 53957.
Miller Nurseries, 1602 W. Lake Rd., Canandaigua, NY 14424 [developers and marketers of the Chojuro and Shinseiki varieties of Asian pear].
Richard Owen Nursery, 2300 E. Lincoln St., Bloomington, IL 61701 [dwarf pear trees].
Page Seed Co., Greene, NY 13778 [broccoli rabe seeds].
Pinetree Garden Seeds, Box 300, New Gloucester, ME 04260.
Wildseed Farms, Inc., 1101 Campo Rosa Rd., Box 308, Eagle Lake, TX 77434.

Product Sources

Bluffton Slawcutter Co., Bluffton, OH 45817 [metal cabbage slicer].
Dymple's Delight, R.R. 4, Box 53, Mitchell, IN 47446 [persimmon pulp].
Gardener's Supply Co., 128 Intervale Rd., Burlington, VT 05401–2850.
Hyde Park Cooperative Society, 55th and Lake Park, Chicago, IL 60615.
Lehman Hardware & Appliances, One Lehman Circle, P.O. Box 41, Kidron, OH 44636 [Amish food grinders, anything non-electric].
Monterey Fruit Market, Hopkins Avenue, Berkeley, CA 94740 [They don't do mail order, but it's a great place to visit. They are located in "Gourmet Gulch" in North Berkeley].
Woodbury Wines, R.R. 1, So. Roberts Rd., Dunkirk, NY 14048 [fine wines and champagnes, sent via UPS].

INDEX

Marian K. Towne was born into a Mennonite farm family in South Dakota during the Great Depression and learned from a large extended family how to garden, prepare, and preserve what precious food resources were available. Wherever she has lived and taught in the Midwest during her adult life (Kansas, Illinois, Ohio, Indiana), she and her family have gardened and bought fresh produce grown by area farmers. She is the author of *Bread of Life: Diaries and Memories of a Dakota Family, 1936–1945, The Onliest One Alive: Surviving Jonestown, Guyana,* and *Dreaming the Impossible Dream: The History of the Edyvean Repertory Theatre at Christian Theological Seminary.*